"The problem with systematic theology is that it wanders too far from the Bible and its inherent narrative structure. 'The Biblical text is not an inkblot into which one can read whatever comes to one's mind,' Witherington insists, or whatever one wants to find there. Witherington calls out several common errors: seeing the Bible as a catalog of doctrines rather than a coherent story; 'denuding the biblical text of its genres'; reading Scripture through the lens of Greek philosophy rather than a Hebrew worldview. Whereas theologians generally put eschatology last among topics discussed, Jesus put it first in his proclamation of God's reign. Anyone reading systematic theology today should have this provocative volume at hand as a corrective companion."

—HOWARD A. SNYDER
Author of *Consider the Lilies: How Jesus Saves People and the Land*

"The modern distinction between systematic theology and biblical exegesis did not exist in the earliest centuries of the church's history. While we might argue about how helpful the distinction has proven, one thing is certain: the division between them has become so deep as to leave each, in different ways, impoverished. Ben Witherington's *Rethinking Biblical and Systematic Theology* offers a critique about the use or neglect of Scripture in contemporary systematic theology that seeks to create a conversation between biblical exegetes and theologians about the right use of Scripture in theology. Scholars in both disciplines should be grateful for this conversation that Witherington initiates."

—J. WARREN SMITH
Professor of Historical Theology, Duke Divinity School

"As a Catholic student of the New Testament, I am happy to recommend Ben Witherington's book on systematic theology. Though I do not agree with his brief treatment of Marian theology, the book helpfully provides a much-needed identification of the problems inherent in Reformed Theology and a welcome illumination of the positive contribution that a well-formed systematic theology can offer. Gerhard Sauter once told me that he and other theologians always looked to the exegetes to provide guidance for their work in systematic theology. This book by Ben Witherington delivers on that expectation."

—MARK REASONER
Professor of Biblical Theology, Marian University

"Witherington holds our attention by his readiness to challenge everybody's sacred cows. He rightly summons us to prioritize the divinely inspired voice of Scripture, understood first in context, as the foundational theological authority around which all churches can unite, despite our variations on detail."

—CRAIG KEENER
Professor of New Testament, Asbury Theological Seminary

"For decades I have appreciated Witherington's scholarship. In an age today of micro-specialization, there are few 'generalists,' and even fewer who can operate across the canon with insight and accuracy. This book draws from Witherington's vast research and teaching career to help those who make an attempt at biblical and systematic theology to learn from others' mistakes and to avoid pitfalls that lead to creating idiosyncratic theologies. This book is chock full of hermeneutical and methodological insights."

—NIJAY K. GUPTA
Julius R. Mantey Professor of New Testament, Northern Seminary

"Precious few scholars know the many twists and turns of the long road of biblical interpretation. Fewer still appreciate the complex relationship between biblical interpretation and biblical and systematic theology. Ben Witherington demonstrates in this present volume that he is one of the few. Indeed, Witherington, with a wisdom only gained by years of living with the text, throws fresh light on the confusion which engulfs many of the Evangelical attempts at a systematic theology. Witherington argues that a systematic theology is not merely biblical theology arranged systematically; nor can systematic theology be reduced to a set of propositions, however much biblically informed. This volume is classic Witherington."

—CAREY C. NEWMAN
Fortress Press

# Rethinking Biblical and Systematic Theology

# Rethinking Biblical and Systematic Theology

By BEN WITHERINGTON III

CASCADE Books • Eugene, Oregon

RETHINKING BIBLICAL AND SYSTEMATIC THEOLOGY

Copyright © 2026 Ben Witherington III. All rights reserved. Except for brief quotations in critical publications or reviews, no part of this book may be reproduced in any manner without prior written permission from the publisher. Write: Permissions, Wipf and Stock Publishers, 199 W. 8th Ave., Suite 3, Eugene, OR 97401.

Cascade Books
An Imprint of Wipf and Stock Publishers
199 W. 8th Ave., Suite 3
Eugene, OR 97401

www.wipfandstock.com

PAPERBACK ISBN: 979-8-3852-6078-2
HARDCOVER ISBN: 979-8-3852-6079-9
EBOOK ISBN: 979-8-3852-6080-5

*Cataloguing-in-Publication data:*

Names: Witherington, Ben, 1951– [author].

Title: Rethinking biblical and systematic theology / by Ben Witherington III.

Description: Eugene, OR: Cascade Books, 2026 | Includes bibliographical references.

Identifiers: ISBN 979-8-3852-6078-2 (paperback) | ISBN 979-8-3852-6079-9 (hardcover) | ISBN 979-8-3852-6080-5 (ebook)

Subjects: LCSH: Theology—Methodology. | Bible—Hermeneutics. | Bible.—Theology. | Bible.—New Testament—Theology. | Bible.—New Testament—Criticism, interpretation, etc. | Theology, Doctrinal.

Classification: BS2397 W58 2026 (paperback) | BS2397 (ebook)

VERSION NUMBER 02/23/26

*This book is dedicated to my long-time editor, friend, and brother in Christ Chris Spinks, who passed away far too soon. May the Lord bless and keep your family and your publishing family at Wipf and Stock, and may the Lord make his face to shine upon you and give you eternal peace and rest.*

*August 1, 2025*
*BW3*

Be careful how you tie down the Word to fit your set and final creeds, systems, dogmas, and organized theistic philosophies! The Word of God is not bound! It is free to say what it will to the individual and no one can outline it into dispensations which cannot be broken.
	—Jim Elliot

I've learned that, in academic scholarship, precious little of it is either "biblical" or "theological."
	—Clifton Black, *Biblical Theology*

As Brian [Daley] emphasizes again and again, early Christian doctrine was never simply the multiplication of propositional teachings in isolation; it emerged directly and was guided by the reading of the Bible.
	—Brian Dunkle, introduction to *Biblical Interpretation and Doctrine in Early Christianity*, by Brian Daley

# Contents

*Prologue: A Text Without a Context . . .* | ix

### PART ONE:
### What Have They Done to Biblical and Systematic Theology?

CHAPTER ONE
Defining *Biblical Theology*: How Does it Differ from Systematic Theology or Canonical Theology? | 3

CHAPTER TWO
*Systematic Theology* by Definition | 14

CHAPTER THREE
The Diatesseron Disease: Synthesis at the Expense of Particularity, and Adding to the Apostolic Tradition at the Expense of Proper Exegesis of That Tradition | 22

CHAPTER FOUR
*Semper Reformanda* or Systemic Problems | 37

### PART TWO:
### Toward a Proper Approach to Biblical and Systematic Theology

CHAPTER FIVE
Abstract Art: Denuding Theology of Its Narrative Thought World | 89

CHAPTER SIX
The Imports: The Promise and Problems of Greek Philosophy vis-à-vis Jewish Ideas and Stories | 106

CHAPTER SEVEN
The Exports: Where Did the Ethics Go? What If They Are Theological Ethics? | 113

CHAPTER EIGHT
Human Logic or the Logic of God? | 127

CHAPTER NINE
Putting the Emphasis on the *Wrong* Syllable: Adjectives at the Expense of Nouns | 133

CHAPTER TEN
Anachronism at the Expense of History: The Problem Revisited | 145

CHAPTER ELEVEN
Tradition at the Expense of Scripture or in the Service of Scripture? | 153

CHAPTER TWELVE
Intertextuality and Dubious Theories of Meaning | 163

CHAPTER THIRTEEN
The Jenson Tonic: A Proper Approach to Systematics | 175

CHAPTER FOURTEEN
Concluding Unscientific Postscript | 185


APPENDIX ONE
Is God Quixotic, and Changing His Mind About Sexual Ethics?
A Review of *The Widening of God's Mercy* (Yale University Press, 2024), by Christopher B. Hays and Richard B Hays | 189

APPENDIX TWO
Toward a More Historical Method to Do Socio-Rhetorical Criticism | 204

*Bibliography* | 213

# Prologue

# A Text Without a Context . . .

I'm sure by now my students (and I have had hundreds over the last forty years) have gotten quite tired of hearing the refrain "a text without a context is just a pretext for whatever you want it to mean." Some have concluded it is my mantra which I chant regularly. Nevertheless, as a basic principle that leads to an accurate interpretation of any piece of literature, including especially ancient literature from a culture very different from one's own, this principle should never be ignored. I say this especially in the age of sound bites, texting, and ridiculously brief advertisements.

Knowing the context is a fundamental principle for exegesis of the Bible, the most published, most studied, most owned book in all of human history. In any given year, despite the *NY Times* best-seller list, the Bible is still the best-selling book—it's hiding in plain sight. And herein lies a major problem with too many forms of Systematic theology and frankly also Biblical theology. Too often, the theologians are too busy talking to each other and spinning out their logic within the narrow scope of their own in-house discourse to actually meaningfully interact with detailed exegesis of the Biblical text.[1] Even when some Biblical texts enter into the discussion, they tend to be used as diving boards into the pool of systematized ideas, most

---

1. All Scripture citations in this study are either taken from the 1984 NIV, which Zondervan has graciously given me permission to use, or are my own translations. Some of the material in this study I have dealt with before in my commentaries or in a study like my *Biblical Theology* and my *Who God Is*. I have taken pains to rephrase things where needed, and in some regards the discussion here is more fulsome than in those earlier studies, reflecting further thinking on these subjects.

of which are either not found in the Bible or do not seem to be reasonable extrapolations from some things the Bible actually teaches.

Let's take a brief example—the Greek term *aseity*. Here's a definition of the term: "the quality or state of being self-derived or self-originated, specifically the absolute self-sufficiency, independence, and autonomy of God."[2] Immediately the question becomes—What does the term *God* refer to in this definition? If it's the Christian concept of God as a Trinity, Father, Son, and Holy Spirit, then already you are raising more questions than you are answering by using this term. For example, in what sense is the Son the only begotten of the Father? In what sense is the Father independent from the Son? Is the Spirit self-sufficient or is the Spirit dependent on the Father and the Son?

If all that is meant by this term *aseity* is that God is not derived from angels, humans, or any mere force or power in the universe that is separate from God, and so God is self-sufficient in this way, then fine. But frankly the Bible does not speak of God in these sorts of terms, terms derived from Greek philosophy. And when such terms are imported into the discussion of Biblical terms and ideas, it is fair to ask—Does this help clarify matters, or does it lead us off into an abstract discourse that is far removed from the way the Bible talks about God? How does this help us to understand the Bible itself and its narrative thought-world? Inquiring minds would like to know.

And here's another question—Why is it that in the Protestant world of the last one hundred plus years, the vast majority of works labeled Systematic Theologies have been done by scholars in the Reformed tradition—for instance, R. C. Sproul, Charles Hodge, Louis Berkhof, G. C. Berkower, John Frame, Norman Geisler, Wayne Grudem, John Webster, and I could go on?[3] This is all the more an issue when one considers the wider and pre-Reformation world of Christian scholarship where there were and are those who do their theology out of the work of Thomas Aquinas, or others out of the work of Augustine, or still others out of the work of the Cappadocian fathers—Basil and the two theologians named Gregory.[4]

2. Oxford English Dictionary Online, "Aseity."

3. When I attended Gordon-Conwell Seminary from 1974–77, I was required to read, among others, Berkhof, Berkower, Hodge, Warfield, as well as Calvin, Jonathan Edwards, some Karl Barth, and more. No Wesleyan theologians like John Wesley or Richard Watson ever entered the discussion.

4. I once had the honor of giving some lectures at the Catholic University in Washington, DC. The subject was Jesus, and I was the only Protestant invited. It turns out, all the other papers were doing Thomist takes on Christology, and I was doing a Biblical take on that. It was interesting, and I learned a good deal about Aquinas's views of Christ. I left with questions about whether several aspects of his views really comported with what the Bible says, not least because I later learned that Aquinas knew little or

It seems worthwhile then to ask the question—What's wrong with this picture? Is there an inherent problem with Systematic Theology, or do we need to make clear the limits of such an approach to theology? Certainly, it is possible to argue consistently within a narrow collection of thoughts or ideas, but not take into account all sorts of data that would lead to different conclusions. Though often misquoted, it is worthwhile to contemplate what Ralph Waldo Emerson once actually said:

> A foolish consistency is the hobgoblin of little minds, adored by little statesmen and philosophers and divines. With consistency a great soul has simply nothing to do. He may as well concern himself with his shadow on the wall. Speak what you think now in hard words, and to-morrow speak what to-morrow thinks in hard words again, though it contradicts everything you said to-day.—"Ah, so you shall be sure to be misunderstood."—Is it so bad, then, to be misunderstood? Pythagoras was misunderstood, and Socrates, and Jesus, and Luther, and Copernicus, and Galileo, and Newton, and every pure and wise spirit that ever took flesh. To be great is to be misunderstood.[5]

My chief concern in this study, as a Biblical scholar, is to help the reader avoid the sin of anachronism, by which I mean imposing later theological ideas on the Bible which in fact distort what the Bible says, or do not meaningfully extrapolate from or amplify the actual theological teaching of the Bible. I will also concern myself with the problems of the synthetic approach to Biblical narrative and the neglect of the Bible's narrative thought world, with the over-reading of the NT into the OT, with the neglect of the nouns predicated of God in the Bible and the over-emphasis on the adjectives, with the pluses and minuses of historical theology, with the neglect of logic and rhetoric in the interpretation of NT texts, and with problematic theories of meaning and more. In essence this book is mainly an attempt to show how NOT to do Biblical and Systematic theology with some clear guidance of how it could properly be done. If I succeed in this attempt, I will be content.

And fair warning: Various of the volumes labeled Systematic Theology by Evangelicals of both the Reformed and Wesleyan traditions are in fact *not Systematic theologies after all*. They are systematized Biblical theologies. And sometimes synthesized versions of historical theologies also are wrongly called Systematic theology. Our first task then is to give a reasonable

---

no Biblical Greek! How does one do Biblical or even Systematic theology that way, especially at a time when a non-Biblical language, namely Latin, is the official language of the church and its academic discourse?

5. *Emerson*, "Self-Reliance."

definition of Biblical theology and after that of Systematic theology, noticing the similarities and the differences. And what must be the basis of any sort of Biblical or Systematic theology is the necessary knowledge of sound contextual exegesis of the relevant Biblical texts.

When texts are stripped of their historical, narrative, rhetorical, ethical, and theological contexts, most any sort of conclusion is possible, but not necessarily warranted by the Bible itself. This is one of the great dangers of doing either Biblical or Systematic theology in a merely topical way without attention to the various original contexts. So, let's be clear first of all how sound Biblical theology should be defined and done, and then deal with definitions of Systematic theology.

PART ONE

What Have They Done to Biblical and *Systematic Theology*?

# Chapter One

# Defining *Biblical Theology*
## How Does it Differ from Systematic Theology or Canonical Theology?

It has long been recognized that the term "Biblical Theology" is ambiguous. It can either denote a theology contained within the Bible, or a theology which accords with the Bible.... The first definition understands the task of Biblical Theology to be a descriptive, historical one which seeks to determine what was the theology of the Biblical authors themselves. The second understands the task of Biblical Theology to be a constructive theological one which attempts to formulate a modern theology compatible in some sense with the Bible.
—Brevard Childs, *Biblical Theology of the Old and New Testaments*

### The Presuppositions of the Church Fathers

The fathers of the church believed that the Bible is one book and that it teaches humanity about the world and ourselves; it is inspired directly by God and demands a reader sensitive to its multifarious meanings and messages.
—Brian Daley, *Biblical Interpretation and Doctrine in Early Christianity*, 2[1]

---

1. I would say that while we can learn from the modus operandi of the Fathers, especially the more Antiochian ones which are more in sync with historical exegesis,

To a very great extent, how one approaches Biblical Theology will determine how one approaches *Systematic Theology,* and it is not too much to say that Biblical Theology, in the last generation of Biblical scholarship, has become something of a *terra incognita*—an all too foreign and unknown land. In part, this is the case because the most recent generation of Biblical scholars have become such specialists in certain aspects of the field, or have confined their research and writing to one or the other of the Biblical Testaments. This means they deliberately avoided attempting or even assessing a subject like Biblical Theology. In an age of specialization and over-specialization, the temptation is to say with St. Paul: "Who is sufficient for such a task" as doing a Biblical Theology?

Furthermore, when one assesses the few recent attempts in the twenty-first century at undertaking such a task—for instance, the recent works by John Goldingay (2016) or R. Feldmeier and H. Spieckerman (2015) or Thomas Schreiner (2013) or further back B. Childs (2012), or at a more popular level C. H. H. Scobie (2002)—one is left feeling one is in the period of the Judges, where "each did what was right in their own eyes." There is not only content diversity in such volumes; there is in addition no agreement about methodology either. There is, however, a good survey textbook by James K. Mead on *how* we got here, and *when* the quest for a Biblical Theology began in the modern era (in the nineteenth century),[2] but there is no consistent definition of *what* Biblical Theology is. For example, for Jewish scholars, Biblical Theology is just Old Testament Theology, and frankly they are not much interested in the Christian attempt at a theology of both Testaments. In terms of a method for pursuing a Biblical Theology, what often happens is just the tracing of themes in a linear way through the canon (see Scobie) or picking a few key themes such as "the living God" or "the God of the living" and unpacking those ideas at great length, and with some profit.

Then there is Brevard Childs's efforts at canonical theology, which involves following the lead of the way NT writers *use* the OT to do Christian readings of the OT that are along the same lines, even though much of the use of the OT in the NT is *not* exegetical in nature, but rather midrashic

---

we cannot simply repeat the Fathers' methods, or if we do, we dishonor the historical context and givenness of the Biblical revelation. Further, God's Word involved inspiration through inspired historical persons. It is unlike the claims made about the Book of Mormon, for example. This is made clear in a text like 1 Pet 1:10, which explains about inspired human prophets offering inspired traditions which became Biblical texts—"the prophets, who spoke of the grace that was to come to you, searched intently and with the greatest care, trying to find out the time and circumstances to which the Spirit of Christ in them was pointing when he predicted the sufferings of the Messiah and the glories that would follow."

2. Mead, *Biblical Theology.*

or homiletical, as we might call it. Sometimes it even involves treating the entire OT as prophetic in character, promising, predicting, foreshadowing a future only brought to fruition in Christ and in the NT eschatological era. And one must say, all of this involves a sort of post-Enlightenment approach where one abstracts certain key ideas such as grace or redemption, or even the doctrine of God, and then tries to connect the dots between said abstract ideas (justification leads to sanctification and finally to glorification).

Though many of these studies are helpful in various ways, what they do not involve is thinking along the lines of the Biblical writers *themselves*, who had a narrative thought world, not a modern or even post-modern abstract thought world. Furthermore, too many of these studies do not take into account the progressive nature of revelation, much less the convergence of the canon when it comes to the doctrine of God (on which more below). Surprisingly, the subject of theology proper, namely the very doctrine of God, often gets *short shrift* in the race to deal with salvation history, covenants, predestination, and the like. This is not true, however, in the case of Robert Jenson in his Systematic theology.

Ideally, the person or persons who would undertake the task of producing a Biblical theology would need to have had years of dealing with the whole of the Scriptures and had done some previous deep exegetical work on both the OT and NT. That, however, would only be prolegomena to doing Biblical theology. One must also think in terms of the larger category of Biblical theology, which deals *with the whole. Biblical Theology is not merely OT theology plus NT theology.* It is not just a *reading of the OT in light of the NT.* When one attempts that latter approach, one needs to ask and answer the questions raised by the *intertextuality* of the canon, particularly the use of the OT in the NT.[3] The intertextual issues alone are quite complex. What counts as a quotation? What amounts to an allusion? Do we consider echoes as well? And why exactly is it that Isaiah, the Psalms, and Deuteronomy (and to a lesser degree Genesis) are over and over again the *go to* sources used by NT writers to make their scriptural cases?

Because of all this, I waited until the evening of my career to even attempt a Biblical theology. It is certainly one of the most daunting tasks imaginable for a Biblical scholar. And I must offer this disclaimer from the outset: I am not, nor is any scholar, an expert in the whole of the Bible, so one must rely on the seasoned veterans who have expertise in the various canonical books. What follows here is an explanation of why and how I have

---

3. On which see my recent series of three books with Fortress Press—*Isaiah Old and New; Psalms Old and New; Torah Old and New.*

approached the task. And I offer a few key insights derived from the study itself.[4]

## *Preparatio Evangelici*

First of all, though I am primarily a NT scholar, I have listened to the pleas of the John Goldingays of this world, as well as my Jewish friends, who focus on what we call the Old Testament, and I largely agree with the plea: *let the Old Testament be the Old Testament*. The OT was not written by Christians, nor is it a Christian book born out of due season. That does not mean one cannot do Christian readings of the OT, but frankly they should *not* be done in a way that violates the contextual integrity of the OT itself or the progress of revelation and salvation history itself.

What I mean by this is that the OT is a book that overwhelmingly focuses on Yahweh and His relationship with His chosen people. It is not about the Holy Trinity—Christ is not the angel of the Lord in disguise in the OT. As the author of Heb 1 rightly insists, Christ is in a whole different category than the angels.[5] Interestingly, when NT writers do want to ask and answer the question about what was the only begotten Son doing during the OT era, they choose to associate Christ with the figure of personified Wisdom (see John 1, Col 1, and in general the Christological hymns, and compare Prov 3, 8–9, Wisdom of Solomon, Sirach) who was involved with God both in the creation of all things, and later in the process of salvation history and the making known of God's redemptions and judgments on His people.[6]

In overly simplistic terms, the OT is about the Father, the Gospels are about the Son, Acts properly introduces the Holy Spirit, and the rest of the NT is an exercise in working out the meaning and roles and collaborations of Father, Son, and Spirit. In short, the canon reveals progressively what came to be called the doctrine of the Trinity, with the full definition of God's divine identity converging or coming to full expression in the latter part of the canon.[7] Yes, there are types and foreshadowings of the Christ in the OT.

---

4. The full study is found in my *Biblical Theology: The Convergence of the Canon*, which won the Association of American Publishers Prose Prize for Book of the Year for books in religion or philosophy.

5. Notice as well that Heb 13 indicates that Abraham was visited by angels, not the Holy Trinity.

6. See my *Jesus the Sage*.

7. It is of course true that Paul has a high Christology and Pneumatology and his is the earliest collection of documents in the NT, but the way the canon ended up being arranged, this only comes into play after the Gospels and Acts.

The NT writers were correct about that. But there was no incarnation before the incarnation. The three visitors to Abraham were not the Holy Trinity, despite Greek Orthodox theology.

The first genuinely Trinitarian text in the Bible is the story of Jesus' baptism. This is, in part, because the term *ruach* in the OT generally refers to the living presence of Yahweh who inspires and empowers human beings along the way. It is not likely a reference to the third person of the Trinity. Indeed, there are only two places in the OT, one in the Psalms ("take not your *Holy* Spirit from me")[8] and once in Isaiah where we even *have* a reference to the *Holy* Spirit.

The Spirit in the NT *is a person*, not merely a power or presence or inspiration of Yahweh, and doesn't properly show up until the Gospels. We could debate whether or not the writers of the OT simply understood the word *ruach* to mean God's living presence, *but* it was the Holy Spirit, just not fully understood yet. The problem theologically with that idea is that it would require a theology of progressive *understanding*, not merely progressive *revelation*.

The concept of progressive revelation is that God reveals Himself in a way that *is* understandable to those first intended recipients, otherwise the perspicuity of Scripture is called into question. At the same time, it is clear that the understanding of God's people did develop over time, for example in regard to the issue of viable secondary causes. In the earlier historical records, including 1 and 2 Samuel and 1 and 2 Kings, there are various things predicated of God that are in the Chronicles predicated of "the Adversary," *ha satan*. Or again, the understanding of the theology of the afterlife clearly develops over time, such that only in Dan 12:1–3 do we first have a clear reference to a literal bodily resurrection, a concept so important in the NT. Earlier in the OT we have the theology of Sheol, the land of the dead, where the spirits of the ancestors are gathered (see the famous story about the spirit or *elohim* of Samuel the prophet and the medium of Endor).

Besides the fact that one needs to have a clear sense of progressive revelation and not interpret the Bible flatly, the second thing to note is that the NT writers are clear that OT revelation was partial and piecemeal (see Heb 1). But *now* God has revealed Himself in His Son, who is the gold standard by which we should interpret the true character of God as revealed elsewhere in Scripture.

In a separate study, I have spent time explaining that when it comes to God's moral character, we should in the first instance focus on the nouns

---

8. Noting the word "your." It is Yahweh's spirit or presence as an anointing and empowering that the psalmist pleads to keep.

predicated of God, not firstly on the adjectives. So, for example, God is love, light, life, spirit, and one. Those are the key Biblical nouns predicated of God. And this has ramifications for how we view the adjectives, namely, almighty, righteous, holy, etc.[9]

If God is love, of course His love is a holy love—not love without holiness but also not holiness without love either. Furthermore, love requires freedom. God is a free agent, but so are we who are expected to respond to God and others in love. Love cannot be coerced or predetermined, or else it ceases to be love. Love must be freely given and freely received and responded to, by grace through faith in our case. And God's moral character, as the nouns make clear, is the same throughout Scripture. It does not change, just as we also hear that Christ is the same yesterday, today, and forever. Such statements are not about God being ontologically immutable, for clearly the incarnation reveals a God who can incorporate change, even incorporating a human nature into the divine identity, without God's character changing.

Further, one must come to grips with the concept of "a surplus of meaning" or *sensus plenior*, particularly when one is dealing with prophetic literature. Often prophets conjured up images and metaphors about the future, sometimes even the remote future (like the wolf will lie down with the lamb without longing for lamb chops), and eventually we discover that they said more than they realized at the time. At the least, it had a significance they had not yet fully grasped. I take it that this is what is being referred to when we read in 1 Pet 1:10–12,

> Concerning this salvation, the prophets, who spoke of the grace that was to come to you, searched intently and with the greatest care, trying to find out the time and circumstances to which the Spirit of Christ in them was pointing when he predicted the sufferings of the Messiah and the glories that would follow. It was revealed to them that they were not serving themselves but you, when they spoke of the things that have now been told you by those who have preached the gospel to you by the Holy Spirit sent from heaven. Even angels long to look into these things.

If they were searching and pondering intently, and if even angels were not fully clued in to the significance, the timing, the circumstances of the fulfillment of the prophecies, then surely the prophets were seeing through a glass darkly, as St. Paul was later to say. A detailed study of OT prophecy reveals that sometimes the prophecies about the near horizon can be quite specific (it's Cyrus who will be God's liberator of His people), but then

---

9. This book is entitled *Who God Is*.

prophecies about the more distant future tend to be imagaic, metaphorical, and far less specific.[10]

The ever-present danger for Christians is anachronism, the reading back into the OT of NT ideas which simply aren't there. For example, the term *salvation* in the OT does not mean right standing with God achieved through the death and resurrection of Jesus appropriated by faith. No, salvation means physical rescue from danger, or disease, or enemies in the OT. It may have a spiritual component as well, that is, salvation from some sort of sin would be included, but it is not Christocentric in character.

Furthermore, election is one thing and salvation is quite another. Many of God's chosen people are not "saved" spiritually or otherwise. Indeed, most of the wilderness wandering generation perished and did not enter the promised land. Their chosenness did not save them. More often than not what election means in the OT is "chosen for some specific historical purpose." For instance, Cyrus the Persian is the only person directly called "my anointed one" (*mashiach!*) in the OT. This does not mean he was "saved" in the NT sense at all. It simply means he was a chosen instrument of God for a particular historical purpose, namely, allowing exiled Jews to go home to the Holy Land and rebuild. Cyrus does not make the hall of faith in Heb 11. Further, in the NT, Christ is clearly the Elect One, the Righteous One of God, but he has no need of being saved! Again, a good and clear sense of the before and after of progressive revelation is a key to understanding Biblical Theology.

It is surprising how few NT scholars actually have studied the nature of covenants in the Biblical world, including ancient Near East (hereafter ANE) covenants, which are often conditional in character ("if my people who are called by my name will repent . . . then I will turn to them"). They further do not understand that when a covenant is *broken*, the covenant maker can either terminate the relationship or renew or even *replace* the covenant. He is under no obligation to continue a particular covenant. Promises of an *olam* covenant simply mean "on an ongoing basis," unless and until the covenant becomes so broken that the covenant curses must be invoked and the covenant dissolved. In other words, in the Bible, only the new covenant is an everlasting covenant according to the book of Hebrews and Paul's letters as well, and the new covenant is *not* merely a renewal of some previous covenant. At this juncture I want to share my own approach to Biblical Theology.

---

10. On this see Witherington: *Jesus the Seer*; and *Isaiah Old and New*.

## The Constructive Task: A Method in This Madness

It became clear to me some time ago that the Biblical writers simply assume the existence of the Biblical God. They do not really argue for it in any sort of extensive way. God is the foundation of their whole thought world and the way they look at life and history and family and so much more. This is why scholars talk about the symbolic universe of the Biblical writers. What were the fixed stars in the sky of their imagination? What were the things they took for granted? Most of these things have to do with a God who is the only true and living God, who is both creator of all things great and small and the redeemer of His people, having a specific and special covenanting relationship with them.[11]

But the second thing that becomes very clear is that the writers of the Bible had a *narrative thought world*, not primarily an abstract concept thought world. They configured the way they looked at God and the universe and human history through narrative, and it was out of narrative, out of story, that they did their theologizing and ethicizing. Theology was not done in the abstract but out of story, and sometimes in the form of story, such as the narrative parables of Jesus. Even in the case of Paul, when Paul thinks of sin he thinks of the story of Adam (see Rom 5). When he thinks of faith he thinks of the story of Abraham (Gal 3, Rom 4). When he thinks of Law he thinks of the story of Moses (2 Cor 3). And when he thinks of salvation he turns to the more recent story of Christ (see 1 Cor 11 and 15).[12]

Trying to think like the Biblical writers themselves, I set up my Biblical Theology volume as follows: Prolegomena, Methodology, *Forschungsberichte* in regard to the development of the discipline of Biblical Theology. This is followed by three chapters on the foundation of the Biblical thought world, including a chapter on God the Father, God the Son, and God the Spirit. This is followed by two chapters, one on the narrative thought world of the OT writers, and one on the narrative thought world of the NT writers. This is followed by a whole series of chapters on the theologizing of these writers about a host of things: covenants, grace, election, salvation, eschatology, and so on. After a chapter summing up findings, the study concludes with some appendices critiquing some of the work of other Biblical theologians

---

11. In a recent essay my colleague Bill Arnold stresses that while the Hebrews believed there were other spiritual beings beyond Yahweh, they also believed Yahweh was the only true God, the only one worthy of worship, for He was both the creator of all things, and the only one who could redeem humanity. Arnold calls this affective monotheism, a belief that Yahweh is unique and the only one deserving worship. See Arnold, *Genesis*.

12. On all of this see Witherington, *Paul's Narrative Thought World*.

and dialoguing with Francis Watson on the issue of the meaning of, and in, texts. There is as well a detailed chapter on the atonement of Christ wrought on the cross.[13]

This methodology, I submit, is more in accord with the way the Biblical writers thought about and did theology, and it is less anecdotal than a study that simply traces *themes* through the canon (sometimes without recognizing that, for example, the term *salvation* in Exodus does not at all mean the same thing as salvation in Romans). Of course, the proof of the pudding is in the eating, or to use a better metaphor, the strength of the building material must be tested with fire to see if it is as strong as it should be.

## Pitfalls and Outcomes

Biblical theology is always a work in progress, not least because for some subjects such as the Trinity, *what we have in the NT is the raw materials of a doctrine of the Trinity, but not the articulation of that doctrine in any detailed or systematic way.* Biblical theology is not Systematic theology, or historical theology, much less is it the retrojection of later theologies such as Patristic or Reformed or Thomistic or Arminian or Orthodox theology into the canon, which sadly all too often happens. There is an incompleteness to Biblical Theology on some topics such as the Trinity, and much depends on how one amplifies or builds upon the raw material in Scripture in order to form these later theologies. If *sola Scriptura* is the battle cry of all good Protestants, this must mean that all later forms of theologizing, including contemporary theologies such as post-colonial theology, philosophical theology, or historical theology and much more, *must be tested against and normed by the Bible, not least because these later constructs were not inspired directly by God.* Because of the open-ended or incomplete nature of Biblical theology, it not only invites further theologizing on its basis, but it prompts the cry *semper reformanda*, since all later constructions of theologies are inadequate human attempts at making sense of the theology in the canon.[14]

At the same time, mere exegesis of the Biblical text, however accurate in ferreting out the contextual meaning of the text, is not the same thing as theologizing on the basis of that meaning, much less the same thing as applying the meaning as a word on target to some contemporary audience and situation. Preaching is not the same thing as teaching the Bible's content. Because, even in the case of so great a theologian as Paul, we are looking at theologizing into specific situations in Galatia or Philippi or Corinth or

13. Witherington, *Biblical Theology*.
14. On sola Scriptura, see my recent study, *Sola Scriptura*.

Rome (and those situations are all quite different in many ways), the later task of systemizing or comparing and contrasting of various Pauline materials is salutary and necessary. One has to allow a certain open-endedness or incompleteness to Biblical theology and the theologizing we do on its basis. And it is very important to bear in mind that the meaning of a text in context may be different than the significance of that text in a later or very different context. Meaning is one thing; significance to a later audience another. An illustration is perhaps in order.

In the summer of 1979, my wife and I were living in England, and preparing to have our first child. Unfortunately, Ann's blood pressure became elevated, and she was admitted to Dryburn Hospital in Durham. The doctor said he was going to induce labor, and this was upsetting because we knew there was some risk to that. Ann and I had been reading through the book of Ezekiel, indeed the doom and gloom chapters of the middle of Ezekiel. On August 13, we read through a dark passage, but one that had these promises embedded in it: "and I will multiply your kindred . . . and I will keep you safe . . . and you will come home soon." I knew this passage's contextual meaning was a promise to exiled Jews that they would finally return from Babylon, but suddenly God had used that ancient prophecy to reassure us in our anxiety. Long story short, I went home to our house convinced the baby would come very soon. I stayed up all night fully dressed, waiting for Bob Raymond to come and get me, as we had no car and no phone in an age before the existence of cell phones (BC standing for Before Cellphone). Sure enough, Bob knocked on the door toward the hour of dawn and was surprised to see me ready to go. He asked, "How did you know to be ready?" I answered, "Ezekiel gave us a clue." That passage in Ezekiel still had its ancient meaning, but it had taken on a new significance or application in our lives in 1979. Sure enough, Christy Witherington was safely born that morning.

To a large extent, asking the right theological questions of the text is crucial. The Bible addresses in detail three intertwined subjects: theology, ethics, and history, and one could add spiritual formation of believers. So, we should not go to the Bible looking for it to teach us *everything* we need to know about science, sociology, psychology, or a host of other subjects of interest to us all.

God keeps acting in human history, even in one's personal history as the illustration above makes clear. Salvation is not an abstract idea; it is redemption in space and time by God, such that salvation history is the real focus of the Biblical writers in various regard. And they would say to us, *nothing can be theologically true and redemptive that is historically false*. If Christ is not raised bodily, then our faith is futile, i.e., we are still in our sins says 1 Cor 15. Of course, not all theological statements in the Bible about God involve a historical component. For example, the discussion in Col 1 about the creation of the universe tells us it involved both the Father and the Son as co-creators before there was a space-time continuum. This is a theological truth that is not grounded or founded on some historical event. But much of the Bible is not of that sort. Much of it is all about *theophany*, God coming down and interacting with His people in space and time in various ways.

Biblical prophecy reveals enough of the future to give us hope, but not so much that we don't have to live by faith every day. Therefore, we must avoid the temptation to try to limit God by giving Him ultimatums and time tables by which he must fulfill this or that promise or prophecy. So also, it is the case that *the Bible reveals enough of the character and will of God to give us hope, but not so much that we need not live by faith, rather than trusting our limited understanding or walking by sight.*

Lastly, doing Biblical theology is a humbling task, and rather like coming into the presence of the Almighty, one realizes that the psalmist is right when he said, "When I consider the sun, the moon, the stars, what is humankind that you are mindful of us or the offspring of human beings that you should care?" (Ps 8:3–4). It is easy to get overwhelmed when contemplating the character of God or His creation and His people. But then one must also remember that God's Son had to humble Himself and take on the form of a servant in order to accomplish God's plan for His life. Perhaps if Biblical theology was always done *coram Deo*, we might see Him more clearly, love Him more dearly, and follow Him more nearly, every day.

# Chapter Two

## *Systematic Theology* by Definition

German liberal theology's method of doctrinal concepts—grouping thoughts expressed by the NT in alignment with dogmatic topics—betrays "scientific criticism" and provokes caricature of NT writers as systematicians in the modern sense. That method's default setting on canonical documents is likewise misguided: a document's canonization makes no difference for either the Protestant theologian or historical investigator . . . none of its subject matter was born canonical.

—Clifton Black, *Biblical Theology*[1]

### Desperately Seeking a Definition

There are numerous definitions of Systematic theology, but what they all seem to have in common is the interpretation of Christian theology using a particular *system* of interpretation. Or, as the folks at Oxford have suggested, "a form of theology in which the aim is to arrange religious truths

---

1. Black, *Biblical Theology*, 18–19. Canonical theology as it is done today by some Protestant scholars is an *ex post facto* approach that is a-historical or in some cases allergic to historical contextual study of the relevant NT texts. This is unfortunate because, as Black goes on to stress, it is not and was not the including of a NT book into the canon which determined its content or intent, and to the extent that the canonical reading of a NT text is at odds with what the text meant in its original historical context it is problematic.

in a self-consistent whole"[2] There's that word *consistent*. But wait a minute—aren't God's ways higher than our ways? Is it ever the case that mere human logic about what counts as *consistent* can possibly encompass the scope and depth of the thoughts of God? Isn't there a book in the Bible called Job where we are truly warned about such thinking? Remember when God finally responds to Job's bitter lament and anger and says,

> "Who is this that obscures my plans
> with words without knowledge?
> Brace yourself like a man;
> I will question you,
> and you shall answer me.
>
> "Where were you when I laid the earth's foundation?
> Tell me, if you understand.
> Who marked off its dimensions? Surely you know!
> Who stretched a measuring line across it?
> On what were its footings set,
> or who laid its cornerstone—
> while the morning stars sang together
> and all the angels shouted for joy? . . .
>
> "Have you ever given orders to the morning,
> or shown the dawn its place,
> that it might take the earth by the edges
> and shake the wicked out of it?
> The earth takes shape like clay under a seal;
> its features stand out like those of a garment.
> The wicked are denied their light,
> and their upraised arm is broken.
>
> "Have you journeyed to the springs of the sea
> or walked in the recesses of the deep?
> Have the gates of death been shown to you?
> Have you seen the gates of the deepest darkness?
>
> Have you comprehended the vast expanses of the earth?
> Tell me, if you know all this." (38:2–7, 12–18)

There is much more along this line, and Job is left almost speechless after this avalanche of questions. In the end in Job 42 he is only able to reply,

> I know that you can do all things;
> no purpose of yours can be thwarted.
> You asked, "Who is this that obscures my plans without

---

2. See Oxford Languages, "Systematic Theology."

> knowledge?"
> Surely, I spoke of things I did not understand,
> things too wonderful for me to know.
> You said, "Listen now, and I will speak;
> I will question you,
> and you shall answer me."
> My ears had heard of you
> but now my eyes have seen you.
> Therefore I despise myself
> and repent in dust and ashes. (42:2–6)

Or perhaps an extended reflection on what Paul says in 1 Cor 13:9–12 ought to bring us all back down to earth.

> For we know in part and we prophesy in part, but when completeness comes, what is in part disappears. When I was a child, I talked like a child, I thought like a child, I reasoned like a child. When I became a man, I put the ways of childhood behind me. For now we see only a reflection as in a mirror; then we shall see face to face. Now I know in part; then I shall know fully, even as I am fully known.

If we only know *in part now*, this entails the notion that our attempts to provide a Systematic theology of God's Word and Truth that we could then count as doctrines set in stone are bound to be flawed or at least incomplete. And especially under suspicion would be any ideas that seem clearly to contradict some things the Scripture *does say* and teach, and some terms and ideas that are not found in the Scriptures at all, even by implication. This in fact has recently been the case with attempts to suggest that when it comes sexual ethics, the God of the Bible (who is said to frequently contradict Himself in the Bible) has now changed His mind about sexual ethics, even though there is absolutely no evidence in the Scriptures themselves of such a volte-face.[3]

I bring this up at this juncture *not* because I'm totally opposed to Systematic theology, but what does bother me is the *hubris* that seems to frequently accompany those who write systematics textbooks as if they have managed to arrange all the *essential* truths of God into a consistent system, and woe betide those who disagree with their approach to the Biblical data.[4] About those who disagree, they intone, "They are not Biblical enough, not consistent enough, and so on." The thing I regularly ask myself, and would

---

3. On this subject see appendix 1 below.

4. Noting the very first sentence in the first volume of Robert Jenson's *Systematic Theology*, 1:vii: "Publishing a system of theology is an irremediably hubristic enterprise."

ask all other theologians of whatever persuasion, is—Have you ever considered you might be wrong, that you might have drawn the boundaries of theological truth too narrowly, or even in some ways wrongly?

But let's consider another definition of Systematic theology, this time with ten major categories:

- Theology Proper. Doctrine of God the Father.
- Bibliology. Doctrine of the Bible.
- Anthropology. Doctrine of humankind.
- Angelology. Doctrine of angels.
- Hamartiology. Doctrine of sin.
- Soteriology. Doctrine of salvation.
- Christology. Doctrine of Christ.
- Ecclesiology. Doctrine of the church.
- Eschatology. Doctrine of future things.
- Pneumatology. Doctrine of the Holy Spirit.

Immediately this arrangement should strike you as odd. Why exactly does the doctrine of God proper not include Father, Son, and Holy Spirit? And why would the Holy Spirit be left until last for discussion? The Pentecostals are bound to ask that question. Where exactly is the discussion of Israel, God's chosen people, and what is Israel's relationship to the church? Why exactly is eschatology simply called the doctrine of future things, when in fact the Dominion of God already broke into human history two thousand years ago in the person of Jesus of Nazareth? What about the interconnection of these subjects? How can one really talk about salvation unless one is also talking about the Savior? And what role does the Holy Spirit play in human salvation?

And where oh where is there any hint that God progressively revealed His truth to His people, so that the climactic revelation of God in His Son Jesus provides the clearest clue about how to interpret everything that came before, especially if all the promises and prophecies of God are fulfilled in or brought to their completion in Christ Jesus? Never mind that the writers of the Bible do their theologizing out of their narrative thought world, not in the abstract by connecting idea A to idea B.

For example, when Paul speaks of sin, he thinks of the story of Adam; when he speaks about faith, he thinks of the story of Abraham; when he speaks about the Law, his thoughts come out of his reflections on the story of Moses, particularly at Sinai. Most of all, Paul does his theologizing out of the story of Christ and its implications. And I could go on.[5]

Sometimes Systematic theology goes well beyond Biblical theology by employing a method that seeks to bring the discussion into interaction with the contemporary discussion on many subjects. Here is what one description of that says: "With a methodological tradition that differs somewhat from biblical theology, systematic theology draws on the core sacred texts of Christianity, while simultaneously investigating the development of Christian doctrine over the course of history, particularly through philosophy, ethics, social sciences, and natural sciences. Using biblical texts, it attempts to compare and relate all of scripture which led to the creation of a systematized statement on what the whole Bible says about particular issues."[6] This is probably the most complete and accurate definition of genuine Systematic theology. That being the case, many volumes labeled Systematic theology don't deserve that label.

Except of course the Bible says exactly nothing about many modern issues: (1) modern cosmology; (2) modern systems of dating ancient artifacts and texts; (3) modern technology; (4) modern systems of mathematics, and I could go on. Something similar to the definition above is what W. Pannenberg has in mind by opening up the discipline to the broad horizons of philosophical, historical, and scientific thought.[7] If that is an essential task of Systematic theology, then what someone like W. Grudem is doing is not Systematics; he is doing systematized Biblical theology of a particularly Reformed sort.

According to Pannenberg, Systematics necessarily involves critically constructing coherent models of reality which render plausible and intelligible to the modern world the Christian confession of God as creator, sustainer, and even final redeemer of the world. In short, there is in-depth engagement with the intellectual discourse of one's age, and an apologetic emerges for the Christian faith in the context of an orderly account of Christian theology. *Frankly, this sounds more like apologetics than just Systematic theology to me, or it is some kind of hybrid of the two.*

Pannenberg suggests that Systematics should take into account the historical development of theological ideas over the course of church history, and also be concerned about the application of Biblical truth to particular issues today. In short, it is not just an exercise in exposition of Biblical

---

5. I have done a whole book on Paul's narrative theology not least because Pauline theology is the sort that has been most often stripped of its narrative thought world and mined for abstract theological ideas. See my *Paul's Narrative Thought World*.

6. Wikipedia, "Systematic Theology," para. 2.

7. See Pannenberg, *Introduction to Systematic Theology*.

doctrine; it is also a discussion of how Biblical doctrine developed over time, and how these truths have interacted with other disciplines of knowledge, and how they can be applied today. In short, it is one part exposition, one part historical survey, one part contemporary application.

And above all, it is about the truth about God. W. Pannenberg puts it this way: "the need for Systematic theology depends on the question of truth. If we suppose that the God of Israel and of Jesus is the one and only true God, then and only then is there sufficient reason for believing in that God, even if one is not a Jew."[8]

But of course, no one attempt at Systematics can be all things to all people, so usually the individual writer focuses on one or another part of these areas of discussion. For example, R. C. Sproul focuses on systematic exposition of key ideas and deals a bit with the historical development in the creeds. Later in this study, I'm going to interact at some length with the way Sproul spins out his definition of Systematic theology because his volume is quite readable and is lay friendly.[9]

## When and Where It Began to Go Wrong

First, however, we need to figure out where things first went wrong, where the synthetic mentality and the "value added" notion began to cause problems in the way the NT (and OT) books were read in the early church. Sadly, both of these trends were already in motion in the second century AD as we are about to see, and often at the expense of what the NT writers were actually claiming about the foundational stories, particularly in the Gospels.

If I were to be asked where these approaches came from, in some cases it came from the attempt to solve problems in regard to the differences between the four original Gospels in various ways and particulars. In some cases, it came from a non-Jewish way of thinking about ancient narratives, in some cases analyzing them on the basis of particular kinds of logic (e.g., syllogistic logic), and in all cases this was because the dominant non-Jewish

---

8. Pannenberg, *Introduction to Systematic Theology*, 4–5.

9. The careful reader will discern that my main concern in this study is offering a critique of conservative Protestant attempts at Systematic theology which turn out to be some sort of highly systematized Biblical Theology, and definitely not what Pannenberg in the main is talking about. No wonder there is confusion about what counts as Systematic theology. Each person seems to be doing what they see as the right limitation and approach that they feel comfortable calling Systematic theology. Or, in the case of someone like Thomas Oden, his work is a recovery project where Protestants and others learn how to integrate the theology of the Church Fathers into a current discussion of canonical theology.

ethos and culture of the empire had already taken over the growing church which before the beginning of the third century had become overwhelmingly Gentile in character.

Not only so, but there was the warning sign of a person like Marcion (AD 85 to 160), who wanted to anathematize the whole OT and accept as sacred texts only Luke and some Pauline letters, for which finally he was excommunicated from the church in Rome in AD 144. The anti-Semitic tide was on the rise in the church already in the second century. Lastly, there was also the simple fact that, almost universally, Gentiles could not read Hebrew,[10] and if they wanted to study and use the OT it was some version of the Greek OT they turned to, a Greek OT that often had different renderings of key texts and ideas than the original Hebrew, not to mention there were several versions of the Greek OT, not just the LXX.[11]

Jerome in the late fourth and early fifth centuries tried to rescue the Hebrew text of the OT for church use, and did indeed use it, but for what—mainly to help produce the *Latin!* text of the Bible, which was already *de facto* the official language of the Western church's faith and praxis. In other words, the Western church based its liturgy, worship, and indeed its Bible on a language which was *not* a Biblical language at all, but the language of a culture very different from early Jewish culture. This problem would be compounded later when Western theology, including Systematics, was done on the basis of a Latin text of the Bible, which not infrequently was not based on an accurate translation of the Hebrew or Greek texts.[12]

---

10. In fact, not only were most Christians dependent on a Greek translation of the OT, but so were the vast number of Jews in the Diaspora which out-numbered Palestinian Jews four million to one million. Stark, *Rise of Christianity*, 58, reminds us, "The Jews outside Palestine read, wrote, spoke, thought and worshipped in Greek." No wonder James wrote his letter or sermon to Diaspora Jewish Christians in Greek.

11. In the second century AD both Aquila of Sinope and Theodotion produced Greek OTs, of which we only have fragments today, and in the third century AD Symmachus also produced a version which again we only have fragments of now. It appears to be the LXX which was the go-to version from which translations into Syriac, Armenian, and many other languages were done, and it also seems by and large to be the form of the Greek OT we find in Codex Vaticanus (B) and Codex Sinaiticus (S) in the fourth century, and codex Alexandrinus (A). Note that these earliest Christian codices included a Greek, not a Hebrew, version of the OT.

12. Two examples will have to suffice from the Johannine literature. In John 21:22–23 a conditional statement, "If I wish him to remain until I come," is turned into a statement, "I wish him to remain until I come," all because a "si" is mistaken for a "sic" (rendering the Greek *ean*) in a manuscript of the Latin Vulgate. Worse still, in 1 John 5:7–8 we have a Trinitarian addition in the Textus Receptus based on a late recension of the Latin Vulgate, which reads, "In heaven, the Father, the Logos, and the Holy Spirit, and these three are One." This is found in NONE of our earliest manuscripts, in fact the earliest Greek MSS that has it is from the eleventh century, nor is it quoted by any

Meanwhile, the Eastern church, while it still had a Greek NT, had begun to accept the LXX as its official Christian OT, which in part explains why Jews by and large abandoned the LXX. *All this is to say, there were problems in both Western and Eastern Christianity in regard to dealing with the Biblical text in its original languages, and these problems without question affected the way they viewed and did theology, including Biblical and Systematic theology.* Bearing this in mind, it's time to turn to Tatian and his attempt to harmonize the four original Gospels.

---

of the Greek Fathers who, if they had known it, would have used it in the Trinitarian controversies against the Arians. And the passage is likewise absent from all ancient non-Latin versions of 1 John 5.

Chapter Three

# The Diatesseron Disease
Synthesis at the Expense of Particularity, and Adding to the Apostolic Tradition at the Expense of Proper Exegesis of That Tradition

> The task of theology is not only to investigate the origin and original content of the Christian faith and of the doctrine of the church or the changes they underwent in the course of history, but also to determine the truth which is contained in that tradition.
> —W. Pannenberg, *Introduction to Systematic Theology*

## Setting the Precedent

Somewhere in the middle of the second century AD, perhaps about 160, a Christian writer named Tatian decided that the church needed a book which blended together all four of the Gospels that would later be part of the NT. Tatian was an Assyrian Christian who became a pupil of Justin Martyr in Rome. Justin read from the memoirs of the apostles each week in church, reading from a harmonized version of the Gospels. It is possible this is where Tatian got his material or perhaps just the idea to create the *Diatesseron* (in Greek διά τεσσάρων meaning "out of the four"). This project of synthesis was understandable, as probably many churches only had access to one or two Gospels, but not four.

Tatian created this volume in Syriac, the language closest to Jesus' Aramaic, but alas, we do not have the original text, only the one reconstructed by Theodore Zahn in 1881. Zahn, however, had a good source, namely the Arabic translation of the book from the twelfth century by Abu Faraj, who worked directly from the Syriac text, and there was a Latin text as well.

While the Greek phrase *dia tesseron* means "made of or created from four," and while Tatian seems to have followed the text of the four Gospels pretty closely, in order to fit it all together he created his own narrative sequence which differs from both the Synoptic and the Johannine sequences. Furthermore, on occasion he created intervening time periods found in no canonical Gospel. In other words, he was both synthesizing existing Biblical material while editing it down, and at the same time adding bits of his own narrative schema. In short, there was both subtraction and addition and synthesis in this process.

The helpful article on the Diatesseron in Wikipedia points out the following salient facts:

> [1] [Tatian's] sequence is coherent and consistent within itself, but not necessarily consistent with that in all or any of the separate canonical gospels; and Tatian apparently applies the same principle in respect of the narrative itself. Where the gospels differ from one another in respect of the details of an event or teaching, the Diatessaron resolves such apparent contradictions by selecting one or another alternative wording and adding consistent details from the other gospels; while omitting apparent duplicate matter, especially across the synoptics. Hence, in respect of the healing of the blind at Jericho the Diatessaron reports only one blind man, Bartimeaus, healed by Jesus when leaving the city according to the account in Mark 10:46ff (expanded with phrases from Luke 18:36–37); consequently omitting any separate mention of two unnamed blind men healed by Jesus leaving Jericho (Matthew 20:29ff), and also the healing by Jesus entering Jericho the previous day of a single unnamed blind man (Luke 18:35ff).
>
> [2] Tatian originally omitted altogether both of the different genealogies in Matthew and Luke, as well as Luke's introduction (Luke 1:1–4); and also did not originally include Jesus' encounter with the adulteress (John 7:53—8:11). The pericope is present in western manuscripts believed to be based on the Diatessaron (e.g., Codex Fuldensis) but is generally considered to be a latter interpolation. This whole passage is also generally considered to be a late addition to the Gospel of John, with the

Diatessaron itself often cited as an early textual witness in support of its omission.[1]

(3) About 72 percent of the four Gospels appear in the Diatesseron, with the omission of the genealogies, Luke's preface (Luke 1:1–4), and John 7:53—8:11 accounting for most of the missing fifty-six verses or 18 percent.

(4) Tatian may have included the long ending of Mark (Mark 16:9–20), and if so, may be the earliest witness to it.

So influential was this work that for a time, in many churches where Syriac was spoken, it became the lectionary text from the second to the fifth centuries AD. But eventually the larger wisdom of the church prevailed that we needed the four different portraits of Jesus, since he was a figure no one biography or portrait could do justice to. Nevertheless, a precedent had been set to produce what came to be called harmonies of the Gospels as a basis for translating the Gospel into new languages. Already in the late second century AD a Latin version of the Diatesseron had been produced and in due course harmonized with or modified by (would be a better way to put it) the Vulgate of Jerome.

The synthetic mentality was in play and would affect many aspects of early Christian theology, especially in regard to the Gospels, on the way to the production of the NT canon in the fourth century AD. While genuinely Systematic theology had not yet appeared in the second century, nor even full-blown Biblical theology (largely because the canon was still in process of being figured out) the *modus operandi* for such an enterprise as Biblical theology or Systematic theology had already gotten a trial run. And it is fair to say that as the church became more and more overwhelmingly Gentile in character, the sense of the Jewishness of not only the Gospels but the other books in the NT was fading, not least because of rising anti-Semitism in the church.

Once the synthetic way of reading the original NT manuscripts was in play, all sorts of problems arose. For example, there was a confusing or blending together of the various Marys—Mary Magdalene was seen to be the same person as Mary of Bethany, and then to top it all off, the same as the sinner woman mentioned in Luke 7:36–50. But no one reading straight through Luke's Gospel would have necessarily assumed that the anonymous sinner woman in Luke 7 was the same person as Mary Magdalene, who is only introduced for the first time by name in the list of women disciples in Luke 8:1–3. And her problem was not immorality, but rather demon possession, which is not the same thing. Or again, the synthetic mentality led to

---

1. Wikipedia, "Diatesseron," paras. 5–6. The quotation stops after (2). I've summarized the rest in (3) and (4).

the blending together of the various Christ-following Johns, such that John son of Zebedee was assumed to be the same person as John of Patmos of Revelation fame, and even the same as "the elder" in 2–3 John, since those letters came to be attributed to someone named John.

The problem is that the Greek of the book of Revelation is worlds apart from the Greek grammar, syntax, and even vocabulary of the Fourth Gospel or 1 John. On top of all this, it was further assumed that John son of Zebedee must be the Beloved Disciple, but as the Synoptics make clear, none of the Twelve were present and observing the crucifixion at the foot of the cross. And in fact, *none* of the special Zebedee stories from the Synoptics recur in the Fourth Gospel, and the term *Zebedee* is not even mentioned until the appendix in John 21 in that Gospel.

Papias, the church father who lived at the end of the first century and into the second century, says he only met John the elder, not the earlier John, and the same was likely the case with Polycarp of Smyrna as well. This being the case, Irenaeus, who was a student of Polycarp, was unlikely to have learned from Polycarp that the John in question on the label of the Fourth Gospel was the Galilean fisherman. But Irenaeus had some urgency to attribute it to one of the Twelve. He wanted to snatch it out of the hands of the Gnostics whose ideas about knowledge and salvation were remote from the original Jewish apostolic teaching. He wanted to claim it must have been one of the original twelve apostles who witnessed most of Jesus' earthly ministry. The synthetic mentality was to lead to all sorts of misinterpretations of early Christian history and its major players.[2] This approach could have been avoided if early Jewish followers of Jesus had actual last names like we do today.

But it was not just persons who got merged with other persons (Mary of Bethany=Mary Magdalene=the sinner woman of Luke 7); there were also rituals that got synthesized with other rituals, for example the merger of the Last Supper accounts in the Synoptics with the account found in John 13. In the first place, John 13:1 begins by stating directly that the meal about to be described in what follows took place "before [Πρὸ] the feast of the Passover," not on the eve of the Passover or during the Passover celebration, but before it. In other words, like the meal in John 12, this meal in John 13 where Jesus reclined with the Beloved Disciple (probably in the Beloved Disciple's house like the meal in John 12) took place earlier in the week than the Last Supper. This immediately explains two conundrums: (1) namely, Why is there no mention of "this is my body broken for you" or "this is my blood

---

2. On all of this and more see my *What Have They Done with Jesus?*, and the two chapters on the Beloved Disciple.

of the new covenant shed for you" *anywhere* in John 13? Answer: Because this meal is not the Johannine portrayal of the Last Supper; it's a meal that transpired earlier in the week at which the Beloved Disciple, who is not one of the Twelve, was not only present but was the host (noting the custom of the chief guest reclining on the couch with the host). (2) Why do none of the Synoptic accounts of the Last Supper include the foot washing episode? Answer: Because it didn't happen at the meal on Thursday night; it happened at a meal earlier in the week and in a different location with a different host. This will come as something of a shock to denominational groups like the Church of the Brethren who almost always have foot washing done in the context of the sharing in the Lord's Supper in the context of a regular meal, having blended those two textual traditions together.

But lest we think that the synthetic mentality is a thing of the past, consider the following paragraph. Harold Lindsell once wrote a famous book entitled *The Battle for the Bible*. It was a big deal in the 1970s. In it he approached various historical questions like a modern historian would. He assumed that the Gospel accounts of Peter's denials of Christ must conform to modern notions of precision. He struggled to figure out the precise relationship between the denials by Peter, and when and where and how often the cock crowed. Wrestle mightily he did, and finally he came to the conclusion that Peter must have denied Christ six times, in order for him to fit the four different Gospel accounts together!

Now this is remarkable indeed since absolutely none of the canonical Gospels suggest that Peter denied Christ any more or less than three times. This sort of false harmonizing of the texts does a disservice to the texts themselves and reflects a frantic and futile effort to explain away the differences between the accounts. Apparently, it never occurred to Lindsell that perhaps the authors were simply giving a *generalized* account of this event and wanted the reader to know that Peter denied Christ three times, and that a cock crowed at some juncture in relationship to the event. It seems never to have dawned on Lindsell that he was imposing a modern standard of precision with which those Gospel writers were not operating. And so, he became guilty of a major interpretive mistake—anachronism.

I was having a dialogue with some colleagues in the Society of Biblical Literature some years back at the Johannine seminar and also at the Evangelical Theological Society, and we were discussing Jesus' cleansing of the temple. One of the scholars on the panel insisted that Jesus cleansed the temple twice, once near the beginning of His ministry and once at the end. And yet NO Gospel has Jesus cleansing the temple twice; they all agree he only did it *once*, and all three Synoptics say this event occurred during the last week of Jesus' earthly ministry, not sometime early on. The synthetic mentality of Tatian is still alive and well.

I went on to point out the historical improbability of Jesus doing it twice. If Jesus had done this at the beginning of His ministry, he would likely never have been allowed into the temple again, to teach or perform other prophetic sign acts, by the Jewish officials. And yet we know he made various visits to the temple during His ministry and taught in the porticos there. The placement of the temple cleansing in John is *theological, not chronological*. It comports with the development of the theme of Jesus replacing or fulfilling the institutions of Judaism in himself—he is the lamb of God, he is the temple or tabernacle (the locus of the living presence of God on earth), he is the heavenly high priest of believers, as Hebrews was later to stress.

Ancient writers of biographies were perfectly happy with less chronological precision than modern historians are, so long as they got the content right, and what we must not do is read the ancient documents in an anachronistic way imposing our own standards on ancient texts. Rather we should seek to learn what standards they wrote by, whether for ancient biographies or historical monographs, and then evaluate them on the basis of their own criteria of precision.

Keeping these missteps in mind we must consider several major attempts at Biblical or Systematic theology[3] that unfortunately do not escape the sin of anachronism or the sin of abstracting ideas from the writers' narrative thought worlds, and then synthesizing the results, imposing a later and rather different theological grid on the Biblical text, and then telling us that it is actually what the Bible teaches us. This problem did not begin with Protestantism, so we will first look briefly at some of the problems with developing Catholic theology from a Biblical point of view.

## Catholic but Not catholic

Perhaps you are familiar with the phrase "hail Mary full of grace the Lord is with you," an English translation of the Latin "*Ave Maria gratia plena, Dominus tecum*." This became a prayer in the Western church which in itself implicitly authorized praying to Mary, in addition to God. Needless to say, this was not a Jewish practice, and did not come from Jewish culture, but few even today realize that this is a *mistranslation* of the Greek text of Luke 1:26–28, which actually reads: "Greetings, you who are highly favored. The Lord is with you." There is nothing in this sentence that suggests Mary was

---

3. Which, as I've already mentioned, are in various cases actually systematized Biblical theologies, not Systematic theologies.

"full of grace" or later a dispenser of grace. It is a statement by an angel that God was highly favoring her, because she was soon to become the mother of the Jewish messiah. God was blessing her and was with her. That is all.

It is certainly also possible to focus on some of the "extra-Biblical" ideas that, especially in the West and in Latin, were added to the Biblical discussion, for instance in regard to the developing ideas about Mary. This train had already left the station in the late second century with works like the Protoevangelium of James, the Gospel of Peter, and the Infancy Gospel of Thomas, which advocated or assumed the perpetual virginity of Mary, but neither Irenaeus nor Justin Martyr, who certainly affirmed the virginal conception of Jesus, say anything about her perpetual virginity.

What this whole notion of perpetual virginity reflects is the rising tide of asceticism that swept over the Western and Eastern churches, *a very un-Jewish and un-Biblical idea indeed.* Early Judaism, like the Hebrews of old, not only embraced the OT commandment to "be fruitful and multiply," but they also had a healthy and positive view of human sexual activity in the context of a heterosexual monogamous marriage. They did not see sex as inherently "dirty" or defiling. To the contrary, they saw it as a gift from God, and did not affirm the theological notion that abstinence from sex inherently made one a more holy person, or was a key to pursuing holiness in one's life.[4] It is not an accident that it was Clement of Alexandria (150–215), already influenced by the rising tide of asceticism in the overwhelmingly Gentile church in Egypt, who was an early supporter of the notion of Mary's perpetual virginity.

This whole approach to Mary as a young Jewish woman not only goes against the historical and religious ethos and ethical values in which she was raised, but goes *against* the evidence of the Biblical text itself. For instance, Matt 1:25 indicates that while Joseph abstained from having sex with his wife during the period of her pregnancy with Jesus, thereafter he took up normal conjugal relationships with her. The Greek text is properly translated in the NIV: "He did not consummate their marriage until she gave birth to a son."

As the text goes on to indicate, thereafter they had more children, six in fact, and they are simply called the brothers and sisters of Jesus (see, e.g., Mark 3 and 6 and par.). They are never called cousins or step-brothers and step-sisters of Jesus, even though there were Greek words for such ideas (e.g., *anepsios* means cousin). Those ideas arise later in the speculations of Jerome and Epiphanius when the notion of holiness=asceticism had taken a

---

4. On other later Wesleyan ideas about holiness, see the critique in chapter 7 below of a recent attempt at a Systematic approach to what the Bible says about holiness of heart and life.

firm grip on the Western church, and some other explanation needed to be dreamed up to explain the other children in Jesus' birth family.

Mary did not need to remain a virgin to be a holy person and a good mother to Jesus, and Joseph did not need to be an old man who had children by a previous marriage which he brought into his relationship with Mary when he remarried after the death of his first wife. This is a tale that no canonical Gospel tells us or even remotely suggests.

But this is not the end of the problem with Marian doctrine. There was also the rise of the use of the term *theotokos* applied to Mary, which literally means the "God-bearer" and was loosely translated as mother of God. This idea arose in the Eastern church, and was taken up in the Latin-speaking church as well. But there was a recognition that the word was problematic. If the Son of God pre-existed in heaven, it was not God that was being born but rather the incarnate Jesus, by which I mean that the Son of God took on flesh in Mary's womb. He was *already* God the Son. She was not mother of His divine identity.

Were this not enough, there then developed the idea of the immaculate conception and sinlessness of Mary, and in some traditions the notion of the bodily assumption of Mary. None of this is found in or suggested by the NT or earliest Christian theology. Unfortunately, in November of 1950 the pope made an *ex cathedra* pronouncement that the notion of the bodily assumption of Mary is a necessary Catholic dogma that all Catholics must embrace. Before that, Mary's immaculate conception was declared dogma by the pope in 1854, but that was before the 1879 pronouncement that the pope was "infallible" in such *ex cathedra* statements.

As C. F. D Moule said, after not being best pleased with the Report of the Anglican–Roman Catholic International Commission,

> Mary, divinely chosen for the unimaginably high destiny and initially heroic and devoted in the extreme, appears seldom after that, and then not conspicuously to her credit. Where, then, in all this, is there so much as a breath of adoration of the Virgin or of assumption into heaven? By all means, let us imagine her tenderly cherishing the precious child. Let us glory in her initial obedience to the stupendous divine mandate and promise. . . . Yet in spite of all this, and in spite of Mary's devout cherishing in her heart of all this witness and prediction (Luke 2:19, 51), the next event reported by St. Luke finds Mary rebuking her 12-year-old son for staying behind in Jerusalem, after the Galilean party, having celebrated Passover, had started back. But it is he who has the last word, with his own gentle rebuke of her. Worse is to follow. Mary is found, with the rest of the family,

trying, unsuccessfully to rescue Jesus from the preaching and healing vocation he has just embarked upon . . . . According to Mark 3:21 some at least of the family even said he was out of his mind, though in this verse his mother is not [directly] mentioned.[5] [So] let us honour and celebrate the divine gift of motherhood. But the Universal Mother, a goddess, a consort for a supposedly male God, one whom one worships, one to whom one offers prayer—for this there is no warrant. Steps in that direction, however discreetly described must surely be resisted. We are told little in the New Testament about the mother of the Lord. Let us rejoice in the glory of her initial stupendous commitment, but not invent what is not evidenced.[6]

The other most prominent area of Catholic theology that has no basis in the NT is the notion that the elements in the Lord's Supper, through the proper ritual of the sacrifice of the Mass, are transformed from bread and wine into the actual body and blood of Christ by a process called transubstantiation. This idea became part of Catholic doctrine in the twelfth century at the fourth Lateran Council and was heavily challenged thereafter, for instance by John Wycliffe, who was himself a Catholic priest.

The idea was meant to guard the notion that one encounters the "real presence" of Christ in the Eucharist while the material bread and wine do not *appear* to have changed. What happened in later Protestant reflections on this is that the idea of the transformation of the bread and wine was not affirmed, but the idea of the real spiritual presence of Christ with the Lord's Supper was affirmed, for instance in the high Lutheran and Anglican traditions.[7]

None of this is based in the careful exegesis of the Greek NT, but reflects later notions that in various ways are read back into the NT anachronistically. For example, a moment's reflection on the Last Supper Gospel accounts reveals not only that Jesus does not say "this becomes my body" or "this becomes my blood," but that, had the disciples understood Jesus to mean that, they would have objected to such an idea, for it sounded like cannibalism, and in any case early Jews did not believe in human sacrifice

---

5. Since Mary is leading her children to go and collect Jesus and take him home, it is perfectly reasonable to assume that Mark 3:21's assessment of Jesus was Mary's as well as perhaps some of the siblings. Much depends on who one thinks the "they" are in the "they were saying" sentence.

6. Moule, *Christ Alive and at Large*, 133–34.

7. Luther seems to have affirmed a notion called consubstantion, namely that the actual body and blood were attached to or accessed by the real bread and wine.

to make atonement for sin.[8] And in fact, in the original Aramaic there would have been no verb to explain what was happening; it would have just been "This my body." "This my blood." Furthermore, all this happened *before* Christ goes to the cross! Jesus is reinterpreting two of the elements of the Passover meal to explain in advance the benefits the disciples will receive from Christ's death, namely new life in Christ. The idea of Christ's spiritual presence with the Lord's Supper is not problematic since Christ said he would be spiritually with His disciples to the end of the age, but the twelfth-century Catholic doctrine is not based in the NT. Notice that in Paul's discussion of the Lord's Supper in 1 Cor 11:27–32 he suggests that there is a sacramental presence of Christ involved in the Lord's Supper elements, and partaking of them in an unworthy manner commits a sacrilege and can have drastic consequences.

As Thomas Oden stresses,

> Among Marian teachings of ancient and modern Roman Catholicism with which other believers have less difficulty are the following: Mary is held as an example to the faithful rather for the way in which in her own particular life, she fully and responsibly accepted the will of God (Luke 1:38) because she received the word of God and acted on it; "because charity and a spirit of service were the driving force of her actions, because she was the first and the most perfect of Christ's disciples. All of this has a permanent and universal exemplary value" (Paul VI) . . . Mary is understood "not merely as a passive instrument in the hands of God, but as freely-cooperating in the salvation of humankind by her faith and obedience" (*Lumen Gentium*, 56).[9]

But was she really the most perfect of Jesus' disciples?

The story in Mark 3:21–35 gives us a reason to challenge the notion of the sinlessness of Mary. She apparently misjudges Jesus, thinks he is "*ekstasis*," that is, out of His mind dabbling with demons, and she and the children come to take Jesus home. And make no mistake Mary is leading this expedition to take Jesus home. Jesus rebukes His physical family when they come

---

8. See, e.g., John 6:51, but very clearly there Jesus is speaking metaphorically of himself as "the bread of life" that came down from heaven, and is mistaken by some in the audience to be speaking literally, which even some disciples quite rightly find repugnant, as they would have done at the Last Supper as well if they had understood "this is my body" literally. The Maccabean stories about warriors giving their lives in battle for their fellow Jews as somehow an atonement for sins is by no means the same idea as the sacrificial offering of a human in an act of worship as an atoning sacrifice (cf. 4 Macc 17:21–22).

9. Oden, *Classic Christianity*, 297.

to get Him, saying, "Then he looked at those seated in a circle around him and said, 'Here are my mother and my brothers! Whoever does God's will is my brother and sister and mother.'" So, the physical family fails in their objective and mission on this occasion, and it is seen to be, according to Jesus himself, against the will of God in this matter, which is the very definition of sin. For Jesus, His primary family is the family of faith by which is meant whoever does the will of God.

Lastly, there is the whole hermeneutical problem with both the Catholic and Orthodox tradition in the following regards: (1) it is quite clear that the NT teaching on "clergy" is ignored. The only priesthoods in the NT are the heavenly high priesthood of Christ in Hebrews, and the priesthood of all believers, not just or even especially the clergy; (2) when it comes to ministers, they are bishops or overseers, elders, deacons, pastors, evangelists in the local churches, and apostles and prophets (and later monarchial bishops) as external authorities providing external accountability to the local churches. What they are not is priests in any special sense that makes them different from other believers.

In other words, there is a hierarchy of leadership in and for the local congregations, but it does not involve priests. Why not? Because priests are those who offer sacrifices to God, as is perfectly clear from ANE, Greco-Roman, and OT religion. But Christians have no need of any such sacrifices since Christ's death has atoned for all sins, past, present, and future, and the only sacrifice all Christians are called to is to present themselves and their service to God as living sacrifices (Rom 12).

The Lord's Supper is a memorial and a way to encounter the living Christ and repent once more of one's sins. It is not a re-enactment of the death of Jesus, nor is the Lord's Supper exactly the same as the Last Supper, as the Lord's Supper is not merely a modified Passover meal.[10] It is, however, a means of grace, through encounter with Christ. There is no transformation of the elements of bread and wine required for the latter. Precisely because ministers are *not* priests distinguished from the priesthood of all believers, there is no reason women cannot be deacons, elders, bishops, or any kind of functioning clergy. There is also no reason ministers can't be married, as the Orthodox tradition has rightly affirmed.

*What happened even before Constantine (but the trend accelerated thereafter) was an OT and patriarchal hermeneutic overwhelmed the new things that were happening in the ministry of Jesus and Paul and their co-workers and their teachings in the first century, and that hermeneutic turned*

---

10. See my little book *Making a Meal of It*.

the Twelve and their successors into priests[11], the Lord's Supper into a sacrifice, the Lord's Day into a Sabbath, and sacrificial giving into tithing. Finally, once Constantine declared Christianity a legal and licit religion, there came the building of public church buildings (by the mother of Constantine in the fourth century in Sille in Turkey, and in Jerusalem and Bethlehem) modeled on pagan Roman basilicas, and some ideas from OT temples. The Byzantines continued all of this, and Christianity in both the East and the West was well on the way to what we see in the medieval church.

This is both sad and ironic because the patriarchal nature of ministry had been left behind when Jesus recruited both women and men to be His disciples, and women were last at the cross, first at the tomb, first to see the angelic messengers, first to see the risen Jesus, first to testify to the resurrection proclaiming "he is risen,"[12] and we probably find them awaiting the coming of the Spirit with the male disciples. Jesus' mother, having been integrated into the family of faith at the cross, when Jesus handed her over to the Beloved Disciple, stays in Jerusalem, praying with the others (Acts 1:14).

The OT approach to worship was left behind when Jesus said what he did in John 4 about worship not being based in some sacred space, on a holy mountain in a sacred building, but whenever and wherever worship was offered in Spirit and in truth, and then the implications of His death made unnecessary a continuation of priests, temples, and literal sacrifices, or even a re-enactment of Christ's once for all sacrifice for all sins and all people on the cross.

Sunday is the Lord's Day (not least because it is the day of resurrection), as we hear in Rev 1:10, not the Sabbath, and there is a specific warning from Paul in Colossians not to get caught up in observing new moons and Sabbaths, both of which are Jewish rituals. In fact, in Rom 14 Paul suggest each should be persuaded in their own minds as to whether every day is the Lord's Day, or that one should observe one day unto the Lord.

The NT teaching on giving does not affirm tithing but rather sacrificial giving, which could be much more than a tenth or, in the case of an impoverished person, less than that. The example of the widow who gave all her coins (i.e., her liquid assets, Mark 12:41–44 and par.) is set forth by Jesus to His disciples as an example of the kind of sacrifice Jesus has in mind. What is a sacrifice for one person may just be a tax write off for another. Each person must prayerfully decide what is a sacrifice for them.[13]

11. Even though the Twelve, not even Peter, are never called priests in the NT.

12. Abelard and also Bernard of Clairvaux once called Mary Magdalene an apostle to the apostles, as did Augustine and later Aquinas using the phrase *apostolorum apostola*. See Wikipedia, "Mary Magdalene."

13. See my book *Jesus and Money*.

In all these cases where things have gone wrong, an OT hermeneutic has been allowed to override the new picture of ministry and sacraments that we are actually presented with in the NT, and it is a problem, both in terms of leadership structures, who can be clergy, the theology of the sacraments, the theology of giving, and much more. These problems existed and still exist in both the Catholic and Orthodox traditions.[14]

Some of these same problems exist in Protestant churches that think the patriarchal model for the physical family is Biblical, and that it rules out women in ministry, confusing the fact that while gender does determine a few roles in the physical family, like bearing children, what determines church roles in the NT age of the Spirit is who is called and who is gifted to do this or that sort of ministry. It has nothing to do with gender, not least because in Christ and His body "there is no male and female" (Gal 3:28).

The Orthodox tradition presents fewer problems than the Catholic tradition because there isn't a celibacy requirement for clergy, and because their theology of the Lord's Supper differs from Catholicism in some respects. What is also interesting about the various Orthodox traditions is that when they do Biblical or Systematic theology, their theology of sanctification is closer to the Wesleyan/Arminian theology of sanctification, nor do they tend to follow the Augustinian or Calvinist tradition in various ways.

The Catholic tradition involves both Augustinians and Thomists, and some of the latter are much closer to Arminians in their theology of salvation by grace through faith in Christ. Indeed, there has even been a joint affirmation of justification by grace through faith by Lutherans and Catholics.[15]

The problems we see in various of these traditions is not merely the *synthetic* tendencies already mentioned, but also the freedom to turn later non-Biblical ideas into doctrines and even dogmas, even when, in some cases, there are scriptural texts that *contradict* such ideas. But it would be well if we turn to Protestant examples that present other kinds of problems when Biblical or Systematic theology is attempted.

---

14. The attempt to use Jesus' discussion with Pharisees who even tithe their condiments as a basis for Christians tithing does not work. Matthew 23:23 reads, "Woe to you, teachers of the law and Pharisees, you hypocrites! You give a tenth of your spices—mint, dill and cumin. But you have neglected the more important matters of the law—justice, mercy and faithfulness. You should have practiced the latter, without neglecting the former." This is Jesus engaged in a discussion with fellow Jews giving advice to Pharisees as to what they should do. This is not advice Jesus gives to his own disciples.

15. This happened on October 31, 1999, and was signed by the Lutheran World Federation and the Catholic Church. Notably, this meeting and signing took place in Augsburg, a place of great importance to the Lutherans.

I have already at length shown in my earlier book *The Problem with Evangelical Theology* that there are problems with Reformed, Wesleyan, Dispensational, and Pentecostal theology, *precisely at the points where they diverge from the ecumenical consensus of what the Bible actually teaches and try to assert something distinctive*. Think of, for instance, the Pentecostal making of speaking in tongues the litmus test of whether one has really been born again, or filled/baptized with the Spirit, or the Dispensational notion of the rapture of the saints into heaven.[16] *But the problems are taken to another whole level when attempt is made to turn these theologies into Biblical or Systematic theologies, and this is the case with some recent Reformed labeled Systematic theology as well as with some Wesleyan attempts.* We will now turn first to two Reformed attempts, one written more for laity, and another written for college and seminary students.

It is important to add at this juncture that it would take another whole book to deal with the problems generated by the modern discipline called canonical theology, which is not the same as Biblical or Systematic theology. In the first place, as Pannenberg and others have rightly emphasized, what gives authority to a document or an idea in a document is whether or not it is *true*, not whether or not it is in a collection of books called canonical. This is the point Clifton Black in the quotation at the outset of the second chapter above is making when he says, "That method's default setting on canonical documents is likewise misguided: a document's canonization makes no difference for either the Protestant theologian or historical investigator . . . none of its subject matter was born canonical."[17]

Secondly, the words and ideas in the NT books had meaning and authority for early Christians in the first through early fourth centuries, not because they were in a twenty-seven-book collection called the canon, but because they were the inspired Word of God, just as was believed about the OT (see 2 Tim 3:16 and cf. 1 Thess 2:13). The meaning in such texts was not determined by what books they were juxtaposed with in the canon formed in the fourth century but by what the original authors intended to say and meant in their original contexts. They, and their writings, were inspired to speak to God's people in particular historical contexts, and the original contexts mattered in regard to the meaning of those texts.

In short, the meaning was in the words of the text, not merely in the eye of the beholders, nor in the way certain canonical texts were juxtaposed with others. The hearers and readers of these inspired texts were not the meaning makers; they were the meaning discerners and receivers of what

---

16. Witherington, *Problem with Evangelical Theology*.
17. See the full quote from Clifton Black at the outset of the second chapter.

the inspired authors had written, and the same applies to the collectors of these documents who eventually formed the NT canon.

Furthermore, who wrote the documents mattered—were they original eyewitnesses and original preachers of the Word (Luke 1:1-4); were they apostles or coworkers of the original apostles? The writers of the NT and their immediate successors were clear enough that these were the criteria that mattered alongside of whether or not a document proclaimed the Good News, the apostolic truth about Jesus Christ. Yes, the texts could have a different significance and application to other people in other settings, and yes, the text could be used homiletically, as we see the OT being used in the NT, but that was not the primary sense and meaning of the text originally.

The church *recognized* the canon, by which I mean they recognized that these documents were inspired, were true, came from the original eyewitnesses and preachers of the Word, and the words already had authority for the church before they became part of a canonical collection. The church did not *give* the documents authority; rather the church *recognized* the divinely inspired authority these early documents (unlike later pseudepigrapha from the second and third centuries) had which came from God through the original inspired human authors. It is a theology of revelation and inspiration that we see at work in these texts producing the truth about so many things, something the inspired writers and church received from God. This inspiration and revelation gave the documents *inherent* authority, not the later recognition by the church that these were their inspired documents, though that became important as well the further the church got from the apostolic era. But this is a subject that deserves a fuller discussion in a later study. Here we must focus on Systematic theology, but first on systematized Biblical theologies that in fact are not Systematic theology by any normal definition of systematics.

Chapter Four

## *Semper Reformanda* or Systemic Problems

[The] truth [is] that in the church there is always much to reform.
—Jodocus van Lodenstein, *Beschouwinge van Zion* (Amsterdam, 1674–78)

Every theological tradition without exception narrows the full range of Scripture and the meaning of Jesus by overlaying a doctrinal schema not found in the Bible itself. Systematic theology typically uses some system or concept from *outside the Bible* to explain what's inside. Strange, when you stop to think about it—as though the Bible can't explain itself.
—Howard Snyder, *Consider the Lilies*

The notion that the church must always be reforming, as the Latin phrase cited above suggests, is somewhat at odds or at least in tension with the idea that the Reformed approach to the Biblical witness can be systematized and promulgated as official doctrine of that tradition, whether we think of the Westminster Confession of Faith or some other formulation of this theology. It is appropriate then that we examine a couple of quite popular attempts to do Systematic theology in this Reformed tradition and examine what the Biblical and theological weaknesses are of this approach.

## A Stroll Through Sproul

A very long time ago, in fact it was BC (by which I mean Before Cellphone), I was a student at Gordon-Conwell Seminary, and I took an apologetics class with a man whose first two initials were R. C.—R. C. Sproul. I also remember listening to many of his cassette tapes from his study center in Ligonier Valley. Much later R. C. took on the behemoth known as Systematic theology. The thing about R. C. is that he indeed had the gift of distilling complex ideas down to a level of discourse that most anyone could understand. And thus, his little *Introduction to Systematic Theology* is worth interacting with as we work through this study.

To begin with, this is what Sproul says about Systematic theology: "Attempts to force Scripture into a preconceived system of thought are similarly misguided, and the result has been an aversion to Systematic theology. However Systematic theology does not attempt to force Scripture into a philosophy or system, but instead it seeks to draw out the teachings of Scripture and understand them in an orderly, topical way."[1] If only this were true!

Sproul is right of course that previous attempts at Systematic theology have often involved Greek philosophy, including the influence of Greek philosophy on doctrinal statements like the Chalcedonian one. And still today the influence of Greek philosophy on systematic theology is evident. One only needs to spend a little time on the modern discussion of Karl Barth's voluminous dogmatics to realize that often the categories, the key terms, and much else besides come from Greek philosophy or a formulation of Greek ideas by the Latin Church Fathers.

Consider for a moment the second half of Sproul's definition—to arrange the teachings of Scripture in an orderly, *topical* way. This frankly sounds more like so many Biblical Theologies, for example that of C. H. H. Scobie.[2] Focus on the term *topical*. The Bible, however, is not a theological dictionary with a bunch of topics alphabetically listed. Nor do the many terms in the Bible have only one meaning throughout the canon. Indeed, many of these words have a considerable spectrum of meaning, with the particular meaning determined *by the context*.

Words don't have meaning in isolation. It is not true that "in the beginning was the dictionary." A dictionary is simply a study of how words are used in various contexts, and the context always matters.

As I was saying, the Bible is not a bunch of topics alphabetically listed. It is instead an epic, a narrative from creation to new creation, from Gen 1

---

1. Sproul, *Everyone's a Theologian*, 6.
2. Scobie, *Ways of Our God*.

to Rev 22. It focuses on the story of God's interaction with His people. Other people groups only come into the discussion as they interact with God's chosen people.[3]

The narrative thought world is the basis out of which theologizing and ethicizing happens. It is not a matter of abstracting ideas from the story and then trying to connect one idea to another. Theology is not just a matter of words or ideas about God. It is as well an exposition on what God has been and is *doing*—God's ongoing salvific actions. Unfortunately, as we will see later in this study the process of abstracting ideas from the Biblical text takes them out of their original contexts and links them together with other concepts or ideas, often in ways the Biblical narrative does not suggest or encourage.[4] Let me give you an example.

I was at a conference with Walter Brueggemann some time ago at Truett Seminary at Baylor, and we were discussing the Hebrew concept of *hesed*, which Walter was insisting meant "covenant love"—God's love for His chosen people. The problem is that the term crops up in Rahab's discussion with the Hebrew spies (Josh 2:12–14), and Rahab herself uses the term *hesed*, translated in the NIV as kindness (or more frequently loving kindness). There is no way a non-Hebrew prostitute was using that word with the meaning "covenant love." My point is that on the lips of Rahab, or later in the story of Ruth the Moabitess, the term *cannot* mean covenant love.

What has happened here is the importing of an idea from later Reformed theological readings of the Bible, particularly the OT, into the Biblical text itself. And one of the major tell-tale signs that this is a mistake can be seen when we look at the various occurrences of how the term *hesed* is translated in the LXX. It is consistently translated as *mercy*, *not* covenant love. And mercy is what God has on all His fallen creatures.

So, all too often we are dealing with a twofold problem—abstraction of ideas from their narrative context but also from their lexical context, and a reading into the terms of later theological ideas, sometimes philosophical ideas, sometimes ideas taken from dogmatic theology that comes from Reformed theology or Thomist theology or elsewhere. You get the picture.

Once again, the sin of anachronism rears its ugly head as later ideas are said to be what the Bible actually means. Going forward in this chapter, and despite what Sproul promised in his introduction to the *Introduction to Systematic Theology*, we will sample some of the discussion in several of his key chapters and we will begin to see that this discussion is by no means

---

3. See the helpful study of OT narrative in Richter's *Epic of Eden*, which also instructs on how to read in a narratival way.

4. See my *Biblical Theology*.

merely an exposition of Biblical texts and concepts, and it is a fair question as to whether the treatment explains or distorts the Biblical text.

The sad truth is that Sproul is much clearer and consistent in his dealing with the Biblical text on the basis of later Reformed interpretations of the Bible, interpretations that mostly didn't exist before Augustine cleared his throat and changed his theology later in life, and did not fully exist before Luther and Calvin re-did late Augustinianism. Such discussions are by no means the same as the discussions prompted by a contextual exegesis of the Biblical texts themselves.

## Covenant

In the course of Sproul's discussions of various covenants, he calls God's relationship with Adam and Eve a covenant, even though no such language occurs in Genesis or elsewhere in regard to Adam and Eve, and then he goes on to talk about the "covenant of redemption" as opposed to the covenant of works and the covenant of grace.[5] By the latter two he primarily means the Adamic covenant as opposed to the new covenant.

Already we are encountering major problems—as various NT scholars, and especially E. P. Sanders has pointed out, the Mosaic covenant also involves grace.[6] Indeed, it is based in the gracious rescue of the Hebrews from bondage in Egypt. And furthermore, the new covenant, both as expressed in Jer 31 and in the NT, involves law—the Law of Christ is what Paul calls it. So already we are dealing with terminology that does not fit the Biblical data.

But the idea that is way off the Biblical chart is the "covenant of redemption," a covenant that Sproul says God made with himself, or within the Trinity. He argues, "It is a covenantal agreement that was made in eternity past among the three persons of the Godhead. In the drama of redemption, we see the activity of Father, Son and Spirit and creation itself was a Trinitarian work. God the Father called the world into being, yet he brought

---

5. For one thing, covenant language comes out of the ANE lord–vassal treaty language, meant to establish a peaceful relationship between the lord and the vassal, and at least initially Adam and Eve were not in a hostile relationship with God before they sinned, any more than Christ as the second or last Adam needed some sort of covenant or treaty between himself and his Abba. Notably, it seems to be only in the case of Yahweh and his chosen people was there a God who did covenants with human beings in the ANE.

6. See the detailed discussion in Sanders's landmark work *Paul and Palestinian Judaism*, and see the further discussion in *Voices and Views on Paul*, a book I did jointly with my former doctoral student Jason Myers.

order out of the darkness, it was because the Spirit of God was hovering over the waters and bringing them into being (Gen. 1:2)."[7]

First of all, as most Biblical scholars would say, the reference to God's spirit in Genesis is not a reference to the third person of the Trinity.[8] It is a reference to the living creative presence of the one Christians call God the Father. Genesis does not articulate a doctrine of the Trinity; that's a later Christian reading into that text of something which is probably not there. The spirit of Yahweh is not the same thing as the Holy Spirit of NT fame.

What is happening in this kind of Christianized reading of the OT is a total ignoring of the progressive nature of God's revelation throughout the canon. Even in regard to Christ's involvement in the work of creation, this is nowhere clearly articulated before passages in the NT. The closest one gets is in the discussion of God's Wisdom in Prov 3 and 8, but those texts are talking about the mind and wisdom of God. The personification there doesn't become an actual person until Paul and the Fourth Evangelist tell us that that language was in fact a shadowy, or foreshadowing, way of talking about the pre-existent Son of God. One must let the OT be the OT instead of trying to read it not only in light of the NT, but in light of a sort of Systematic theology that runs roughshod over the original context of the Hebrew Scriptures.[9]

Sproul goes on to argue, "The Father initiated the plan of salvation, this means the Father is behind the eternal decrees of election."[10] One has every right to ask where this kind of soteriological language is in Scripture, and the answer is *nowhere*. Nor is it even consistent with the language we find in Scripture. Scripture doesn't paint a picture of God electing some to be saved before the foundation of the universe, nor does it anywhere talk about the "eternal decrees" about saving only the elect, as if it were written in stone, before there even were stones!

In the first place, the language of redemption is applied quite literally in the book of Exodus to God's rescue of His people from bondage in Egypt. And frankly this is not the same thing as the soteriological language in the NT which tells us that the Son of God came to provide spiritual liberation from the bondage of sin, in the first place for Israel (for the Good News is for the Jew first—Rom 1), and then also for Gentiles. And there is a further major confusion in this language.

---

7. Sproul, *Everyone's a Theologian*, 122.

8. Jenson and other Systematics scholars are wrong about this.

9. This should not be confused with the *modus operandi* of various NT writers who do look at all sorts of things in light of the Christ event.

10. Sproul, *Everyone's a Theologian*, 122.

Election is the language of choosing, and in the first place God chose the Hebrews to be His chosen people. It is a *corporate* concept, though it can also be used in Isaiah of an individual like Cyrus the Persian for some specific historical purpose. It's certainly not about Cyrus's personal salvation. In any case, election has to do with God's historical purposes as he seeks to get His will done on earth as it is in heaven. But in neither case is the election of a group which came to be called Israel, or of a pagan agent of deliverance called Cyrus, the same thing as salvation. One could be an Israelite, part of the corporate community of Israel, and not be saved. One could be called Yahweh's *mashiach* (Isa 45:1; cf. Isa 44:24, 28), the anointed one of God (that specific phrase only used of Cyrus in the OT), and not be saved.

In the NT, as Eph 1–2 indicates, election happens "in Christ," God's truly Chosen One who was indeed destined in advance to be the savior of the world. Election happened in Israel, but that did not determine the salvation of particular Israelites, and election in the NT happens in Christ—the Chosen One of God. But a minute's reflection about Christ will make clear that salvation is one thing and election is another—*Christ did not need to be saved, and yet he is the Elect One of God.*

Christians are only elect if and when they are saved by grace through faith in Christ. It is only when they are "in Christ" that they can be called among the elect. And the means of salvation is not by God's eternal decrees issued from before the foundation of the world. It is by grace through faith in Christ. The Son of God existed before the foundations of the world, and was there to be destined in advance to be the world's savior. We were not there before the foundation of the world to be destined one way or another. Christ is the pre-destined one, and we are only destined in Him to be conformed to His image through the full process of salvation which ends with conformity to Christ's image in the flesh by means of resurrection, as Rom 8:28–30 suggests.

There are further problems with the Calvinist theology of seeing covenants all over the place in the Bible. The writers of the NT only talk about three covenants—the covenant God made with Abraham, the covenant made with Moses, and the new covenant.[11] That's all. Furthermore, all of these covenants involved God's grace and also God's commandments. And there is more.

Paul tells us that the Mosaic covenant was *temporary*, and that the Abrahamic and Mosaic covenants were fulfilled or completed in Christ (cf. Gal 4 and Rom 10). In other words, there was not and is not just one

---

11. The covenant made with Noah after the flood (see Gen 9) is not even mentioned in the NT and really has little or no bearing on NT theology except perhaps in the sense that God promised not to destroy the earth again.

covenant being renewed again and again, with some fresh aspects, like a doughnut that already existed to which later was added a sugar glaze, or chocolate sprinkles.

The new covenant is not merely a renewal of older ones, though there is some overlap. And it needs to be borne in mind that as with ANE covenants, if the subordinate persons in the covenant agreement seriously violate the covenant, the covenant maker, in this case God, is under *no* obligation to keep His *conditional* promises. He can dissolve the relationship and, if he chooses, start over with a new agreement, a new covenant, and even presumably a new people. The conditional nature of covenants and the conditional promises within them should be evident from statements like the following:

Second Chronicles 7:14 says, "If my people who are called by my name humble themselves, and pray and seek my face and turn from their wicked ways, then I will hear from heaven and will forgive their sin and heal their land."

This verse is part of a speech God gives to Solomon at night after the temple's dedication. In it, God tells the king how the nation should respond if he sends drought, locusts, or pestilence. Notice the "if" at the beginning of the statement.

The new covenant is a genuinely new covenant, and there is only some theological and ethical overlap with the various iterations of the old covenant. And it is the only truly permanent covenant, inaugurated by Christ himself. The author of Hebrews even says that the Mosaic covenant is, or is becoming, obsolete (Heb 8:13). *And the covenant of redemption between the members of the Trinity which Sproul talks about is nowhere to be found in Scripture.*

As a Biblical scholar and a Biblical theologian one has to be extremely wary of the attempt to read into the Bible later theological systems that, rather than clarifying the Biblical data, distort it. This sort of approach puts the dog back in dogmatics. It is not surprising that Biblical scholars often have an allergic reaction to various sorts of Systematic theologies that do not do exegesis on the basis of the original context of a Biblical text, but rather on the basis of a system of interpretation that has abstracted ideas from their original historical context and inserted Biblical ideas into a preexisting theological or philosophical schema.

Sproul goes on to suggest that the covenant of works in the first place refers to the covenant God had with Adam and Eve. If they obeyed God, they would receive the gift of everlasting life. Strictly speaking, the story of Adam and Eve says nothing about a covenant God had with them, and the commandment given to them was to *avoid* doing something—eat of the tree of the knowledge of good and evil. It is hard to see how *avoidance* can be counted as a covenant of *doing works*, and in any case, Sproul admits that there was grace involved in God's relationship with Adam and Eve, as is true of all those relationships actually called covenants in the Bible. What the Adam and Eve story *does* suggest is that Adam and Eve had an intimacy with God that they lost by disobeying the one commandment God gave them. Nothing is said in this story about how avoiding eating from the tree of moral knowledge could be rewarded with allowing them to eat from the tree of life. To the contrary, God said from the outset they could eat of any trees except the one that was forbidden. Eating from the tree of life is not said to be some reward for obedience.

And perhaps more importantly the creation story does not suggest that Eve was brought into the world to be subordinate to Adam. That idea first shows up in the curse on Eve: "Your desire will be for your husband and he will lord it over you." To the contrary, Eve was created as "bone of my bone and flesh of my flesh" as Adam exclaimed. Eve was created as Adam's equal partner in life, and since she is the last thing God created, one could say she was the crown of all creation. The key term *kenegdo* simply means a suitable helper, and parallel terms like *ezer* are used of God as a helper of His creatures. No subordination or inferiority is implied in using a term like *kenegdo* to describe Eve. It simply means someone who corresponds to Adam and can be his partner, his counterpart.

Patriarchy, as it turns out, is when to love and to cherish degenerates into to desire and to dominate after Adam and Eve have sinned. In other words, it is what Christians call a result of Adam and Eve's Fall from grace. It is no accident that patriarchy and patriarchal genealogies only show up after the account of the Fall in Gen. 3.

What ensues immediately after that account is men behaving badly: Cain slays his brother Abel, and then we have the grizzly tale of Lamech vowing all sorts of revenge, and on and on the chaos goes. Jesus in Matt 18 makes clear that the antidote to all such revenge taking and chaos is forgiveness, and notice it is in the same proportions as Lamech swore to take revenge (cf. Gen 4:24 to Matt 18:22). The failure to read the Creation and Fall accounts properly often leads to the misreading of the Redemption accounts.

Christ did not come to reinstall patriarchy and male headship as the solution to the human dilemma. He came to create a people of God in which neither ethnic, nor racial, nor social, nor sexual identities determine who is what in Christ. As Paul puts it—in Christ there is neither Jew nor Gentile, slave nor free, and no male and female, for all are one (Gal 3:28). In the age of the Spirit-filled life, roles in the church, in the family of faith, are determined by who is called and gifted by God to do the task.[12]

## Sproul on Christology

It is part of the Calvinist system to argue that the life of obedience that Christ lived is part of what saved human beings.[13] It was not just Christ's death on the cross. Christ's life of obedience saved humankind—but from what? Saved them from having to obey God to stay in a state of grace or a right relationship with God? This notion, which again is not to be found in Scripture, provides the background for the idea that Christ's own righteousness must be imputed to the believer for them to be reckoned as righteous. But again, it is debatable whether one can find the imputed righteousness idea in the NT, as we shall see. Initial right standing with God comes from trusting God as Abraham did, as Paul emphasizes both in Gal 3 but also in Rom 4, with Abraham being the paradigm for the Christian.

This whole approach comes from the insistence on a radical reading of the term *sola gratia*—salvation is purely of grace, and not of works, lest anyone should boast. But in fact, since salvation is more than just justification, since salvation part two involves sanctification and we are called upon in Phil 2 to work out our salvation with fear and trembling, working out what God's Spirit has been working in, it is not at all clear that Christ's obedience during His earthly ministry is any sort of substitute for our obedience. And while an unblemished and sinless life of Christ is the presupposition for His death to be genuinely atoning for the sins of others, it is not the life of Jesus which atones, but rather only the death of Christ, because there is

---

12. Obviously, there are some roles in the physical family that are gender specific, like carrying a child or breastfeeding one, but these roles do not determine who can perform non-gender specific roles in the church. The problem with complementarian language is that it is right in regard to a few physical family realities, but wrong in regard to the implications of that reality for roles in the church. The concept of male headship is literally turned on its head by Christ himself, who makes clear that He came to be the head servant, not to follow the patriarchal role models of rulers who lord it over people, which again is a result of human sin. What we see in the household codes is the attempt to reform an existing fallen structure that *de facto* was already in place. Notice for example Eph 5:21–22 where Paul clearly teaches mutual submission of all Christians to one another, and then in v. 22 there is no verb, so one has to assume it from the previous verse, namely that the wife's submission to her husband is a form of mutual submission, just as the husband's loving self-sacrificial service to the wife is likewise a form of mutual submission.

13. Sproul, *Everyone's a Theologian*, 124.

no atonement and no remission of sin without the shedding of blood (Heb 9:22). Suffering or obedience alone does not provide atonement.

Not surprisingly, in his discussion of "the two natures of Christ" Sproul dodges the exegetical issues raised in Phil 2:5–11, and instead gives an exposition of the Chalcedonian formula about Christ's two natures. While the latter may be a place to end up when dealing with the implications of what the NT says, it is certainly not the place to start, not least because the NT says nothing about Jesus Christ having two natures—one divine and one human.[14]

In his recent discussion of this matter, Richard Bauckham has quite rightly suggested that perhaps a better way to talk about this issue, in Biblical terms, is by saying that the Son is an essential part of the divine identity. Bauckham insists that we need to see the discussion of these crucial matters not, in the first place, in light of Greek Church Fathers' discussions about two natures, but rather from a Jewish point of view. Bauckham helpfully puts it this way: "When we think in terms of divine identity, rather than of divine essence or nature, which are not the primary categories for Jewish theology we can see that the so-called divine functions which Jesus exercises are intrinsic to who God is. The Christology of divine identity is already a fully divine Christology, maintaining that Jesus Christ is intrinsic to the unique and eternal identity of God."[15]

The sort of "Systematic" theology we find scholars like R. C. Sproul or Wayne Grudem doing doesn't in fact adequately take into account the Jewish nature of the discussions about Jesus in the NT. Instead, it depends on Greek formulations and Greek philosophical distinctions. Interestingly, this is not what Cyril of Jerusalem was doing when he made the following distinction, speaking of Jesus: "He did not say I and the Father *am* One, but I and the Father *are* One, that we might neither separate them nor confuse the identities of Son and Father. They are one in the dignity of the Godhead, since God begot God" (*Catechism Lecture* 11 FC 61:226). Cyril is sticking to the Greek text of the NT itself, not importing later ideas into the discussion. And frankly, there is quite enough Christology in the NT to keep us on track, for instance in the Christological hymns.

Let's take a minute to examine the high Christological statement found in the form of a Christological hymn fragment in Phil 2:5–11. It begins with the clear assumption that Christ pre-existed in heaven before he became incarnate or took on human flesh. The Greek term *morphe* does not merely mean the outward appearance of someone or something; it refers to what

---

14. See pp. 130–34 below of Tom Morris's work on the two natures idea.
15. Bauckham, *Jesus and the God of Israel*, 185.

someone inherently is, by his very nature. So, the hymn begins, "being in very nature God, Christ did not take advantage of this, but rather emptied himself and took on the very nature of a human being." Paul does not mean nor did he believe that we are talking about the pre-existent Son of God exchanging His divinity for humanity. Rather, there is an additive process of taking on flesh and become a human being.[16]

But at the same time there is a *kenosis*, a stripping or emptying. I take this to mean that Christ chose to limit himself so He could be fully and truly human, not merely appearing to be human. In short, He took on the natural human limitations of time, space, knowledge, power, and mortality. These are indeed the normal limitations of human beings. Christ did not take on the limitation of sin or having a fallen human nature. The Good News is that sin, while characteristic of fallen human beings universally, is not an inherent or necessary quality of being truly human as God originally made the human race. He made them good, indeed very good.[17] Being human is one thing, but being fully human as God intended from the beginning we only see in Christ, for sinning is not a *necessary* quality of being genuinely human according to the divine design.

A note on Christ's obedience is in order. As Paul indicates in Phil 2:5–11, the focus of this obedience is not His life in general, but rather His acceptance in the garden of Gethsemane of the divine cup of God's judgment on sin,[18] and His willingness to be obedient even unto death on the cross. In other words, it is not Christ's general obedience to God during His life, but rather His obedience unto death on the cross that has to do with atonement for sin, making it possible for sinners to gain not only right standing with God, but in fact to be sanctified by the Holy Spirit, and have moral righteousness and holiness of heart and life.

Why is this way of reading Phil 2:5–11 so important? It's important because it comports with the Gospel portrayal of Jesus as living a genuine

---

16. It is worth stressing as well how that whole passage begins—"have this mind in yourself that was also in Christ Jesus who . . ." In other words, this profound theological Christ hymn in Paul's hands has an ethical function of telling the believer they are to think and behave like Christ is depicted in this passage—as a self-sacrificial person who obeyed God. Paul is quite clear that we should not radically separate theology from ethics, not least because belief and behavior go together; indeed, believing is a form of behavior.

17. Various of the Church Fathers asked the pertinent question—Is the virginal conception meant to be God's attempt to protect Jesus from inheriting a fallen nature from Joseph? This assumed that fallenness was seminally transmitted, from one person to another.

18. On the cup of God's wrath poured out because of sin, see Jer 25:15–16; Isa 51:17, 22; Ezek 23:28–34; Hab 2:16.

human life. As the author of Heb 4:14–15 says, He was tempted like us in every respect but without sinning.

When Jesus asks a question like "Who touched me?" in the episode of the woman with the issue of blood, He is actually asking for information. His life is not a charade and He is not merely pretending to be human. Divine condescension, or divine self-limitation, is the decision the pre-existent Son chose before taking on flesh.

In other words, while He remained the Son, a part of the divine identity, He put the omnis on hold—omniscience, omnipotence, omnipresence. He experienced the human limitations of time, space, knowledge, power, and mortality. Jesus performed His miracles by the power of the Holy Spirit, as He Himself says, which is why His disciples were later able to do the same sort of miracles. And above all, Jesus really died!

Only He was the Son of Man who was foretold in Dan 7:13–14, and since that figure is said to be worshiped and rule forever, it is clear He is not only human but also part of the divine identity. The latter is why He has authority to forgive sins, to change the rules of the Sabbath, and so much more. He is Adam gone right, starting the human race over again with Himself, and others becoming new creatures in Him, given a fresh start, as the old has passed away. As the sinless God-man He was able to provide the atonement for the sins of the world, the ransom for all (as 1 Tim 2:6 says).

All the actions of Jesus during His earthly ministry are predicated of Jesus the person, not this human nature or that divine nature. He is both part of the divine identity, indeed He was a part of that before He ever took on flesh and became Jesus of Nazareth, and He also became a genuinely human being who could even be killed.

The Chalcedonian formula came to the fore as result of Christian theologians not being able to figure out the relationship between the person with an ongoing divine identity and the person who became a human being. In the end, they concluded the two natures idea was the best solution the church could come up with. Of this solution, the NT says nothing. It might have been better if the early church had stopped after forming the Apostles' Creed and the Nicene Creed, for at least in the case of the relationship of the Son to the Father, the NT has quite a lot to say and the Nicene Creed amplifies what the NT actually says.

At the end of the Christology chapter, R. C. Sproul stresses that Christ is the theme of the OT as well as the NT. Really? In my *Biblical Theology* volume, I have shown at length the problem with over-reading NT ideas back into the OT, rather than letting the OT be the OT, and taking seriously the contextual exegesis of OT scholars. There was no incarnation of Christ in any form before the one described in the NT.

As the author of Hebrews says, Christ was of a higher order than the angels (see Heb 1), so He is not the angel of the Lord in the OT. Nor is He one of the three angelic visitors to Abraham in Genesis. While it is certainly true that the OT prepares for, prophesies about, and foreshadows the coming of a messianic figure, especially in Dan 7:13–14 and Isa 52–53, it has its own tale to tell about Israel as God's people and God's relationship with Israel. This OT story is preparatory for but not in the main about Christ just as the OT institutions such as temple, sacrifice, and priesthood prepare for Christ to come and fulfill their purpose, but they have a function in themselves for God's Hebrew people, so they are not merely preparatory for Christ.

It is not an accident that writers like the author of Hebrews portray Melchizedek not as an appearance of Christ in the OT but rather as a prototype of Christ, a historical foreshadowing. Typology, however, is one thing; identification is another. Persons or things that are types of persons or things that will show up later in salvation history are never identical with the person or thing that comes later. They are simply previews of coming attractions. In other words, typology honors the notion of there being a before and after to history and in narratives about salvation history.

In the following chapter about "One Person, Two Natures" Sproul argues that Jesus had both a human mind and a divine mind, mirroring the idea of two natures in Christ. He wants to suggest that there were things the human mind did not know, that His divine mind did know. But was Jesus really a person with two minds and two natures? The NT does not say so, and frankly this makes Christ sound bipolar if not schizophrenic (cf. what James says about being double-minded in Jas 4:8; cf. 1:8—δίψυχοι, which is hardly a compliment). Consider what Cyril of Alexandria (412–44) said in critiquing the Nestorians: "If anyone distributes between two characters or persons the expressions used about Christ in the Gospels . . . applying some to the man, conceived of separately apart from the Word . . . others exclusively to the Word . . . let him be anathema."[19]

This sort of idea is not really helpful to understanding the NT. Much better is the idea of self-limitation by the Son of God before His incarnation, the Son who is a part of the divine identity from before the foundation of the universe.[20] The *kenosis* (self-emptying or self-limiting) mentioned in

---

19. Bettenson, *Documents of the Christian Church*, 46.

20. If one is looking for a philosophical discussion of these matters, see the excellent book *The Logic of God Incarnate*, by Thomas V. Morris, my old classmate at UNC in the early 70s. The book is now available in reprint by Wipf and Stock. Morris uses the idea of Christ having access to all knowledge like a computer having access to material in an extra hard drive, or in the cloud. But Christ did not draw on it. But then Morris succumbs to the two minds idea about Christ. See pp. 130–34 below.

Phil 2:5–11 must be taken seriously. The Son did not cease to be part of the divine identity when He took on flesh and became a human being called Jesus, but at the same time, He accepted the normal limitations of what it meant to be human. The reason Paul and others can urge their disciples to be imitators of Christ is because it is possible to do so in a limited, non-salvific way, since Jesus was "truly human." It is His humanity that can be imitated, at least to some degree.

Jesus as a human being was really tempted by Satan, but He resisted temptation by quoting Scripture and relying on the power of the Spirit of God with which He had just been anointed at baptism. And part of the point of that story in Luke 4 and par. is that Christ's followers can also resist temptation by drawing on the Word and the Spirit (see 1 Cor 10—"no temptation has overcome you that is not common to humanity . . ."). Jesus did not take advantage of His divine identity in a way that would have obliterated His true humanity. He did not, for instance, say to Satan, "I'm God. God can't be tempted, ergo this encounter is not a real temptation. God is never inclined to sin."

Another way we see the divine self-limitation is in statements like we find of the twelve-year-old Jesus in Luke 2:41–52 where we hear He *grew in wisdom* and in stature. That is, Jesus learned things over time. He had access to all knowledge, just as He had access to all power, but He did not draw on these things during His earthly ministry lest He cease to be genuinely human, and cease to be an exemplar for His disciples to follow. We can also emphasize that Jesus performed His miracles by drawing on the power of the Holy Spirit within Him, which His disciples could also do later (Matt 12:28).

It is largely who Jesus reveals Himself to be, as the Son of Man, and as the unique Son of God (Matt 11:27), that makes clear He is a part of the divine identity, and by His ability to forgive sins or declare all foods clean, and also by His being the one human being who could be the mediator between God and humankind and take the place of humanity in enduring the punishment for human sin on the cross, and thereby provide a ransom and redemption for those who embraced Him later, by grace through faith.

Notice that Jesus speaks on His own authority, and He never speaks merely as a prophet, never using the formula "thus says Yahweh . . ." He does not quote God (except when He recites Scripture); rather He speaks as a person who is a part of the divine identity and can speak for Himself. He feels no *need* to quote other Jewish teachers or earlier non-scriptural traditions.[21]

---

21. It is interesting, however, that Christ does draw on ideas from Sirach and Wisdom of Solomon in his self-presentation. See my discussion of this in *Jesus the Sage*.

As Paul would later indicate in Rom 5 and 1 Cor 15, Christ is the last Adam, Adam gone right, starting the human race over again and making possible reconciliation between God and humankind. Jesus did not come to *be Israel*, but rather to *free* the lost sheep of Israel, as well as the nations. Yes, Jesus fulfills the mission of Israel to be a light to the nations, but as both Jesus and Paul make clear, the church is not Israel, and God is not reneging on His promises to Israel. They are still part of God's future plans (see especially Rom 9–11).

More helpful, and more focused on actual Biblical statements and concepts, are Sproul's three chapters on the death of Christ and its meaning and significance. Referring to John 19:30, Sproul points out the Greek term translated as "it is finished" is in fact often used as a commercial term meaning paid in full.[22] The question is whether it means that in this text, or whether it has the simpler sense that something has been completed. The idea of payment seems clear in 1 Cor 6:19–20—"you've been bought with a price." The idea is we have been bought out of bondage, slavery to sin presumably. Sproul is right that there is no hint in Scripture of a ransom paid to Satan, not least because God owes Satan nothing. But who is the ransom paid to? As Sproul suggests, it is paid by the Son to the Father.

Sproul is also right that there are various strands to atonement theology, and no one theory encompasses them all. For instance, the *Christus victor* theory stresses Christ's triumph over the powers and principalities on the cross, an idea which may be present in Eph 4:7, or 1 Pet 3. But does Colossians actually suggest that by His death Christ has pacified the powers? Possibly Col 1:20 could be read that way, in tandem with the earlier mention of Christ being ruler over all of creation (1:16). Ephesians 6:10–20 suggests, however, that Satan and his minions are still alive and well, and at work attacking Christians, so whatever Col 1 may suggest, it does not mean that the principalities and powers are out of business. One of the problems we have is that there never was an ecumenical council to hammer out a doctrine of atonement, and so various theories have flourished throughout church history as a result. I like O. Cullmann's suggestion that we see the cross as D-Day in the battle with evil and the powers of darkness, the turning point in the war against the powers and principalities, but VE Day does not arrive before the return of Christ.[23]

Ever since the time of Anselm the satisfaction theory has been prominent and in modern times under heavy attack. The idea that God's wrath has to be propitiated if God is going to be reconciled to sinful humanity has

---

22. Sproul, *Everyone's a Theologian*, 155.
23. See Cullmann, *Christ and Time*.

been objected to, sometimes vehemently. This is partly based on the false notion, in an extreme caricature, that the God of wrath and judgment is just found in the OT, whereas the NT is all about a God of grace and forgiveness.

This is pretty much what Marcion tried to assert in the second century AD and was rightly condemned for it. In fact, we find the judgment of God, including the final judgment of God, both in the OT and the NT, and God's righteous wrath against sin is a proper expression of the holiness of God in both Testaments. As I have shown at some length in my *Biblical Theology*, the idea of God needing propitiation is found in both Romans and 1 John, and it is suggested strongly in Revelation as well. God's holiness, including His holy love, cannot be set aside. It is inherent to who God is. Nor does God change His mind about fundamental things.[24]

The character of God does not change from the OT to the NT. As Paul clearly says, God could not pass over sin forever. A just God had to deal with it at some point. God accepts the death of His righteous Son as the substitute payment for the sins of the world, and note that it was the Father who sent His Son into the world to provide such an atonement. God is both righteous and the one who sets the sinner back into right relationship with Himself.

As far as the substitutionary aspect of Christ's death, this seems clear enough from Mark 10:45—the Son of Man came to serve and provide a ransom *in the place of the many*. The contrast here is between the one who provides the ransom and the many who benefit from it. The contrast here is not between the "many" and "all humans." In other words, this saying is not about God limiting the scope of the atonement to the elect.

What is interesting about the atonement of Christ is that it combines two OT ideas—the idea of the sacrificial lamb who provides atonement and so forgiveness, and the idea of the scapegoat who takes away the guilt and punishment for the sinner. So, for example, in John 1, John's exclamation "behold the lamb of God who takes away the sin of the world" combines these ideas. In some ways, Hebrews best explains these mysteries (see Heb 10). It is well to keep in mind that it is not merely the fact that Jesus shed blood, and so atonement was accomplished. No, it was life poured out *in death* that amounts to the sacrifice that atones. The lamb had to die to pay for the sins of the offerer.

Sin is not a substance; it involves actions and attitudes. So, when we are talking about our sins were borne by Christ on the cross, what we mean is that the punishment for our sins was borne by Christ, just as the scapegoat bore the punishment, being sent off into the wilderness. Likewise, when we

---

24. See my detailed critique of the book by R. B. and C. Hays entitled *The Widening of God's Mercy* in appendix 1 below.

talk about being cleansed from sins, which classically has been called expiation (God is propitiated, the saved are expiated), we mean being cleansed from the guilt and other effects of sins. Hebrews 9:14 calls it the cleansing of the conscience (i.e., a cleansing from guilt).

What about the extent of the atonement? Did Christ die for the sins of the elect, or did He die for the sins of the world? Here, Sproul is clearly wrong in suggesting Christ just died for the ones God had already chosen to be saved. His interpretation of key texts requires exegetical gymnastics. For example, 1 John 2:2 says explicitly that Christ died for the sins of the whole world. Sproul takes this to mean that Christ died for people in all parts of the world.[25] This is not what the Greek text says. The world as a place is not who Christ died for. First John 2:2 is not about geography; it's about Christ dying for people. One could just as well translate this sentence as "Christ died for all the world's people."

What limits the atonement is not God's plan or desire, but rather who responds to the offer of salvation. Second Peter 3:9 is clear enough—"God does not desire that any should perish, but rather that all should come to repentance." First Timothy 2:6 is just as clear—Christ gave Himself as a ransom for *all persons*. God did not send His Son into the world to condemn the world, but rather to save the world. God's desire and intent is clear from these sayings, and they do not match up with the Reformed theology of election of only some unto salvation.

The epitome of a closed Systematic theological system is one which appears to be internally consistent but depends on the accuracy of ALL its major points; for example, consider this statement by Sproul:

> Holding to the L in TULIP is the litmus test of whether one really believes what the other letters represent. People say they believe in total depravity—the T—but they do not believe in limited atonement. They say they believe in unconditional election—the U—meaning that God has sovereignly chosen from all eternity those whom He will save merely out of his own good pleasure, but they do not hold to limited atonement. However, we cannot believe one and not the other. If we believe that election is unconditional and that it is grounded in God's sovereign mercy and grace from all eternity, then we must also see the purpose of the cross. The *value* of the cross extends universally, but God's *design* and *purpose* for the cross were to save only some of fallen humanity by satisfying the demands of his justice.

---

25. Sproul, *Everyone's a Theologian*, 168.

He determined to apply the work of his Son to the benefit of those he chose from the foundation of the world.[26]

What R. C. does not say is that if one of these major points is wrong, then the whole superstructure falls down like a house of cards. This is so because each major point fundamentally depends on the other ones also being true. If not, abandon hope.

Undergirding all this is a theology of how God's sovereignty is necessarily exercised, not to mention a theology which confuses election, a corporate concept, with salvation. But leaving that aside for a moment, of the five major points, limited atonement and perseverance of the saints are exegetically quite weak.

And the idea of grace always being irresistible violates the very nature of God as love, a God who desires that His creatures respond freely in love to Him. Real love cannot be predetermined. There may be moments when grace overwhelms a person, for instance at conversion or in a revival experience after conversion when the Spirit does a mighty work in the life of a believer. By and large, however, grace enables a person to freely respond to God again and again and again.

God in His wisdom has enabled His creatures, whether celestial or terrestrial, to have a measure of self-determined will. This is not the secular notion of free will, as if angels or human beings have that innately. Rather since human beings and some angels are fallen creatures, it is a grace enabled power of contrary choice. Salvation is by grace through faith, but faith has to be exercised by the person in question. Faith is a gift from God, indeed one of the gifts of the Spirit, but it does not work automatically and apart from the conscious choice of the individual involved.

Notice what Paul asks his new converts in Gal 3—"Did you receive the Spirit by the works of the law, or by believing what you heard?" *Believing* is an activity of a believer. It is not enough to have the gift of faith. One must freely exercise that gift. No one else can do it for you. Notice that Paul both in Gal 3 and in Rom 4 cites the example of Abraham who "trusted God and it was credited to him for righteousness." Whether we translate the verb believed or trusted, in either case we are talking about a chosen *activity* of the person in question. This is not some automatic or programmed response of a robot. But more needs to be said about God's grace in response to the errant ideas found in the TULIP theology.

---

26. Sproul, *Everyone's a Theologian*, 169.

## God's Grace—Common, Special, and Variegated

Certainly, the very best study on Paul's view on grace in recent years has been John Barclay's *Paul and the Gift*.[27] He has helped us see the various ways Paul has used the term *charis* and its cognates, and to distinguish the meanings in differing contexts. The most basic meaning of the word is "gift," and it was used regularly in patron–client relationships and other contexts. But in the NT in general and in Paul in particular it regularly refers to a gift from God.

Barclay very successfully dispels various modern myths about grace; for example, in Paul's context grace does not mean "giving with no thought of return" or anonymous giving. To the contrary, God's grace is meant to prompt and enable a human response and an ongoing relationship. Furthermore, while this grace is not given on the basis of merit or on the basis of something someone deserves, and so it is "incongruous" as Barclay puts it, this does not mean it was meant to be unilateral.

To the contrary, it was intended, as I said, to prompt a response, a relationship. Barclay in his final conclusions puts it this way: "[Paul] simultaneously emphasizes the incongruity of grace and the expectation that those who are 'under grace' (and wholly refashioned by it) will be reoriented in the 'obedience of faith.' What has seemed in the modern world a paradoxical phenomenon—that a 'free' gift can also be obliging—was entirely comprehensible in ancient terms."

He adds, "Although Christian theologians (and modern dictionaries) regard it as self-evident that 'grace' means a benefit to the unworthy, in ancient terms this was a striking and theologically dangerous construal of the concept." Normally, a gift was given to someone deemed worthy of receiving it, but with Paul, and when it came to salvation, this is not how Paul used the term. Here Paul is striking out in a direction that distinguished him from his Greco-Roman contemporaries.

Barclay is able to set up a taxonomy of grace where it is perfected in different ways in different contexts. "We identified six possible perfections of grace, which we labelled superabundance, singularity, priority, incongruity, efficacy, and non-circularity. Each of these configure gift in some maximal form, but none are necessary features of the concept, and, crucially, none requires or even implies another. They are distinguishable perfections and do not constitute a 'package deal.'" Barclay traces how various commentators along the way including Augustine, Luther, Calvin, and Wesley

---

27. All of what follows in these next few paragraphs of Barclay's views comes from *Paul and the Gift*, ch. 18, 562–74, used by kind permission of Eerdmans.

"perfected" the concept of grace in ways that Paul himself did not, and in some cases would not have agreed with.

Barclay is right that Paul has a Christological focus to his theology of grace, with Christ Himself being the big "gift" of God to humanity, a theology that changes the way he looks at the Mosaic covenant, as Gal 4 makes quite clear. It is fair to say that Christ has reconfigured the way that Paul looks at most things, including grace, the Law, salvation, and much more. Barclay puts it this way:

> The starting-point is the framing of the Christ-event as gift. Christ's death "for our sins" (e.g., 1 Cor 15:3–4) is interpreted by Paul in the language of gift (God's gift of His Son, or Christ's gift of Himself). The life, death, and resurrection of Jesus are thus, for Paul, the focal point of divine beneficence: the witness of Scripture and the history and identity of Israel are interpreted in this light. Grace is discovered in an event, not in the general benevolence of God, and its focal expression lies not in creation or in any other divine gift, but in the gift of Christ, which constitutes for Paul the Gift.

Notice the disclaimer—Paul doesn't have some sort of theology of common grace, a grace that restrains the sin of the non-elect and blesses them in some non-salvific way. Nor does Paul say anything about the grace he does talk about, the grace in and of Christ, as *irresistible*. At times, Calvin extended or "perfected" Paul's theology of grace in ways that are probably not consistent with what Paul actually teaches.

And make no mistake, Paul's theology of grace is not merely about "spiritual" matters. As Barclay stresses, "In figuring believers as 'dead to the world' and as expressions of a 'new creation' (Gal 6:14–15), he articulates the birth of dissident communities which are capable of disregarding distinctions between Jew and Greek, slave and free, male and female (Gal 3.28). Such social identities continue to exist, but they are declared insignificant as markers of worth in a community that is beholden to Christ and operates 'at a diagonal' to the normal taxonomies of value (Gal 1:10–11). Ancestry, education, and social power are subordinated to a common 'calling' that disregards previous assumptions of worth (1 Cor 1:26–31)."

And what about a theology of particular grace for those predetermined by God to be part of the elect? Barclay says the following: "Paul's theology is anchored not in a determined creational past, but in an eschatological future: if the past is important, it is only for what it foreshadows and points forward to in the future. As Paul reads it, the purposes of God run towards mercy (11:32), though what that looks like in practice he is unable to say (hence 11:33–36!)." Thus, the plan is, as Barclay says, oriented to the worldwide spread of grace. If that is not finally and fully effective, "it will be not because God did not want it to be so, but because his grace will have been rejected by some in unbelief."[28]

Just so, and this means that God's grace is not irresistible. Every time someone sins, God's desire and will for humankind is violated, because God's desire is that none should perish and all be saved. And this in turn means that God has not predetermined all these outcomes from before the foundation of the world. God does not will sin or evil, nor is He the author of sin or evil. Absolutely not. A careful reading of Barclay's instant classic makes clear that the TULIP theology wilts when the searchlight of detailed exegesis of what the Bible really says about grace and salvation is shone upon it.

It is not necessary to go further with Sproul's analysis, since we have seen that at the most basic level in its soteriology and Christology it is fundamentally flawed. But there are more detailed attempts to approach systematic theology this way, and we will now turn to the best-selling one, the work of Wayne Grudem, in the next portion of this chapter. In Grudem we find a much more detailed, consistent, and insistent Reformed reading of Biblical theology.

## Grudem's Grand Gambit

Systematic theologies are rarely best-sellers, but Wayne Grudem's large volume on the subject, now in an even bigger second edition (topping out at over one thousand pages) has become one—selling at least 750,000 copies in its two editions. At the very outset of this huge work, Grudem has this to say about the nature of systematic theology:

> Systematic theology is any study which answers the question, "What does the Bible teach us today about any given topic?" This definition indicates that Systematic theology involves collecting and understanding all the relevant passages in the Bible on various topics and then summarizing their teaching clearly so we know what to believe about each topic.[29]

The word *topic* keeps coming up, as if the Bible was not largely a grand narrative, but rather a collection of theological ideas. And how does one

---

28. The other voice in the last couple of sentences was me, as I was having a dialogue with John Barclay for my blog. The remarks in quotation are those of Barclay.

29. Grudem, *Systematic Theology*, 1.

decide which passages are relevant on a given topic? Does it involve assuming that the topics listed in a Systematic theology like this one are the crucial ones, or all the major ones? Further, does this approach assume that wherever we find similar terms or phrases we must be dealing with the same subject throughout the Bible? How much development or change is allowed in the use of this or that term or idea?

For example, the language of salvation clearly has different meanings in different places in the Bible. In the OT it tends to refer to someone being healed, or rescued from danger or from some kind of bondage or slavery. What it does not tend to refer to is a conversion experience, much less "salvation by grace through faith in Jesus." The earlier use of the language is not at odds with the later use, but one could not simply collect all the passages which use salvation language, summarize them, and come up with a particular doctrine of salvation, except in the very broad sense that God is providing this benefit to those in question.[30]

One of the great dangers of doing Systematic theology the way Grudem describes it is it ignores the progressive nature of revelation in the Bible, and indeed also the fact that God's *approach* to humanity, including His chosen people, has changed over time. For instance, the theology of the afterlife in the Pentateuch does not include a theology of bodily resurrection or even dying and going to heaven. Instead, one goes down into the land of the dead, Sheol, and is gathered to one's ancestors.[31] There is no robust literal theology of the afterlife involving bodily resurrection and further living on earth beyond death before we get to the exilic prophets like Daniel (see Dan 12).

It is simply not possible, based on similar or same language or topics, to gather up all the passages on said predetermined topic and treat them as if they all were talking about the same thing. The Bible is a more complex book than that. It involves all sorts of different genre of literature, and God's revelation is progressively revealed, such that one must be careful not to read later ideas *back* into earlier texts where those ideas are not present.

It is not clear to me that there is much difference between Biblical theology and Systematic theology for Grudem, except that he says that Biblical theology "traces the historical development of a doctrine and the way one's place in the historical development affects one's understanding and

---

30. On this matter in regard to the discussion of this sort of terminology just within one author, for instance in Luke–Acts, see the appendix to my *Acts of the Apostles*. For instance, when Jesus says to the woman with the issue of blood, "Your faith has saved you," He most likely means her faith has healed her.

31. The only possible exception in the Pentateuch is apparently Enoch, and in the historical books Elijah. It looks like your name needs to begin with E to get beamed up (and yes, of course I'm kidding).

application of that particular doctrine."[32] That certainly is needed in Biblical theology, but the need is not absent from Systematic theology. But let's consider another related matter.

When Jesus gives His own teaching about marriage and divorce, He is then asked why exactly did Moses *permit* divorce (and by implication why was Jesus' teaching apparently at odds with this dictum). Jesus' reply in Matt 19:8 is crucial: "Moses permitted you to divorce your wives *because your hearts were hard.* But it was not this way from the beginning." In other words, God in His mercy gave His OT people *less* demanding standards in various ways than Jesus was offering to His own disciples, and Jesus was returning to God's original creation order intent for marriage.

Why did God do that? Jesus says because of the hardness of the hearts of God's OT people. Jesus is not allowing divorce for that reason anymore. He has come, the Dominion of God is breaking in, and new occasions teach new duties. You cannot simply lump together Biblical topics and not take into account the progressive nature of the revelation in the Bible. But there is more. Even within the OT itself there is development of revelation and of the OT writer's understanding of things.

Most scholars would agree that the account in Chronicles was written a long time after the account in 1–2 Samuel and 1–2 Kings, maybe even several centuries later. During that time, the light dawned on some of the Biblical writers that there was something we would call secondary causes. Even though there was only one God in the universe, God was not the cause of everything, and especially He was not the author of sin and evil. In the earlier account in 2 Sam 24:1 we are told that the Lord incited David to take a census of Israel, due to God's anger with Israel at the time. But then, paradoxically, in 24:10 David quite rightly concludes he has sinned by taking the census and then God exacts punishment as a result!

When we look closely at the parallel passage in 1 Chr 21:1 we hear, "Satan rose against Israel and incited David to take a census." What is going on here? The best answer is that when 2 Samuel was written there was not yet a clear understanding of the concept of secondary causes. Yes, of course, God is the first cause of everything that happens in the universe, being the creator of the universe, but this notion becomes problematic when wicked things are then attributed to God.

And the writer of 1 Chronicles understands this, and so he points out that it was Satan that incited David to take the census. This author clearly understands that while God *allows* lots of things to happen that are not His specific will or desire, God is not the author of everything that happens

---

32. Grudem, *Systematic Theology*, 3.

in a fallen world. In this case, we are told plainly it was Satan who was the influencer of David in this matter, and clearly the text goes on to show that this was a sin and against God's will.

One more similar point from the same context is helpful. Consider the story of Saul trying to pin David to a wall with a spear. Here the Hebrew of 1 Sam 19:9 reads, "Now an evil spirit from the Lord came on Saul," leading to his trying to spear David. Who is apparently said to send this evil spirit on Saul? Yahweh, and yes, the adjective *ra'ah* does mean evil in numerous OT texts. Again, what in the world is going on in 1 Samuel?

Granted that in the broadest sense God is the creator of all creatures great and small, even angels that go over to the dark side of the force, but as the Chronicler helps us to see, the author of 1 Samuel did not yet have a clear understanding of the difference between primary and secondary causes. How is this relevant to our discussion? In two ways.

First of all, it reminds us that a flat or unnuanced reading of all texts in the Bible that have a bearing on what God does and does not do is *not* adequate because there is a developmental understanding of that reality reflecting in the earlier and later portions of the canon, even just in the OT itself.

Second, there is a difference between what God directly wills and causes to happen, and what He allows to happen by secondary agents who have a modicum of freedom of choice—whether angels or human beings. This is what we should have learned from reading the text in Chronicles about the Davidic census, but even in 1 Samuel there is a realization that David sinned in taking the census.

Now the crucial upshot from all this is that we must reject a theology of God's sovereignty that suggests or even hints at God being the author of evil or wickedness. As James rightly stresses, God cannot be tempted and never tempts anyone; in Him is no shadow of turning (Jas 1:13). This is simply not the correct way to read texts, especially texts from the early part of the OT in regard to the issue of God's will. Evil and sin are violations of the will of a good and loving God, and in His sovereignty He has permitted His angelic and human creatures to have a modicum of the power of contrary choice.

God did not predestine before the foundation of the universe some of His creatures to sin or to do evil, to be eternally lost, and to end up in outer darkness, in the place we call Hell. This involves a serious misreading of what it means to talk about what the Bible says about God's sovereignty, and this misreading flatly contradicts many Biblical texts, especially many NT ones. The clearest revelation of God's character is found in Jesus, who was not sent into the world to condemn humanity, but rather to save it. *The issue is not—Is God sovereign or not? The issue is—How does God exercise His sovereignty? Bearing this in mind we are prepared now to work through some of Grudem's arguments in his systematized Biblical theology.*

## Doctrine and the Outline of *Systematic Theology*

It is rather surprising that Grudem doesn't define what he means by "doctrine" right from the outset. For example, is a doctrine a theological idea or concept that is *normative*, something that *must* be believed? Is the concept of Sheol a doctrine that must be believed? Is this place of the dead in the afterlife the same thing as Hell? If not, what are we talking about? Where for example is the spirit of the prophet of Samuel that is summoned *up* by the medium of Endor? *One suspects that, when one comes to the list of theological topics to be covered in this massive volume, they have been selected on the basis of certain theological presuppositions, various of which the writers of the OT did not share.*

But aren't we supposed to think along with the inspired Biblical writers about these things? After all, they are mediating God's thoughts to us in some sense, since this is a revelation from God through human beings, human language, human concepts. And it is constantly a good idea to bear in mind the warning of the author of Hebrews that God spoke in different ways in the past, and the revelation was partial and piecemeal, but now we have the fuller and clearer revelation in Christ.

We will have much more to say about this as we go, but let's consider the major topics covered in Grudem's tome: (1) the doctrine of Scripture; (2) the doctrine of God (these first two sections of the book take up about one-third of the content of the whole book!); (3) the doctrine of humankind in the image of God; (4) the doctrines of Christ and the Holy Spirit; (5) the doctrine of the application of redemption, and here especially Calvinistic ways of presenting soteriology come to the fore; (6) the doctrine of the church; and finally, (7) the doctrine of the future.

One of the things that stands out immediately as problematic about this outline is that for the most part it does not take the approach of any of the NT writers! By this I mean that the writers of the New Testament believed they were already living in the eschatological age, already living in what we might call the End Times, and the inauguration of this eschatological situation begins with the coming of Jesus, including the beginning of His ministry where we learn that "the Dominion of God is at hand, repent and believe the Gospel" (Mark 1:15). The whole of the NT is suffused with a belief that in some ways "the future is now," though this is an already and not yet situation. It is not helpful to talk about the end of the end times, or the future of something that has already begun, without taking full account of its origins in the Christ event which has already transpired.

And the second thing to note about the NT writers is their Christocentric focus, even to the extent that they look at the Father and the Spirit through their Christocentric lens. The incarnation, life, death, resurrection, ascension, and sending of the Spirit all depend on Christ, and these Christological events shape how everything else is being viewed. There is a Christological revolution in their thinking about all things as a result of the Christ event, including how they view the OT itself as the book that prepares for, promises about, prophecies about the One who is to come who will fulfill the promises and prophecies and indeed the major OT institutions, such as temples, priests, and sacrifices.

There are tell-tale signs in our earliest NT documents, namely the letters of Paul, that a Copernican revolution in the thinking of these early Jews had taken place because of the Christ event. Paul in what is probably his earliest letter, Galatians (see Gal 1), indicates that, while "the present evil age" is still in progress, "the age to come," the eschatological age, has already broken into this evil age and is changing things. Consider for a moment what Paul says in 2 Cor 7:29–31:

> What I mean, brothers and sisters, is that the time has been shortened. From now on those who have wives should live as if they do not; those who mourn, as if they did not; those who are happy, as if they were not; those who buy something, as if it were not theirs to keep; those who use the things of the world, as if not engrossed in them. For this world in its present form is passing away.

All too often v. 29 is mistranslated as "the time is short," but that is not what Paul says or means. The proper translation is "the time has been shortened," and one must ask by what. He is talking about a game-changing event that has *already* happened and should change the worldview of Christ followers such that they should live with a sense of detachment from the things and institutions of this world (like marriage or property) because the *schema* of this world is already passing away. What caused that to happen? The Christ event set in motion the end times.[33]

---

33. See my *Conflict and Community in Corinth* on all this. Note that for Paul, as Rom 7:1ff. confirms, marriage is an institution for our earthly good, and when a partner dies, the marriage is no longer extant, and so the remaining spouse is free to remarry. In the Dominion there is neither marrying nor giving in marriage, but instead persons are like the angels, which doesn't mean sexless, but probably means deathless, remembering that the purposes of marriage were: (1) so a person would not be alone, but in the Dominion one has millions of fellow believers; and (2) so the command to be fruitful

Any view of doctrine that ignores or gives only lip service to how the writers of the NT operate with their new eschatological and Christocentric worldview is likely to place the emphases in the wrong places in various ways. It is no accident that both of the first two major ecumenical councils in 325 and 450 focused in the main on Christology.

If you begin your discussion of doctrine with the doctrine of a canonical collection, the NT, when the twenty-seven books of the NT were not yet widely agreed upon by Christians before the fourth century AD, then you are beginning where *none of the OT or NT writers began when they wrote!*[34]

Let me be clear that I don't have large quibbles with Grudem's high view of the authority and truthfulness of Scripture in its sixty-six books. In fact, I largely agree with him. But I don't think any Biblical Theology or *Systematic Theology* should *begin* somewhere the authors of the Bible would not begin.[35] No, we must begin with contextual exegesis of texts that existed in or before the NT era.

But more fundamentally, the tendency to synthesize terms and concepts together from diverse passages from varied historical contexts and settings is a problem, a problem we can trace back to Tatian himself and his Diatesseron, as we have already seen. To illustrate these issues, we will focus on Grudem's section entitled "The Doctrine of the Application of Redemption."

## About That Theology of Redemption

The discussion begins with a bang with a treatment of what Calvinists call common grace (something John Wesley in a moment of anger called damning grace). Grudem's definition of common grace is as follows: "Common grace is the grace of God by which he gives people innumerable blessings *that are not part of salvation*."[36] What this assumes is that God has predetermined before all creation to save some and not others, but nevertheless God still blesses these eternally lost souls in this life presumably because

---

and multiply could be fulfilled to ensure the perpetuation of the species. But that purpose is no longer necessary anymore either in the Dominion.

34. Canonical theology tends to make the huge mistake of ignoring that these scriptural documents had been the Word of God spoken into numerous settings for centuries before the canon was finally agreed upon in the fourth century. There is all too often in canonical theology an anti-historical bias against historical criticism and the attempt to understand the Bible in its original historical contexts as words on target for some specific audience well before Constantine made Christianity a legal or licit religion.

35. See my *Sola Scriptura*.

36. Grudem, *Systematic Theology*, 803; emphasis added.

He is a gracious and merciful God. The term "common" refers to blessings common to all people, whether they are among the elect or not. The rain falls on the sinner and the saint.

We already have had occasion in this study to point out the major problem with amalgamating the concept of election, which is a corporate concept for the most part, with the concept of salvation. Israel is God's chosen or elect people in the OT, but this does not guarantee the salvation of particular Israelites. That depends on whether they respond to God in faith and trust God as Abraham did and avoid idolatry and immorality.

As for the NT, the Son of God is the only person who existed before the foundation of the universe (other than the Father and the Spirit, and some angels) and could be destined in advance by God the Father to become a human being, and *He was*—He was destined to be the savior of all those who are saved by grace through faith in Him. But as Paul stresses, this salvation happens "in Christ," because Christ Himself incorporates believers into Himself as His body, and they become part of the Elect One.

Christ as the Elect One, chosen before the foundation of the world to be its savior, did not need be saved Himself. Ergo, election is one thing, salvation is another, just as was true of Israel. Election is corporate; salvation is individual.

But there is more to say. The whole assumption that God desires and chooses the salvation of only some human beings and that Christ only died for them is flatly contradicted by numerous texts. Not only does John 3:16 say that God loves the world of humanity and sent His only begotten Son to save "whosoever will" and that He did not send His Son into the world to condemn anyone to eternal punishment, but also 1 Tim 2:5–6 is clear enough that Christ gave His life as a ransom for all. God did not limit the atonement in regard to whom it might benefit. The universal atonement, however, only benefits those who respond positively to God in faith, or to use NT language, who respond by grace through faith in Christ.

Sometimes, at this point in the discussion it is objected that God's sovereign will cannot be frustrated by mere human decisions and sin. The problem with this notion is that all the evidence of Scripture says that sin and evil are indeed violations of God's will for humankind.[37] God in His wisdom gave both angels and human beings a modicum of grace enabled will, including the power of contrary choice. The question is not whether

---

37. And it's no good trying to make a distinction between God's revealed will and his hidden or secret decrees, as if the revealed will tells one story, but really behind the scenes God had willed something else. Though we do not by any means know everything about God's will, what we do know is that his revealed will, which is God's truth, certainly should not be seen as contradicting what we don't know about God's will.

God is sovereign but rather *how He has chosen to exercise His sovereignty*, and since He wants His creatures to freely choose to love God and their neighbor, to which Jesus added and even love their enemies, He had to enable them to do so. Freely they have received the grace of God, and freely they are enabled to respond in love and obedience to God. Not apart from God's grace, but by God's grace.

It makes sense that if: (1) God loves the world; and (2) He desires that no one perish but all have a chance at everlasting life; and (3) Christ died to atone for the sins of all, providing a ransom for all; then (4) God by His grace, call it prevenient grace, the grace that comes before saving grace, has enabled His fallen creatures to freely respond to the Gospel and be saved.

It is quite amazing to see Grudem's exegetical tap dance around what 2 Pet 3:9–10 actually says. He takes it to mean that God is patient with humankind because He intends to redeem "those who will be saved."[38] If that sounds like a redundant statement, it is. What 2 Pet 3 actually says is that "God is not wishing *any* should perish but that *all* should reach repentance." Any of whom, and all of whom? The only appropriate answer is anyone and everyone.

Even if the author simply addresses anyone in the audience of those many, many house churches he is addressing in several huge regions in Turkey that Peter had dealings with, what the author is talking about is *why the second coming and final judgment have not happened yet*. The reason is not merely so that those who are already believers will keep on believing. It is because God desires the repentance of the fallen world *in general*. The second coming is not delayed because of those who are already in Christ!

In this regard, however, Grudem and Wesleyans would agree that there is such a thing as God being gracious to those who are not yet saved. So, Wesley would say that prevenient grace is not saving grace, but it enables a person to respond to the Gospel positively if they choose to do so. In this regard, it is a sort of common grace, and Wesley would say that God's grace does indeed restrain sin in the unbeliever, as Calvin said about common grace. Common grace is not just a blessing; it is a retardant in Reformed theology. And like common grace, prevenient grace does not guarantee a person will respond positively to the Gospel. Wesley believed that texts like John 1:9 refer to this prevenient grace—"the light which enlightens *everyone* was coming into the world." Perhaps so.[39]

---

38. Grudem, *Systematic Theology*, 810.

39. See the full treatment of the subject of prevenient grace in Shelton, *Prevenient Grace*.

The following chapter in Grudem's volume treats in detail election and reprobation. It is clear he is on the defensive in this chapter, because he insists he is not really talking about double predestination, because there is a distinction between someone being chosen by God to be saved, and someone being passed over for salvation.[40] This is a distinction, however, without a difference, for whether a lost soul is passed over and goes to Hell, or is chosen to go to Hell, either way the outcome is the same for that poor lost person, and God is still ultimately responsible.

If someone stands by and allows a person to be killed, when in fact they could have intervened and prevented that death, they still have major responsibility for not doing something to prevent a disaster, even if they did not directly cause that outcome. Again, what God allows to happen, in a Reformed system where God is *actively involved in the cause of everything*, even in what He simply permits, does not escape the odium of besmirching the good, loving, and merciful character of God, never mind rejecting the clear scriptural teaching that God loves the world and desires that no one should perish but all should come to repentance.

## What About That Predestination Text in Romans 8?

Perhaps here is the right place to deconstruct the Calvinist view of Rom 8:28–30. Here is what the text actually says:

> God works all things together for the good for *those who love God*, for they are the ones who God has called according to his purpose, they are the ones whom he foreknew and destined in advance to be conformed to the image of his Son that he might be the first born among many brothers and sisters. For those he destined in advance, he also called, those he called, he set right, those he set right he also glorified.

The problem with Calvin's (and Grudem's) reading of this text is that it ignores who the antecedent is for the term *who* in v. 28. The phrase "those who love God" is clearly enough referring to Christians and their love for God. It is not referring to the antecedent love God has for people, and as such it is a rare phrase in Paul who most often talks about God's love for humanity when the subject of love comes up.

In that very same verse we can compare τοῖς ἀγαπῶσιν τὸν Θεὸν (literally "those loving the God") to the following phrase, τοῖς κλητοῖς οὖσιν, "those who are called." Clearly the antecedent of the second phrase, "those

---

40. See Grudem, *Systematic Theology*, 816–17.

being called," is "those who love God." The calling is for those who love God. If we move on to v. 29 we have the words οὖσιν προέγνω, and clearly again, the antecedent for "those whom he foreknew" is "those who love God." Here is where we need to make clear that God's knowing something doesn't necessarily mean He has already caused it to happen.

A moment's reflection will show that in the very next chapter in Romans we hear about God foreknowing the wickedness and sin of some, but He did not cause that to happen. Indeed, there is a clear distinction made between the vessels that God has prepared in advance for mercy, and the vessels that have prepared themselves (middle/passive verb) for destruction.[41] God's knowing something, even knowing it in advance, doesn't cause it to happen. Nor can it be said that God knows it because He had already willed it. God knows all things, all realities, and all possibilities. God knows our sin and the evil that exists in the world caused by Satan and his minions and by human beings.

None of that evil is something God desires or wills. And what this necessarily means is *that there is more than one volitional actor in the universe*—there is God in three persons, but there are also angels, and there are human beings. God in His sovereignty has chosen to give angels and human beings a measure of freedom of choice, which in the case of fallen creatures requires, in addition, not just being made in God's image, but also enabling grace so the power of contrary choice is partially restored to those in the bondage of sin. Bearing this in mind we can now return to the discussion of Rom 8:28–30.

There is a good reason to follow the logic of those crucial verses *in order*. It is a mistake to start with Rom 8:30, because doing so can give the false impression that predestination is behind everything that happens to a lost person, including his or her response to the Gospel call. This is to ignore the fact that Rom 8:28–29 says otherwise. It says that God has called those who love God, or put another way, God calls those He knows in advance will respond in love to the call. Again, we must bear in mind that love has to be freely given, freely received, and freely responded to. It can't be predetermined, or else it's simply not the love talked about in the Bible, which is

---

41. While he was writing his ICC commentary on Romans, Charles Cranfield was also teaching Romans at Durham University, and I was fortunate enough to take that class in 1978 or 79. Now, Cranfield was absolutely committed to Reformed theology, but he was also quite clear in his reading of the relevant phrases in Rom 9 that a distinction between the vessels of mercy and the vessels of wrath was being made by Paul in terms of the latter fitting themselves for destruction, not being predetermined for it.

required as our wholehearted response to God, our neighbor, and even our enemies.[42]

As W. Pannenberg puts it, "According to Christian theology the nature and power of God is love. This is not first expressed in his sustaining and redeeming activity but in the very act of creation. To grant existence to creatures is an act of love, if it does not serve another purpose but is itself the purpose of the creative act. *But God cannot be at the same time loving and omnipotent (as one must suppose the all-determining reality to be) if he left his creatures to the power of evil and destruction.*"[43] Exactly so, God is not only love in His creation but also in His work of salvation. But this would not be true if God created some to be excluded from the work of redemption.

Notice, finally, that v. 30 begins with the reference to the antecedent; it begins with the word οὖς. It is appropriate once more to fill in who the "those who" are, namely those who love God and are called according to purpose or choice. The bottom line is this—those who love God are destined in advance by God to be conformed to the image of His Son through a process of justification, sanctification, and glorification, and only that last stage of salvation, the bodily conformity to the image of the risen Christ, is unilaterally the activity of God on and for the believer. Before that, justification is by faith and so is sanctification where the believer actively works out what the Spirit is working in them (Phil 2). In short, the willing and decision making of Christians enabled by grace has a part in the working out of salvation in their lives. Salvation is not like being strapped into a roller coaster by God from which one cannot escape, and taken for a ride to the end of the line. Saving faith is indeed a gift from God, but it is a gift that the believer must actively receive and use to benefit from it.

## The Order of Salvation

This brings us to the way Grudem lists the *ordo salutis*, or order of salvation:

1) Election (God's choice of some to be saved)
2) The Gospel call
3) Regeneration (being born again)
4) Conversion (faith and repentance)
5) Justification (right legal standing)

---

42. See my *Who God Is*.
43. Pannenberg, *Introduction to Systematic Theology*, 11–12; emphasis added.

6) Adoption (membership in God's family)

7) Sanctification (right conduct of life)

8) Perseverance (remaining a Christian)

9) Death (going to be with the Lord)

10) Glorification (receiving a resurrection body)[44]

We've already dealt with the problems with the Reformed view of election, and Grudem's failure to see it's a corporate concept, and in the Christian sense it applies only to those who are "in Christ," having been incorporated into the body of Christ by God's Spirit (see 1 Cor 12). Here we must deal with the mis-ordering of (3) through (5) in the chart above.

Consider for a moment what Gal 3 asks of those new Christians— "Did you receive the Spirit by the works of the law, or by believing what you heard?" They were not regenerated by God's Spirit *before* hearing and responding to the Gospel positively. No indeed, they first responded positively to the Gospel and then received the Spirit, not unlike the first disciples at Pentecost according to Acts 1–2.

Or consider 1 Cor 12 that says that those who received the Gospel were baptized by the Spirit into the one body of Christ, and were given the Spirit for their spiritual nourishment. Or consider 2 Cor 5:17, if anyone is "in Christ" new creation has happened and the old has passed away.

Or consider the "born again" passage in John 3. Nicodemus is already a pious, believing Jew. He has faith in God, and he believes Jesus is a teacher sent from God. To him Jesus says—you must be born again, you must be born from above. Clearly regeneration did not precede Nicodemus's belief in God and his beginning belief in Jesus. This is why theologians quite rightly point out that justifying faith and the new birth are probably coincident in time with each other, they are the objective and subjective sides to one thing—conversion, but clearly regeneration and the new birth do *not* precede trusting God.

The reason the Calvinist argues that way is not only because he does not believe in the concept of universal prevenient grace that enables anyone to respond positively to the Gospel if they will, but he also does not believe that God wants to save the world, or in some case he doesn't even believe that Christ's death provided a ransom for all. No, the Reformed view is that the sinner is dead in trespasses and only irresistible grace could possibly bring him or her to new life. This is definitely not what the balance of the witness of Scripture teaches.

---

44. Grudem, *Systematic Theology*, 817.

Part One: What Have They Done to Biblical and Systematic Theology?

What about Grudem's exegesis of Rom 9:11–13?[45] Let's set forth the whole relevant passage itself first which reads,

> For not all who are descended from Israel are Israel. Nor because they are his descendants are they all Abraham's children. On the contrary, "It is through Isaac that your offspring will be reckoned." In other words, it is not the children by physical descent who are God's children, but it is the children of the promise who are regarded as Abraham's offspring. For this was how the promise was stated: "At the appointed time I will return, and Sarah will have a son."
>
> Not only that, but Rebekah's children were conceived at the same time by our father Isaac. Yet, before the twins were born or had done anything good or bad—in order that God's purpose in election might stand: not by works but by him who calls—she was told, "The older will serve the younger." Just as it is written: "Jacob I loved, but Esau I hated."
>
> What then shall we say? Is God unjust? Not at all! For he says to Moses,
>
> "I will have mercy on whom I have mercy,
> and I will have compassion on whom I have compassion."
>
> It does not, therefore, depend on human desire or effort, but on God's mercy. For Scripture says to Pharaoh: "I raised you up for this very purpose, that I might display my power in you and that my name might be proclaimed in all the earth." Therefore God has mercy on whom he wants to have mercy, and he hardens whom he wants to harden.
>
> One of you will say to me: "Then why does God still blame us? For who resists his will?" But who are you, O man, to talk back to God? "Shall what is formed say to him who formed it, 'Why did you make me like this?'" Does not the potter have the right to make out of the same lump of clay some pottery for noble purposes and some for common use?
>
> What if God, although choosing to show his wrath and make his power known, bore with great patience the objects of his wrath—having prepared themselves for destruction? What if he did this to make the riches of his glory known to the objects of his mercy, whom he prepared in advance for glory—even us, whom he also called, not only from the Jews but also from the Gentiles? As he says in Hosea:
>
> "I will call them 'my people' who are not my people;
> and I will call her 'my loved one' who is not my loved one."

---

45. Grudem, *Systematic Theology*, 818–19.

First, if we ask what is the subject of this passage, the answer is that it is clearly about God electing a people, a chosen people, Israel. And within that corporate group there is a further selection of a specific line of Israelites, through Jacob. Paul tells us that this choosing is not done on the basis of anything the person who is chosen has done, nor is it on the basis of pure heredity. Not all Israel is the chosen line within Israel. It has to do with God's historical purposes just as the hardening of Pharaoh had to do with God's historical purposes. In none of these cases does it have to do with God choosing some individuals to be saved, and others not. Election of a people is one thing; salvation of an individual is another, and choosing a line of "elect" persons to fulfill the historical purpose of being a light to the nations does not guarantee the salvation of all those in that line.

It is also interesting what Paul then adds about election. Not only does he talk about a selection within the elect group, he even says only a remnant will be saved. On what basis are they saved? When Paul finishes his discussion of Israel in Rom 11:25–27 he states clearly enough that all Israel will be saved in the same manner by which Gentiles were saved—by grace through faith in Jesus. Jesus will return and turn away the impiety of Jacob, and they will embrace their messiah.

Returning for a minute to Rom 9, let's re-emphasize the distinction in the Greek between vessels of mercy prepared in advance for glory, and vessels of wrath who have "prepared themselves for wrath." The former phrase is speaking to the same issue as Rom 8:28–30—God has destined those who love God to be conformed to the image of His Son. The middle passive form of "prepared" as used with "vessels of wrath" makes clear that those who will face the final judgment of God's wrath on sin have "cooked their own goose." It is not what God desired or designed for them. Finally, we also learn in Rom 9 that there is a relationship between election and salvation. One needs to be in the sphere of "the elect" to be saved. In the case of the OT that means being within the sphere of Israel the elect people of God, and in the NT it means being within Christ, the elect one of God.

## Imputed or Imparted Righteousness?

But what about this idea of "imputed righteousness"? Grudem has much to say about this, and we need to deal with it in some detail.[46] First of all the language in question involves a series of related terms—*dikaios* means righteous, *dikaiosune* means righteousness, and *dikaioo* has the sense of making or declaring someone righteous. This language is not inherently

---

46. Grudem, *Systematic Theology*, 884–96.

legal language, but in ancient Greek it is often used in the sense of "just" according to the law, or rendering "justice." In my view, it is important to stick to the context of how these terms are used in the NT itself. Let us look at the parade of examples Paul uses to explain the terms in question.

He summons up the example of Abraham twice over, once in Gal 3 and once in Rom 4. The Galatian text reads as follows and involves the citation of Gen 15:6: "So also Abraham 'believed/trusted God, and it was credited to him as righteousness.'" And in Rom 4:2–3: "If, in fact, Abraham was justified by works, he had something to boast about—but not before God. What does Scripture say? 'Abraham believed/trusted God, and it was credited to him as righteousness.'"

You will notice that nothing is said in either of these texts about someone else's righteousness being imputed to the believer. To the contrary, it is Abraham's faith or trust in God which is reckoned or credited as Abraham's righteousness. If this is the paradigm for the Christian situation, then we should conclude that our trust/faith in the Lord is credited or reckoned as righteousness. We could debate whether this is referring to being given right standing with God, or whether it is some sort of legal fiction. Faith is credited as righteousness, but is it actually only about one's legal standing, not also about one's condition?

Now I understand this traditional Reformation argument served up by both Luther and Calvin, who was by the way a French lawyer, but what is being forgotten here is that the beginning of sanctification in the believer is the new birth which seems to coincide with the being given right standing with God. Grudem is right that since the opposite of this term is condemnation, we must at least in part be talking about a legal judgment on us as not guilty. Why not? Because Christ has already paid the price for our sins and there is now no condemnation. Instead, there is forgiveness. It is also important to point out that Paul the businessman uses the language of reckoning credits and debits, when talking about this matter. This is not mainly legal language, so it is a mistake to over-emphasize the legal side of what is going on here.[47]

My point is that what came to be called justification does not happen in isolation from the new birth. The sinner needs not merely to be cleared of his previous sin debt; he needs to have his conscience cleansed by the work of the Holy Spirit in the new birth. When Paul says in 2 Cor 5 that if anyone is in Christ they are a new creature, the old has passed away, he does not merely mean that they have a new right standing with God. He means there

---

47. See Ps 106:31; 1 Macc 2:52; and Phlm 18 for the use of this business language of human conduct.

has actually been a conversion, a change in their life, and they are no longer the old person. This requires the internal work of the Holy Spirit.

It is not an accident that Paul adds in 1 Cor 12 that it is by the one Spirit that everyone is baptized into (i.e., spiritually joined to) the body of Christ and given the Spirit as an ongoing resource in one's Christian life. This happens at the point of the new birth. God actually expects and indeed requires that Christians lead righteous lives, and Paul makes this clear in many places. Christ is not righteous in the place of the believer in such a way that they are not required to be righteous.

Even worse would be the notion that when God looks at us, He simply sees Christ's righteousness, not our actual condition. This would mean that God is deceived about our actual condition, or is willing to look the other way and will no longer hold us accountable for our behavior. But one has to ask, does God require more of His people under the Mosaic covenant or under the new covenant? The answer is—to whom more is given (including the indwelling Holy Spirit), more is required. And there is a reason why believers are told they must appear before the judgment seat of Christ to give an account of the deeds they have done in the body (2 Cor 5:10).

Where then did the idea of the imputation of Christ's righteousness come from? Let's take a couple of examples—Phil 3 says this:

> What is more, I consider everything a loss because of the surpassing worth of knowing Christ Jesus my Lord, for whose sake I have lost all things. I consider them garbage, that I may gain Christ and be found in him, not having a righteousness of my own that comes from the law, but that which is through the faithfulness of Christ—the righteousness that comes from God on the basis of faith. I want to know Christ—yes, to know the power of his resurrection and participation in his sufferings, becoming like him in his death, and so, somehow, attaining to the resurrection from the dead.

Paul had just said that in regard to a righteousness that is according to the Mosaic law, he was blameless. This meant he was not a law-breaker. It did not mean he was faultless or perfect. I would add that if Paul had thought that Rom 7:13–25 was about himself, he could never had written such a statement about blamelessness in Philippians, but in fact Rom 7 is a Christian view of the pre-Christian condition of those outside Christ.

Paul goes on in Phil 3:9–11 to add that he wants to be found in Christ, not having a righteousness of his own, but rather one that derives from God on the basis of faith. The righteousness in question comes through the faithfulness of Christ, an allusion to His obedience even unto death on the cross.

But is this righteousness that comes from Christ merely imputed, or is it in fact imparted? I would insist it is imparted, which is what Paul is talking about in 2 Cor 5 when he talked about a believer having *become* a new creature, with the old self *having passed away*. That is not merely a *positional* change in relationship to God; it is a change of *condition*. Yes, the believer is granted right standing with God, but as a result of Christ's work on the cross, there is also a real change—one becomes a new creature in Christ.

One other text is important at this point, which is also often misread. It is found in 1 Cor 1 and reads as follows: It is because of him [i.e., God] that you are in Christ Jesus, who has become for us wisdom from God—that is, our righteousness, holiness and redemption." But in fact, after the phrase "wisdom from God" the Greek is *not* translated properly in the NIV cited here. Here is what it actually says: "Out of Him [God] *you are* in Christ Jesus (who has been made our wisdom), righteousness, and sanctification, and redemption." Notice then the emphatic placement of the main verb *you are*. Paul is explaining what believers are in Christ, not what Christ is on their behalf. And the proof that this is the correct way to render that Greek sentence can be found in 2 Cor 5:21, which reads literally, "The One having not known sin was made sin for us so that we might *become* the righteousness of God in Him." Let us focus on that last clause for a minute—"so that *we might become* the righteousness of God in Him." This does not say that He becomes the righteousness of God *for* us. It says WE become the righteousness of God in or through Him. I would submit that this is also clearly what Paul is getting at in 1 Cor 1:30 as well, though the sentence is complex. In any case, Christ didn't need to become righteous or the righteousness of God because He already was that. Paul is clearly talking about believers becoming examples of the righteousness of God on earth.

In what sense was Christ MADE sin? ἐποίησεν is a strong verb, and it is unlikely to mean He was merely counted as sin. Probably, this language refers to Him actually being the sin-bearer, like the scapegoat in the OT, or better said, the bearer of the sinners' guilt, such that He was punished in our stead for our sins. He actually bore the penalty for our sin. This was not a mere reckoning; it was an execution based on substitution!

True enough, the believer only becomes the righteousness of God in and through Christ, but Christ is not doing this for us; He is transforming us into His image. The goal is actual righteousness, actual holiness, actual redemption happening in us through Christ. And here is where I note that the word *our* is not there in the Greek before the words *righteousness*, etc. in 1 Cor 1. The sentence properly reads, "You are in Christ Jesus, . . . righteousness, and also sanctification and redemption." This is not about His being this on our behalf. It is about the change that happens to us if anyone is in Christ Jesus.

And this is one of the main places where Wayne Grudem goes wrong.[48] It is not true that *either* God sets us right and declares us not guilty on the basis of the work of Christ alone, *imputing* Christ's righteousness to us, *or* it is based on some goodness or holiness within us. In fact, it is neither of these things because justification, or being given right standing, happens at the same time as the new birth. Regeneration doesn't precede having right standing with God; these things come at the same time. No Wesleyan theologian that I know of would ever say that the right standing with God was given on the basis of some goodness or holiness already resident within the recipient. Grudem's either/or does not take into account the third option.

Christ's death on the cross not only is the basis of our obtaining right standing with God; it is also because of that death that we can be born again, and internally transformed. In short, righteousness doesn't *just* have to do with our objective standing with God; it *also* has to do with what has been done by the Spirit to us imparting holiness to us, the beginning of a righteous character in us. The Spirit convicts, convinces, and converts, and we respond in faith and trust, a faith God graced us with. This has nothing to do with works righteousness, because we did nothing at all to deserve or merit it; we simply had to receive it and believe it. This is of course different not only from Grudem's view, but also from the traditional Catholic view he critiques, namely that justification and sanctification come through the sacrament of baptism. Grudem's critique of the traditional Catholic view of baptism is basically correct.

It is worthwhile to point out that 1 Cor 12 is not about the ritual of water baptism that the church performs. It is in fact the only place in the NT we hear about a baptism by the Holy Spirit into the body of Christ, and it happens at the juncture of conversion, when one first becomes part of the body of Christ, by grace through faith in Jesus. In 1 Cor 1, Paul is even able to say that he is glad he didn't water baptize more of the Corinthians, because clearly many of them had interpreted the ritual the wrong way (1 Cor 1:14). He would never say, "I thank God more of you were not baptized into the body of Christ by the Spirit." Water baptism is one thing; Spirit baptism in conversion is another.[49]

---

48. Grudem, *Systematic Theology*, 889.

49. Grudem, *Systematic Theology*, 895–905, spends no little time critiquing in detail N. T. Wright's view of justification, found in Wright's book simply called *Justification*. Grudem also critiques the new perspective on Paul. Some of this critique of both subjects is helpful and correct, but a good deal of it is not. See now Witherington and Myers, *Voices and Views on Paul*.

And while we are at it, water baptism by immersion, according to Paul in Rom 6, is an image of the old person dying and being buried with Christ. It is not in the first place about rising to resurrection life, which only the Spirit can give. Paul is perhaps thinking about the story of Christ's baptism in which the water baptism by John was one thing, and thereafter, God sent the Spirit upon Him. Similarly, Christian water baptism is performed by humans, but it is God alone who can baptize someone in and with the Spirit at conversion.

## The Perseverance of the Saints

We have already dealt with the major problems with the notion of Christ's death only atoning for the sins of the elect, which Grudem equates with the saved, but here a critique of his view of perseverance of the saints is necessary. The exegetically weakest links in the TULIP chain are limited atonement and perseverance of the saints, and as I said, if these things are wrong, the whole interconnected TULIP system is flawed. As I like to put it—a person is not eternally secure until they are securely in eternity. Short of that, apostasy, however rare, is possible for the true believer.

Here a definition of apostasy is needed. In the first place, the phrase "lose your salvation" is not accurate. You cannot lose your salvation like you can lose a pair of glasses. Apostasy is not something that happens by accident. It is a willful and deliberate rejection of the work of God in a person's life.

Here is how Grudem defines perseverance: "The perseverance of the saints means that all those who are truly born again will be kept by the power of God and will persevere as Christians until the end of their lives, and that only those who persevere to the end have been truly born again."[50]

On the surface of things, it appears a strong case can be made for this view being grounded in Scripture. Romans 8 is often appealed to when it says: "For I am convinced that neither death nor life, neither angels nor demons, neither the present nor the future, nor any powers, neither height nor depth, nor anything else in all creation, will be able to separate us from the love of God that is in Christ Jesus our Lord."

No angel, no devil, no third party human being, no force of nature can separate a Christian from the love of God in Christ. But one needs to ask the question—What or who is missing from this list? And the answer is *yourself*! *You* can wrench yourself free from the strong grasp of God, you

---

50. Grudem, *Systematic Theology*, 970. It is interesting to contrast this with the published form of I. H. Marshall's dissertation, *Kept by the Power of God*.

can grieve and quench the Spirit in your life, you can reject Christ after wholeheartedly embracing Him. And this is precisely what is being warned against in multiple NT texts.

Take for instance Paul's warning to his spiritual child Timothy to follow his guidance: "So that by recalling them you may fight the battle well, holding on to faith and a good conscience, which some have rejected and so have suffered shipwreck with regard to the faith. Among them are Hymenaeus and Alexander, whom I have handed over to Satan to be taught not to blaspheme."

As John Wesley once said, you can't make shipwreck of something you never had. Paul says he has handed these two men over to Satan to be taught not to blaspheme. Perhaps they had not committed an unforgivable sin, and so Paul hoped that they could be sobered up by being expelled from the community and into Satan's realm. Compare this to what Paul says in 1 Cor 5: "So when you are assembled and I am with you in spirit, and the power of our Lord Jesus is present, hand this man over to Satan for the destruction of the flesh, so that his spirit may be saved on the day of the Lord" (vv. 4-5).

Let's deal now with the text that is the *bête noir* of Reformed thinking about apostasy. Hebrews 6 reads as follows:

> It is impossible for those who have once been enlightened, who have tasted the heavenly gift, who have shared in the Holy Spirit, who have tasted the goodness of the word of God and the powers of the coming age and who have fallen away, to be brought back to repentance. To their loss they are crucifying the Son of God all over again and subjecting him to public disgrace.

Let's take a close look at the special pleading by Grudem. Hebrews 6:4 says that the persons in question have *shared* in the Holy Spirit. This same term *metochos* occurs in Heb 3:14 where "to share in Christ" means to have a "close participation with Him in a saving relationship" as Grudem himself has to admit.[51] Ignoring this close contextual parallel, he resorts to pointing out that in some texts like Luke 5:7 *metochos* simply refers to a looser connection, like an associate or companion for instance who helps with the fishing. But surely the Holy Spirit that one shares in is a very different and more intimate and personal matter than having a fishing buddy who helps you! Sharing in the Holy Spirit refers to the indwelling of the Spirit in a person. The context itself in Heb 3:14 suggests the author is talking about someone who shares in Christ.

Sometimes we also hear the artful dodge that merely tasting the heavenly gift doesn't mean one has taken it into one's self. There are two major

---

51. Grudem, *Systematic Theology*, 982.

problems with this. (1) Here and elsewhere, "tasting" need not imply a superficial encounter with something. For example, in Acts 10:10 and 23:14 the cognate term is translated *eat*, not a superficial encounter with food at all. Notice that both here and in Heb 6:5 this same verb (γευσαμένους) is used to refer to the encounter with both the heavenly gift and the good Word of God, and in regard to both these references we are reminded of Ps 34:8, "taste and see that the Lord is good," which in the LXX reads γεύσασθε καὶ ἴδετε ὅτι χρηστὸς ὁ κύριος. The psalmist is not suggesting one should have a superficial encounter with the Lord any more than the author of Hebrews is talking about someone who is not saved. Indeed, there could hardly be a more fulsome description of the saved persons—they have been enlightened by the Gospel, have taken into themselves the heavenly gift (likely the gift of salvation) and the good Word, and experienced the powers of the eschatological age, and they have shared in the Holy Spirit, and even their prior repentance is mentioned.

(2) And it is precisely because all this is true that then the author warns that if they turn away *after all this*, they will be crucifying Christ afresh! This surely must imply that they have already accepted the death of Christ and its benefits, and to renege on that is tantamount to joining those who had Him crucified in the first place! One has to bear in mind the author is addressing Jewish Christians in Rome who are feeling pressure to retreat back into their Jewish origins and forsake Christ. And notice that our author talks about the impossibility to restore them AGAIN to repentance, which implies they had repented previously, presumably when they joined the Christian community in Rome.

Grudem, however, appeals to the warning analogy about fruitless land in v. 8, but this is to ignore that this is a warning against what the author thinks they are *considering doing*, NOT what was already true about them. He then suggests that the more positive tone, of "we are convinced of better things that have to do with salvation in your case," indicates the author is speaking to the elect. Grudem doesn't seem to realize the rhetorical character of Hebrews as a sermon. The author is using both the stick and the carrot approach to make sure they *don't* commit apostasy, not because it is impossible, but because he is worried it might happen!

And notice he doesn't just warn *some* in the audience; he warns them *all*. There would be no point in warning the elect about such an outcome if it were impossible. And there would be no point in warning the non-elect if they are never going to be in right relationship with God. Sometimes you hear the argument that the writer doesn't know who's who in the audience so he has to warn them all. Why then would someone like Paul *presume* that the Corinthians, with isolated exceptions, *are Christians*, even though they are Christians who are immature and having several different kinds of problems and commit various different kinds of sins, some ethical, some theological? And the same applies to the author of Hebrews. We presumed these writers are inspired by God to write what they wrote, so why would we also presume that their spiritual judgment that some genuine Christians are in danger of committing apostasy is wrong or is based on ignorance of the character of those they are addressing?

A problem we have not mentioned with the Reformed approach to these matters is that it vitiates the power and character of the ethical exhortations *which presume again and again that people can change. That those currently manifesting the fruit of the Spirit, if they keep on committing serious sins like those listed in Gal 5:19-21*, shall not enter the Dominion of God when it comes fully on earth when Christ returns. In other words, it is possible for the converts in Galatia to revert to their previous course of behavior.

And a text like Gal 5 reminds us that there are three tenses to salvation: (1) I have been saved (justification and the new birth); (2) I am being saved (sanctification); and (3) I shall be saved (glorification when we are fully conformed to the image of Christ when we are raised and made like Him). Until one gets through the first two stages of salvation, being faithful unto death, or until Christ comes before one dies, the situation is still requiring the believer to move on faith and be faithful. Yes, there is *assurance* of salvation if one follows that faith journey. Assurance is for those who do persevere. If we were to read Heb 11–12 we would learn that perseverance requires human effort as well as God's assurance and grace. We will have something to say about Eph 1 in a bit.

The second passage in Hebrews which requires exegetical gymnastics to fit into a Calvinistic scheme is Heb 10:26–31, which reads,

> If we deliberately keep on sinning after we have received the knowledge of the truth, no sacrifice for sins is left, but only a fearful expectation of judgment and of raging fire that will consume the enemies of God. Anyone who rejected the law of Moses died without mercy on the testimony of two or three witnesses. How much more severely do you think someone deserves to be punished who has trampled the Son of God underfoot, who has treated as an unholy thing the blood of the covenant that sanctified them, and who has insulted the Spirit of grace? For we know him who said, "It is mine to avenge; I will repay," and again, "The Lord will judge his people." It is a dreadful thing to fall into the hands of the living God.

> Remember those earlier days after you had received the light, when you endured in a great conflict full of suffering. Sometimes you were publicly exposed to insult and persecution; at other times you stood side by side with those who were so treated. You suffered along with those in prison and joyfully accepted the confiscation of your property, because you knew that you yourselves had better and lasting possessions. So do not throw away your confidence; it will be richly rewarded.
>
> You need to persevere so that when you have done the will of God, you will receive what he has promised.... But we do not belong to those who shrink back and are destroyed, but to those who have faith and are saved.

Let's start with the last verse—the author is confident that he and his audience have faith and are saved. Notice as well the echo of Heb 6 in v. 32 which talks about the audience in general having received the light during a period of great suffering (I suspect he is talking about the persecution of Nero in 64–65), which included the confiscation of property, but they knew they had "better and more lasting possessions." Again, the author as a Christian is writing to those who are Christians and have gone through all sorts of trials and tribulations, and he is warning them not to commit apostasy. He reminds them that if they keep on sinning after having received and believed the knowledge of the truth, if they turn back now, they face judgment. In vv. 28–29 he contrasts the judgment that Mosaic lawbreakers faced, which pales in comparison to the abandoning of one's Christian faith—it amounts to trampling the Son of God underfoot, and rejecting the shed blood of Jesus, which already sanctified them, insulting the very spirit of grace by which they were accepted by God into Christ's community!

The warnings here are severe, and all too real. Some Christians were abandoning Christ, and all the benefits of the relationship with Him, and the author fears that at least some in his audience are in danger of doing the same. He is warning that they are not eternally secure until they are securely in eternity.

This is akin to John of Patmos's warning that those whose name have been written in the Lamb's book of everlasting life will not be blotted out, *if* they endure faithfully to the end of their lives (Rev 3:5). That is, this is a conditional promise contingent on them following the examples of those in the hall of faith in Heb 11. Typically, Grudem takes this sentence in Rev 3:5 as an ironclad guarantee, but it definitely is not. It says literally, "The one who overcomes ... I will not blot out of the book of life." The latter is dependent on the former, and so clearly this is a conditional promise contingent on a Christian persevering to the end.

Now on the showing of Reformed thinking, the elect can't possibly fall from grace, and the lost can't possibly repent and become part of the saved. It doesn't matter that no human knows for sure who is in which category, because God has already predetermined the outcome either way. That being so, such warnings can neither help the currently lost nor threaten the currently elect. In short, they are ultimately pointless, or at least they are not warnings against the serious sin of Christians committing apostasy. But surely that is exactly what Heb 6 and Heb 10 are warning against. And it does not matter that the human who wrote this may not know who's going to be among the saved at the end. The writer is inspired by God, and God certainly does know, and God is the one who inspired the human writer to say this! We now need to consider in more detail the collateral issue in Eph 1.

## In Christ in Ephesians 1

The phrase "in Christ" or "in Him" (ἐν αὐτῷ) used interchangeably occurs some thirty-nine times in the NT, mostly in Paul's letters, eleven examples of which are found in the opening 202-word sentence in Eph 1. Paul does not use the language we find in Acts, namely the term Χριστιανος, which means a partisan of Christ, or belonging to Christ, but which we simply translate as "Christian." Paul never uses this term. Instead, he talks about believers being "in Christ" or "in Christ Jesus" or "in Him." But what exactly would such a phrase actually mean?

The first thing to be said about this sort of language is that God, including God in Christ, is an incorporative personality, by which I mean because God is omnipresent, people can be said to be "in Him" regardless of where they are on earth. This is not merely metaphorical language; it refers to a reality which can also be expressed as "in the body of Christ," where it is clearer we are talking about a group of people baptized by the Spirit into Christ and His people (1 Cor 12). This is organic, not referring to an organization called "church." We are talking about a spiritual reality, according to Paul, again an organism, a living thing, not an organization.

So when we get to the some eleven occurrences of "in Him" in Eph 1, we need to keep this concept in mind. It is related to the idea of corporate personality, by which is meant that one's group identity is primary, and one's individual identity is secondary. As we have mentioned before, this becomes obvious in the Gospels where people do not have last names, the way we moderns distinguish one person from another. Instead, they are identified by who their father is, "Simon bar Jonah," or what religious group they are part of, "Simon the Pharisee," or where they come from, "Jesus of Nazareth," and the like. Our modern obsession with individual identity and individuality makes understanding incorporative personality or group identity as primary hard to grasp.

The recurring use of "in Him" in Eph 1 is important for many reasons, not least because it implies that there is salvation in no one and nowhere else than "in Christ" for either Jews or Gentiles. But Eph 1–2 wants to say more than that. Ephesians 1–2 says that before the beginning of creation God had a *predetermined plan* of salvation for fallen human beings. Note that it is the *plan* that was predetermined by God, who foreknows all things, and knew we would sin and become fallen creatures. But there is also the language of predestination. God predestined someone or someones before the universe began for election.[52]

In the Augustinian/Calvinistic schema of things this refers to God choosing some individuals to be saved, not on the basis of something good about some humans as opposed to others, but simply because God chose to do so, apparently arbitrarily. Ephesians doesn't talk about what happens to those not so chosen. But this is to forget that both Calvin and Luther were children of the Renaissance, which is to say the intellectual movement that placed far more emphasis on individuality and individuals in general. Markus Barth, in his landmark Ephesians commentary, is on the right track when he stresses that it was Christ whom God destined in advance, and believers are only elect if they are in Him, the Elect or Chosen One of God.[53]

## The Seal

We are all by now familiar with the famous reference in Eph 1:13–14 about the Holy Spirit and the seal, which reads, "When you believed, you were marked in him with a seal, the promised Holy Spirit, who is a pledge/earnest of our inheritance until the redemption of those who are God's possession—to the praise of his glory." The Greek word *arrabon* does *not* mean "guarantee." The King James quite rightly renders it as "an earnest," something given in advance as a sort of promissory note of something to be given later, all being well. Or the NASB rendering is good here—"a pledge." Interestingly, in modern Greek the term *arrabon* is used for an engagement ring! In other words, it refers to something that foreshadows something big

---

52. Origen, it is true, accepted the Platonic idea of the pre-existence of human souls, as well as the Greek idea that the soul is immortal. See pp. 134ff. below. See also pp. 112–14.

53. Barth, *Ephesians 1–3*, especially the detailed discussion of Eph 1–2.

later. As we all know, the ring is not the consummation of the relationship; it is a promissory note, a preview of possible coming attractions.

The same applies to *arrabona* in 2 Cor 1:22 and 2 Cor 5:5, and again in both cases the reference is to the Holy Spirit as this "pledge." There are no other references to this word in the NT. But let us focus on the reference to a seal—not, mind you to a *sealing*, a verbal idea, but to a *seal* (a noun idea).

Surely most everyone in antiquity knew about seals—seals on amphoras, seals on documents, and so on. The seal on an amphora not only indicated who it was doing the sealing, but it protected the wine from contamination, just like shrink wrapping does today on bottles of pills. But such seals could be and were broken (cf. Rev 5:1-5).

So most everyone knew that such a seal could be compromised, could be broken open. Bearing in mind that it is the person of the Holy Spirit who is said to be this seal, this pledge of future good, we need to ask the question raised in the NT repeatedly—Is it possible to so grieve the Holy Spirit or blaspheme or quench the Holy Spirit that one nullifies the pledge or earnest? And the answer surely is yes.

This is exactly what Heb 6, for instance, indicates as we have already seen. Hebrews 6:5-6, it will be remembered, says the following: "It is impossible for those who have once been enlightened, who have tasted the heavenly gift, who have shared in the Holy Spirit, who have tasted the goodness of the word of God and the powers of the coming age and who have fallen away, to be brought back to repentance. To their loss, they are crucifying the Son of God all over again and subjecting Him to public disgrace." What is being described here is apostasy—a willful rejection of the work that God has already done in a person's life. Notice the reference to "having shared in the Holy Spirit," and *then* having rejected all those benefits that one already had.

In short, the reference to the Holy Spirit as the seal, and as the pledge or earnest, reminds us that salvation is not finished until one goes through all three stages of "I have been saved (justification and the new birth), I am being saved (the process of sanctification), and I shall be saved (full conformity to the image of Christ even in the flesh at the resurrection)." The presence of the Spirit in a Christian's life is a pledge that more is coming and *needs to happen*, but it is not a guarantee that apostasy cannot happen (which is why in Rev 3:5 we hear the warning to the church that their names could be erased from the Lamb's book of life if they don't "overcome" and persevere).

One more thing about a seal—it protects something from an *outside* danger. This is why we have promises like that in Rom 8 that no external power or force or principality or angels or demons or circumstances in life can separate us from the love of God in Christ. That is a great assurance. But remember the one thing not in the list of things that can separate you from God is *yourself*, an internal source of trouble, hence the textual warning in various places about apostasy.

Again, apostasy is not about "losing one's salvation"; it is about deliberately, willfully rejecting the work of God in your life. Apostasy doesn't happen by accident or when you are sleeping, as Heb 6 makes perfectly clear. No one can steal your salvation, no circumstance can cause you to lose it. No temptation that comes to you cannot be resisted and escaped from (see 1 Cor 10), if you draw on the power of God already resident in your life. This is what assurance is about, but what it is not about is some sort of guarantee that no matter what you do after conversion you are once saved and always saved. That is not a NT idea.

I could go on at much greater length about the problems with traditional Reformed theology of the sort promulgated by Sproul, Grudem, John Piper, and others, but this must suffice, as we have shown at some length that the TULIP wilts because it is exegetically flawed especially in regard to limited atonement and perseverance of the saints, but if that theology is wrong about those things, then by definition they are wrong about irresistible grace and unconditional election, and also in various cases about what or who limits the atonement.

One also has to ask whether total depravity is the best way to describe fallen human beings in the bondage to sin. It clearly cannot mean they are unredeemable or that the image of God in them has been erased. Defaced yes, distorted yes, erased no. But sin has tainted every aspect of who they are. And if there is such a thing as prevenient grace, then God, who desires that none should perish, has given the lost person the means to respond positively to the Gospel if they will. Some other approach to Biblical and Systematic theology must be taken that involves less serious exegetical errors than the Reformed theology we have considered in this chapter.

What we have seen in this chapter is neither systematic theology as we saw it defined in previous chapters, nor systematic Biblical theology of an historic or apostolic sort, but rather *a reading of the Biblical evidence in light of later Reformed theology.* You will look in vain to find this sort of systemic theologizing in the Apostolic Fathers, or the Patristic Fathers. Indeed, you will not find even a reasonable facsimile of this sort of theology before the later reflections of St. Augustine. It is not accidental that Martin Luther was an Augustinian monk, nor that Calvin likewise was profoundly influenced by Augustine and the Augustinian tradition. But Biblical theology proper should be done on the basis of the Bible itself, not on the basis of readings of the Bible that did not really arise for many centuries after the inspired Biblical writers were dead and gone.

In order to explain how to do Biblical and Systematic theology properly, we are going to step back for a bit from analyzing existing examples of systematized Biblical theology, and explain some of things that should be, or should have been, taken into consideration before undertaking such a daunting task. I'm going to point out that one must *first* take into account the writers' symbolic universe and narrative thought world as we have been intimating right along in this study. But what does that look like if done properly? After that we will consider other factors that have led to flawed approaches to Biblical and Systematic theology.[54]

---

54. There will also be a place in the ethics chapter below to do a critique of recent Arminian attempts to produce a Systematic theology of holiness, looking at all the canonical books.

PART TWO

Toward a Proper Approach
to Biblical and *Systematic Theology*

## Chapter Five

# Abstract Art
## Denuding Theology of Its Narrative Thought World

The first qualification for judging any piece of workmanship from a corkscrew to a cathedral is to know what it is—what it was intended to do and how it was meant to be used.
    —C. S. Lewis, Preface to *Paradise Lost*

At this juncture, having looked at some sample theologies that bear the label Systematic theology but aren't, it will be well to ask *how*, besides making better *exegetical* judgments about the meaning of Biblical texts, the enterprise of Systematic theology (and Biblical theology) could be done much better than what we have seen so far. This will take several chapters to unpack, beginning with the issue of the Bible's narrative thought world, which if taken seriously would prevent one from treating the Bible as just a collection of ideas or theological topics arranged in various configurations.

So, to begin with, to understand the Bible, one must start with the symbolic universe that all the Biblical writers lived in and were influenced by. In that universe there were fixed stars like God, revelation, redemption, holiness, mighty works (or miracles) to mention but a few things which were *taken for granted* by all the authors. All of our authors were Jews, or perhaps in the singular case of Luke and perhaps the compiler of 2 Peter, God-fearers. Their symbolic universe was formed and shaped by things like the books we call the OT, and in the case of the NT writers also by the Jesus tradition, the apostolic tradition, new prophetic revelation, and the like.

None of them really felt the need to argue for the things mentioned above as fixed stars. But the new thing in that symbolic universe was Christ and the Christ event and its sequel. About these new things, they realized they did indeed need to persuade human beings (see 2 Cor 5:11).

There was a shift in the symbolic universe between the time of the OT and the time of the writing of the NT. As for the OT writers, their symbolic universe was shaped by the gradually emerging monotheistic worldview involving a singular deity—Yahweh and a chosen people, the Hebrews, later called Israel, and Yahweh's revelations to His people, which involved both what we call theology and what we call ethics.

Out of that shared symbolic universe was formed their narrative thought world. And here I am suggesting that the Biblical writers not only shared certain big ticket *ideas* in common, they also shared a narrative thought world in common as well. They made sense of God and His revelation through telling stories, in particular stories about God's interaction with them in history, in particular salvation history. They even told the story of God's creating as a story, a story that climaxes with the creation of human beings in Gen 1–2.

They all were convinced, for example, that history was going somewhere, that God was guiding it and working things together for good for His people, and in the case of the NT writers, they thought they were all writing late in the story, trying to get the Good News out in time for the final edition to be published before the "Deadline" was reached. These NT writers all stood on tiptoe utterly convinced that they already lived in the eschatological age and were looking for a consummation devoutly to be wished. The failure to recognize the common narrative thought world that is presupposed by the various NT writers is a very significant failure indeed.

Finally, out of that narrative thought world, the writers theologize and ethicize into particular contexts. The commonality lies as much or more at the presuppositional level as at the articulation level. What we have in the Bible is theologizing and ethicizing out of a shared narrative thought world. What we don't have is a systematic theology textbook, or even a dictionary of Biblical thoughts and ideas.

It is important to stress as well that there was a seismic shift in the symbolic universe and the narrative thought world as a result of the Christ event, not just because of His coming but especially because of the death and resurrection and Spirit sending of Jesus. Among other things, this involved re-envisioning the divine identity so that it included both the Father and the Son, and in due course the Spirit, which was seen as personal, and more than just the living presence of Yahweh, the latter being what we probably find in the OT where the reference to spirit comes up.[1]

Certainly, *none* of the writers of the NT envision what had happened and was happening since Jesus came and inaugurated the eschatological age as *not* involving Jesus when it comes to salvation. If one tries to do Biblical or Systematic theology without recognizing the symbolic universe, and the shift that Christ caused in it, and without recognizing the narrative thought world which also got reconfigured because of the Christ, and finally by failing to realize that what we have in the Bible is theologizing and ethicizing out of and into specific situations and contexts, one is bound to make serious mistakes in the theological discussion. Early Jews prior to the time of Jesus were not looking for a crucified, much less a crucified and then raised and thus vindicated, messiah. Indeed, the notion of a crucified messiah would have seemed to be an oxymoron to most of them.

Bear in mind nothing is said in Isa 52–53 about a *crucified* suffering servant. Crucifixion happened to someone who was cursed, not anointed and vindicated by God (cf. Gal 3:13 based on Deut 21:23, which is clearly referring in the latter case to the public display of a corpse after execution as a shaming exercise). This verse in Deut 21 by itself did not lead to a theology of crucifixion as some kind of atonement for sin, never mind a *human* execution as an atonement for sin. Rather it was Christ's death on a cross that caused a *re-evaluation* of Deut 21:23. The Christ event caused a rethinking about numerous OT texts. A change in the narrative thought world led to a change in the way the OT was read—now with Christological glasses.

Unfortunately in some Biblical and Systematic theologies where OT and NT ideas are simply analyzed and systematized as if there was no development in understanding by the inspired writers, or even worse that nothing really significant *changed* before or when Christ showed up, there is little or no reckoning with the Christ revolution and how it was a game changer (see 1 Pet 1:10–12).[2] But we know, to give but one example, that the theology of the afterlife changed dramatically during the Babylonian exile and thereafter, not because the ideas about Sheol were left entirely behind, but because the new ideas involving resurrection of the dead, among other things, changed the landscape of the beliefs about the afterlife. Justice and

---

1. Only twice does the phrase "Holy Spirit" clearly turn up in the OT (see Ps 51:11 and Isa 63:10), and it is clear in both cases that it refers to Yahweh's spirit, Yahweh's living presence, that for instance David begs God not to take from him.

2. With apologies to my friend Tom Wright and the excellent and thought-provoking title about the cross and related events in *The Day the Revolution Began*. I would say that the revolution began when Christ came, and particularly when He began his ministry, but of course the cross and resurrection were the major game changers.

redemption would indeed be done on the earth, and God's reign would finally come on the entire earth surprisingly brought about by one "like a son of man" (see Dan 7:13–14).

Analyzing only the articulated similarities between the various OT and NT witnesses is like analyzing and comparing the tips of what appear to be several different icebergs and noticing their similarities in shape and hew and size, all the while failing to note that they turn out to all be united below the surface of the ocean in which they are floating. In other words, they are all individual peaks of one much larger common mass.

Beneath the surface and sometimes above the surface is the narrative thought world. It is not a set of consistent, abstract theological ideas which unites the Biblical witness; it is the shared worldview of the narrative thought world, and its values, implications, and possible applications. And this involved what we call theology and also ethics not in the abstract, but as words on target for a specific audience in a specific setting at a specific time. To denude the text of its historical context is, to some degree, to change the meaning of the material abstracted.

It is no accident that much of the OT and the NT involves narrative, historical narrative. God operates in the human sphere, and relates to His people there. This is why we find theologically rich narratives in the stories we find in the Pentateuch, in Joshua, Judges, Ruth, Esther, 1–2 Samuel, 1–2 Kings, 1–2 Chronicles, and substantial bits and pieces in the prophetic books (cf., e.g., Jonah). Even the Wisdom literature gives us the story of Job.

In the NT the first five books are *all narratives*, and Jesus' preaching is often narratival—drawing analogies in story form that we call parables. Then there are stories embedded in various of the letters in the NT, not to mention in sermons like Hebrews, and closing out the Bible is the grand narrative in the form of apocalyptic prophecy of where God's plan was heading, and how the issues of justice and redemption would be resolved finally at the return of Christ, and the appearance of the new Jerusalem.

The Biblical story begins in Genesis with creation and the beginning of God's relationship with humankind and it ends with the new creation and the final dwelling of God with His people on earth. Finally, "thy kingdom come, thy will be done on earth as it is in heaven" will come to pass as Jesus' disciples had learned to fervently pray from Jesus Himself.[3]

Part of paying attention to the historical context involves studying the Gospels as examples of the ancient genre of biographies (Matthew, Mark, and John) and ancient historical monographs (Luke–Acts). There was some overlap between these two ancient genres, but the focus of the *bioi* was on a

---

3. See my extended discussion of all this in my *Biblical Theology*, 1–265.

person or persons, whereas the focus of historical monograph was on *"the things* that have happened among us," i.e., the significant events that shaped the history being recounted. Let me be clear that ancient biographies did not work just like modern ones, and the same can be said about ancient historical monographs. So, the failure to study the theological content of these documents in light of their ancient genre is *a big mistake*. A text without a context is just a pretext for whatever you want it to mean.

Ancient biographers were, and had to be, content with less precision about things like time. For example, the phrase "on the third day" often means the same thing as "after three days." This is not a contradiction; it's just the use of imprecise language. Or take Mark's incessant use of the adverb *euthus*, which translates as "immediately," but really means "next," or "soon after that."

It really isn't a mystery as to why Acts doesn't record the end of Paul's missionary life in Rome. The goal of the history was to tell the story of the spread of the Word, the Good News about Christ, from Jerusalem to Rome, the heart of the empire, not to tell Paul's full story. Again, genre and its ancient conventions matter, as does the way theologizing and ethicizing happen in narrative, in speech material, in marginal or parenthetical comments by the writer. For example, notice how Luke indirectly highlights the theological and ethical implications of ignorance in the speech material in Luke–Acts. "Father forgive them, for they know not what they do," says Jesus of His executioners (Luke 23:34), and Peter reiterates this theme in Acts 3:17. With more knowledge comes more moral responsibility. Or one can look for positive repeated patterns in the stories, which suggest this was or should be the norm (e.g., cf. Acts 2:42–47 to Acts 4:32–37). One can always ask about narratives—Is this a go and do likewise story, or a go and do otherwise story? Normally, these stories are all about theological ethics, not just theology or just ethics.

Furthermore, it will not come as a surprise that in an oral culture, actually most of the NT letters were meant to be read aloud, and conform more to the conventions of ancient speeches, acts of rhetorical persuasion, than they do to ancient letter conventions. In fact, I would argue that almost all of the letters and sermons we find in the NT, to one degree or another, are shaped by the oral conventions of rhetoric.[4] They are documents that were meant to be read aloud and heard, and their oral and aural dimensions are crucial.

---

4. Maybe not so much 2–3 John.

I quite agree with Francis Watson that the Bible is irremediably theological in character.[5] It is all about God, and God's relationship with various human individuals and groups. *The Bible's history cannot be readily abstracted from its theologizing or vice versa.* There is of course a good reason for this—God is committed to involvement in the messiness and contingencies of human history and always has been. Indeed, it should be said that God, as the creator of all things including all human beings, is the one who made history possible, viable, having purpose and a goal, and so on.

Further, I quite agree with Watson that the segregation of Biblical studies from theological studies has led to the impoverishment of both fields. Exegetes are working on inherently theological texts! Biblical theologians require exegetical study to come to grips with the subjects of their own fields of interest and inquiry. Watson is right to complain about the rigid divisions of these fields in the guild.

Watson also urges a "dialectical" interdependence between the OT and the NT, decrying the tendency to see the OT as merely background for the NT. He urges "the notion of a dialectical unity between the two bodies of writing, constituted as 'old' and 'new' by their relationship to the foundational event that they together enclose and attest, only makes sense from a theological standpoint."[6] I would agree with this assertion in principle, but I would add that such an assertion only makes sense from a historical viewpoint as well.

After all, the terms 'old" and "new" refer to time and space, and events that happen in time and space and objects that are created in time and space, such as the various parts of the Bible. Here is where I must insist, however, that unless one does justice to the historical, narratival, and theological character of these texts, *one will not be doing theology properly, nor doing history justice, nor adequately dealing with the genre of the literature.* What do I mean by this?

Well for one thing I mean that the OT does not cease to be Christian Scripture simply because it mostly tells us about God the Father and His relationship with the universe, the world, a people. Patrology in the more antique and theologically loaded sense of that term is just as much a part of Christian theology as Christology is. The fact that with benefit of hindsight and further revelation Christians came to view the Father through the lens of the Son and the Spirit does not mean that we cannot appreciate what is going on in the OT on its own terms, and furthermore recognize that the Christian doctrine of God would be severely and seriously impoverished

---

5. Watson, *Text and Truth*.
6. Watson, *Text and Truth*, 5.

without what the OT has to say about the matter. For example, the holiness, justice, mercy, and indeed the love of God would be far less clear if we did not have the Hebrew Scriptures.

So what are the implications of all this for Biblical and Systematic theology? The first is a cautionary word. Not only should such theology be well grounded in detailed exegesis of the Biblical text, and recognize its contextual and historical nature, but one must also take account of the narrative thought world in which the theological discussion is embedded and emerges from and the rhetoric writers such as Paul use to present the material. A failure to do this leads to bad theology. One detailed illustration showing why a detailed interaction with the original rhetorical context and content of the text is crucial for doing Biblical and Systematic theology must suffice.[7]

Romans 7 demonstrates not only Paul's considerable skill with rhetoric, but his penchant for using even its most complex devices and techniques. This text proves beyond a reasonable doubt that Paul did not use rhetoric in some purely superficial or sparing way (e.g., using rhetorical questions).[8] To the contrary, the very warp and woof of his argument here reflects, and indeed requires an understanding of, sophisticated rhetorical techniques to make sense of the content of this passage and the way it attempts to persuade the Roman audience.

"Impersonation," or *prosopopoeia*, is a rhetorical technique which falls under the heading of figures of speech and is often used to illustrate or make vivid a piece of deliberative rhetoric (Quintilian, *Inst.* 3.8.49; cf. Theon, *Progymnasta* 8). This rhetorical technique involves the assumption of a role, and sometimes the role would be marked off from its surrounding discourse by a change in tone or inflection or accent or form of delivery, or an introductory formula signaling a change in voice. Sometimes the speech would simply be inserted "without mentioning the speaker at all" (Quintilian, *Inst.* 9.2.37).[9] Unfortunately for us, we did not get to hear Paul's discourse delivered in its original oral setting, as was Paul's intent. It is not surprising then that many have not picked up the signals that impersonation is happening in Rom 7:7–13 and also for that matter in 7:14–25.[10]

---

7. This material can be found in another form in my Romans commentary, Witherington and Hyatt, *Paul's Letter to the Romans*.

8. Against several of the essayists in Porter and Stamps, *Rhetorical Criticism and the Bible*, who continue to misjudge Paul in this regard, as has rightly also been noticed by M. M. Mitchell in several publications. See, e.g., *Heavenly Trumpet*.

9. For an earlier and simplified version of this discussion, see Witherington and Hyatt, *Paul's Letter to the Romans*.

10. "Impersonation" was a rhetorical device used to train those learning to write letters (see Theon, *Progymnasmata* 2.1125.22).

Quintilian says impersonation "is sometimes introduced even with controversial themes, which are drawn from history and involve the appearance of *definite historical characters* as pleaders" (*Inst.* 3.8.52). In this case Adam is the historical figure being impersonated in Rom 7:7–13, and the theme is most certainly controversial and drawn from history. Indeed, Paul has introduced this theme already in Rom 5:12–21, and one must bear in mind that this Roman discourse would have been heard *seriatim*, which means they would have heard about Adam only a few minutes before hearing the material in Rom 7.

The most important requirement for a speech in character in the form of impersonation is that the speech be fitting, suiting the situation and character of the one speaking. "For a speech that is out of keeping with the man who delivers it is just as faulty as a speech which fails to suit the subject to which it should conform" (*Inst.* 3.8.51). The ability to pull off a convincing impersonation is considered by Quintilian to reflect the *highest skill in rhetoric*, for it is often the most difficult thing to do (*Inst.* 3.8.49). That Paul attempts it tells us something about Paul as a rhetorician. This rhetorical technique also involves personification, sometimes of abstract qualities (like fame or virtue, or in Paul's case sin or grace—*Inst.* 9.2.36). Quintilian also informs us that impersonation may take the form of a dialogue or speech, but it can also take the form of a first person narrative (*Inst.* 9.2.37).

Of course, since the important work of W. G. Kümmel on Rom 7, it has become a commonplace, perhaps even a majority opinion in some NT circles, that the "I" of Rom 7 is not autobiographical.[11] This, however, still did not tell us what sort of literary or rhetorical use of "I" we do find in Rom 7. As S. Stowers points out, it is also no new opinion that what is going on in Rom 7 is the rhetorical technique known as "impersonation."[12] In fact, this is how some of the earliest Greek commentators on Romans, such as Origen, took this portion of the letter, and later commentators such as Jerome and Rufinus take note of this approach of Origen's.[13] Not only so, Didymus of Alexandria and Nilus of Ancyra also saw Paul using the form of speech in character or impersonation here.[14]

---

11. See Kümmel, *Romer 7 und das Bild des Menschen*.

12. Stowers, *Rereading of Romans*, 264–69.

13. Unfortunately we have only fragments of Origen's Romans commentary. See the careful discussion by Stowers, *Rereading of Romans*, 266–67. Origen rightly notes that: (1) Jews such as Paul do not speak of a time when they lived before or without the Law; (2) what Paul says elsewhere about himself (cf. 1 Cor 6:19; Gal 3:13 and 2:20) does not fit this description of life outside Christ in Rom 7.

14. See Stowers, *Rereading of Romans*, 268–69.

The point to be noted here is that we are talking about Church Fathers who not only know Greek well but who understand the use of rhetoric and believed Paul is certainly availing himself of rhetorical devices here.[15] Even more importantly, there is John Chrysostom (*Hom. Rom.* 13), who was very much in touch with the rhetorical nature and the theological substance of Paul's letters. He also does not think that Rom 7 is about Christians, much less about Paul himself as a Christian. He takes it to be talking about: (1) those who lived before the Law; (2) and those who lived outside the Law or lived under it. In other words, it is about Gentiles and Jews outside of Christ.

But I would want to stress that since the vast majority of Paul's audience is Gentile, and Paul has as part of his rhetorical aims effecting some reconciliation between Jewish and Gentile Christians in Rome,[16] it would be singularly inept for Paul here to retell the story of Israel in a negative way, and then turn around in Rom 9–11 and try to get Gentiles to appreciate their Jewish heritage in Christ, and to be understanding of Jews and their fellow Jewish Christians. No, Paul tells a more universal tale here of the progenitor of all humankind, and then the story of all those "in Adam," not focusing specifically on those "in Israel" that are within the Adamic category.[17] Even in Rom 7:14–25, Paul can be seen to be mainly echoing his discussion of Gentiles in Rom 2:15 who had the "Law" within and struggled over its demands.[18]

What are the markers or indicators in the text of Rom 7:7–13 that the most probable way to read this text, the way Paul desired for it to be heard, is in the light of the story of Adam, with Adam speaking of his own experience?[19] Firstly, from the beginning of the passage in v. 7 there is reference to one specific commandment—"thou shalt not covet/desire." This is the tenth commandment in an abbreviated form (cf. Exod 20:17; Deut

---

15. It appears that the better a commentator knew both Greek and rhetoric, the more likely they were to read Rom 7 as an example of impersonation.

16. See Witherington and Hyatt, *Paul's Letter to the Romans*, intro.

17. See Quintilian, *Inst.* 9.2.30–31: "By this means we display the inner thoughts of our adversaries as though they were talking with themselves . . . or without sacrifice of credibility we may offer conversations between ourselves and others, or of others among themselves, and put words of advice, reproach, complaint, praise or pity into the mouths of appropriate persons."

18. The sensitive analysis by Aletti, "Rhetoric of Romans 5–8," 300, deserves to be consulted. He makes clear that Paul is not talking about Christians here.

19. Some commentators, such as Barrett, *Romans*, 134–35, attempt a combination interpretation. Barrett avers the text is about Adam and also autobiographically about Paul. The rhetorical conventions suggest otherwise, but of course Paul is retelling the story of Adam because of its relevance for his audience's understanding of themselves. They are not to go back down the Adamic road.

5:21). Some early Jewish exegesis of Gen 3 suggested that the sin committed by Adam and Eve was a violation of the tenth commandment.[20] They coveted the fruit of the tree of the knowledge of good and evil.

Secondly, one must ask oneself, who in Biblical history was only under *one* commandment, and one about coveting? The answer is Adam.[21] Verse 8 refers to a commandment (singular). This can hardly be a reference to the Mosaic law in general, which Paul regularly speaks of as a collective entity. Thirdly, v. 9 says, "I was living once without/apart from the Law." The only persons said in the Bible to be living before or without any law were Adam and Eve.

Fourthly, as numerous commentators have regularly noticed, Sin is personified in this text, especially in v. 11, as if it were like the snake in the garden. Paul says, "Sin took opportunity through the commandment to deceive me." This matches up well with the story about the snake using the commandment to deceive Eve and Adam in the garden. Notice too how the very same verb (in the LXX) is used to speak of this deception in 2 Cor 11:3 and also 1 Tim 2:14. We know of course that physical death was said to be part of the punishment for this sin, but there was also the matter of spiritual death, due to alienation from God, and it is perhaps the latter that Paul has in view in this text.

Fifthly, notice how in v. 7 Paul says, speaking as and for Adam, I did not know sin except through the commandment. This condition would only properly be the case with Adam, especially if "know" in this text means having personal experience of sin (cf. v. 5). As we know from various earlier texts in Romans, Paul believes that all after Adam have sinned and fallen short of God's glory. The discussion in Rom 5:12–21 seems to be presupposed here. It is, however, possible to take *egnon* to mean "recognize"—I did not recognize sin for what it was except through the existence of the commandment.

If this is the point, then it comports with what Paul has already said about the Law turning sin into trespass, sin being revealed as a violation of God's will for humankind. But on the whole it seems more likely that Paul is describing Adam's awakening consciousness of the possibility of sin when the first commandment was given. All in all, the most satisfactory

---

20. See 4 Ezra 7:11; Babylonian Talmud San. 56b; and on the identification of Torah with the pre-existent Wisdom of God, see Sir 24:23; Bar 3:36—4.1.

21. See Kasemann, *Romans*, 196: "Methodologically the starting point should be that a story is told in vv.9–11 and that the event depicted can refer strictly only to Adam.... There is nothing in the passage which does not fit Adam, and everything fits Adam alone."

explanation of these verses is if we see Paul the Christian re-reading the story of Adam here, in the light of his Christian views about law and the Law.[22]

Certainly, one of the functions of this subsection of Romans is to do something of an apologia for the Law. Paul is asking, is then the Law something evil because it not only reveals sin, but has the unintended effect of suggesting sins to commit to a human being? Is the Law's association with sin and death then a sign that the Law itself is a sinful or wicked thing? Paul's response is of course "absolutely not"! Verse 7 suggests a parallel between *egnon* and "know desire," which suggests Paul has in view the experience of sin by this knower. Verse 8 says sin takes the Law as the starting point or opportunity to produce in the knower all sorts of evil desires.[23]

Stowers reads this part of the discussion in light of Greco-Roman discussions about desire and the mastery of desire, which may have been one of the things this discourse prompted in the largely Gentile audience.[24] But the story of Adam seems to be to the fore here. The basic argument here is how sin used a good thing, the Law, to create evil desires in Adam.

It is important to recognize that in Rom 5–6 Paul had already established that all humans are "in Adam," and all have sinned like him. Furthermore, Paul has spoken of the desires that plagued his largely Gentile audience prior to their conversions. The discussion here then just further links even the Gentile portion of the audience to Adam and his experience. They are to recognize themselves in this story, as the children of Adam who also have had desires, have sinned, and have died. The way Paul will illuminate the parallels will be seen in Rom 7:14–25, which I take to be a description of all those in Adam and outside of Christ.[25]

---

22. See the earlier discussion of this view at some length by Lyonnet, "Histoire du salut selon le ch. 7 de l'epitre aux Romains," 117–51; and the helpful discussion of Elliott, *Rhetoric of Romans*, 246–50, who comes to the same Adamic conclusion on the basis of rhetorical considerations.

23. Barrett, *Romans*, 132, puts it vividly: "The law is not simply a reagent by which the presence of sin is detected: it is a catalyst which aids or even initiates the action of sin upon man."

24. See Stowers, *Rereading of Romans*, 271–72. He suggests the tragic figure of Medea might be conjured up by what Paul says, but surely Adam is a more likely candidate to have come to Paul's mind and his audience as well.

25. It simply complicates and confuses the matter to suggest Paul is also talking about Israel as well as Adam here. Paul is addressing a largely Gentile audience who did not identify with Israel, but could understand and identify with the progenitor of the whole human race. That Israel might be included in the discussion of those who are "in Adam" in 7:14–25 is certainly possible, but even there Paul has already described earlier in Rom 2 the dilemma of a Gentile caught between the law and a hard place. My point would be that even in vv. 14–25 he is not specifically focusing on Jewish experience or the experience of Israel.

Paul then is providing a narrative in Rom 7:7–25 of the story of Adam from the past in vv. 7–13, and the story of all those in Adam in the present in vv. 14–25. In a sense what is happening here is an expansion on what Paul has already argued in Rom 5:12–21. There is a continuity in the "I" in Rom 7 by virtue of the close link between Adam and all those in Adam.

The story of Adam is also the prototype of the story of Christ, and it is only when the person is delivered from the body of death, it is only when a person transfers from the story of Adam into the story of Christ, that one can leave Adam and his story behind, no longer being in bondage to sin, and being empowered to resist temptation, walk in newness of life, as will be described in Rom 8. Christ starts the race of humanity over again, setting it right and in a new direction, delivering it from the bondage of sin, death, and the Law. It is not a surprise that Christ only enters the picture at the very end of the argument in Rom 7, in preparation for Rom 8, using the rhetorical technique of overlapping the end of one argument with the beginning of another.[26]

Some have seen v. 9b as a problem for the Adam view of vv. 7–13 because the verb must be translated "renewed" or "live anew." But notice the contrast between "I was living" in v. 9a with "but Sin coming to life" in v. 9b. Cranfield then is right to urge that the meaning of the verb in question in v. 9b must be "sprang to life."[27]

The snake/sin was lifeless until it had an opportunity to victimize some innocent victim, and had the means, namely the commandment, to do so. Sin deceived and spiritually killed the first founder of the human race. This is nearly a quotation from Gen 3:13. One of the important corollaries of recognizing that Rom 7:7–13 is about Adam (and 7:14–25 is about those in Adam, and outside Christ) is that it becomes clear that Paul is not specifically critiquing Judaism or Jews here, any more than he is in Rom 7:14–25.

Verse 12 begins with *hoste*, which should be translated "so then" introducing Paul's conclusion about the Law that Paul has been driving toward. The commandment and for that matter the whole Law is holy, just, and good. It did not in itself produce sin or death in the founder of the human race. Rather sin/the serpent/Satan used the commandment to that end.

---

26. This has confused those who are unaware of this rhetorical convention and have taken the outburst "Thanks be to God in Jesus Christ" to be a cry only a Christian would make, and that therefore Rom 7:14–25 must be about Christian experience. However, if 7:14–25 is meant to be a narrative of a person in Adam who is led to the end of himself and to the point of conviction and conversion, then this outburst should be taken as Paul's interjected reply or response with the Gospel to the heartfelt cry of the lost person, a response which prepares for and signals the coming of the following argument in Rom 8 about life in Christ.

27. Cranfield, *Romans 1–8*, 351–52.

Good things, things from God, can be used for evil purposes by those with evil intent. The exceeding sinfulness of sin is revealed in that it will even use a good thing to produce an evil end—death. This was not the intended end or purpose of the Law.

The death of Adam was not a matter of his being killed with kindness or by something good. Verse 13 is emphatic. The Law, a good thing, did not kill Adam. But sin was indeed revealed to be sin by the Law and it produced death This argument prepares the way for the discussion of the legacy of Adam for those who are outside of Christ. The present tense verbs reflect the ongoing legacy for those who are still in Adam and not in Christ. Romans 7:14–25 should not be seen as a further argument, but as the last stage of a four-part argument which began in Rom 6, being grounded in Rom 5:12–21, and will climax Paul's discussion about sin, death, and the Law and their various effects on humankind.

It will not be necessary for us to go into as much depth with Rom 7:14–25 as we have with the tale of Adam in 7:7–13. Rather we will focus on the points of rhetorical significance that should have guided the interpretation of this text all along. Firstly, once it is realized that there is a fictive "I" being used in 7:7–13, to create a "speech in character," then it requires a change of rhetorical signals at 7:14 or thereafter if that were to cease to be the case in 7:14–25. We have no such compelling evidence that Paul is now using "I" in a non-fictive way in these verses now under scrutiny. There is, it is true, a change in the tenses of the main verbs; here we have present tenses, signaling that Paul is talking about something that is now true of someone or some group of persons, but it must be some group that has an integral connection with the "I" of 7:7–13.

Fortunately, Paul had already set up such a link in Rom 5:12–21, in particular at the outset of that *synkrisis* or rhetorical comparison—one man sinned and death came to all people, but not just because he sinned but also because they all sinned. The link has been forged, and we see here how it is played out as Adam's tale in 7:7–13 leads directly to the tale of all those who are in Adam in 7:14–25. Kasemann puts the matter aptly: "*Egō* [here] means [hu]mankind under the shadow of Adam: hence it does not embrace Christian existence in its ongoing temptation. . . . What is being said here is already over for the Christian according to ch. 6 and ch. 8. The apostle is not even describing the content of his own experience of conversion."[28] This comports completely with Rom 7:5–6 where Paul contrasts what the audience once was before they became Christians, and what they are now—free in Christ. It comports as well with what Paul stresses in Rom 8:1–2 where

---

28. Kasemann, *Romans*, 200.

he tells us that the Spirit has already set the believer free from the law of sin and death.

It is telling that most of the Church Fathers thought as well that Paul was adopting and adapting the persona of an unregenerate person, not describing his own struggles as a Christian. Most of them believed that conversion would deliver a person from the dilemma described here, deliver them from the bondage to sin or the law of sin and death, as Rom 8:1–2 puts it.[29]

But what about the reference to the struggle with the "law of the mind" here? Does not that suggest a person, perhaps a Jew, under the yoke of the Mosaic law? While not an impossible interpretation of the struggle described here, there is a better and more likely view if we are attentive to the rhetorical signals of the whole document. In Rom 2:15 Paul is quite explicit that Gentiles not beholden to the Mosaic covenant or its Law nonetheless have the generic law of God written on their very hearts, and therefore they do from time to time do what God requires of them.

Notice that the struggle described in Rom 7:14–25 is between a law residing in one's mind, and a quite different ruling principle residing in one's "flesh" or sinful inclinations. Nothing is said here about rebellion against a known external law code, nor is the book of the Law nor Moses mentioned here. Remember too, that it was said that even Adam himself had a singular commandment of God to deal with, well before Moses, such that when Adam violated that one commandment sin and death reigned from Adam to Moses, even prior to the existence of the Mosaic code (Rom 5:14). Notice the difference between Rom 7:14–25 and debates in Rom 2–3 with the Jewish teacher over the meaning of the external Law code.

It is thus most likely that we have here a more generic description of the condition of those who are in Adam, and are fighting but losing the battle with sin in their lives. The only way out of their dilemma is deliverance. Paul is speaking as broadly as he can in this passage, addressing the human plight outside of Christ in general, and is not singling out Jews for special attention here. That would have been rhetorically inept in any case since the great majority of his audience for Romans is likely Gentiles (see Rom 11:13).

We must bear in mind, as well, that we are dealing with a Christian interpretation of a pre-Christian condition. Paul does not assume that this is how either Gentiles or Jews themselves would view the matter if they were not also Christians. But clearly Gentiles could relate to this discussion. For example, Ovid, in his famous work, *Metamorphoses* speaks in very similar

---

29. Bray, *Romans*, 189–90.

terms of the struggle with sin: "Desire persuades me one way, reason another. I see the better and approve it, but I follow the worse" (7.19–20). Even closer are the words of Epictetus: "What I wish, I do not do, and what I do not wish, I do" (*Ench.* 2.26.4). Paul has not traipsed into terra incognita for his largely Gentile audience; rather he is standing on familiar ground. The effect of law, law of any sort, on a fallen human being, whether the law of the heart, or the law in a code, is predictably the same, in Paul's view.

In the earlier parts of Romans, and especially in Rom 2–3, Paul was resorting to the rhetorical device of the diatribe—a rhetorical debate with an imaginary interlocutor. Romans 7:7–25 has just a taste of that at Rom 7:25a where Paul himself, in his own and most pastoral voice, responds to the heart cry of the lost person—"Who will deliver me from this body of death?" His answer is swift and powerful—"Thanks be to God—through Jesus Christ our Lord!" What was lost on Luther is that the voice in v. 25a is not the same voice as the one which preceded it, or indeed which follows it in 25b. What was lost on Augustine is that this is not Pauline autobiography however well it may have suited Augustine. It is to Augustine and Luther that we owe being led down the wrong garden path in the interpretation of this text, and in some cases led to a wrong view altogether of Pauline anthropology.

At the end of Rom 7, Paul is following a well-known rhetorical technique called chain-link, or interlocking construction, which has now been described in detail with full illustration of its use in the NT by Bruce Longenecker.[30] The basic way this technique works is that one briefly introduces the theme of the next argument or part of one's rhetorical argument, just before one concludes the argument one is presently laying out. Thus in this case Rom 7:25a is the introduction to Rom 8:1 and following where Paul will once more speak in his own voice in the first person. Quintilian is quite specific about the need to use such a technique in a complex argument of many parts. He says that this sort of close-knit ABAB structure is effective when one must speak with pathos, force, energy, pugnacity (*Inst.* 9.4.129–30). He adds, "We may compare its motion to that of men, who link hands to stead their steps, and lend each other their mutual support" (*Inst.* 9.4.129). Failure to recognize this rhetorical device, where one introduces the next argument before concluding the previous one, has led to all sorts of misreadings of Rom 7:14–25.[31]

---

30. Longenecker, *Rhetoric at the Boundaries*.

31. Longenecker, *Rhetoric at the Boundaries*, 88–93, shows in great detail how this works in Rom 7:14–25 and his argument answers every question or possible objection to this view of this passage.

As Longenecker goes on to stress, this reading of Rom. 7:25a comports completely with the thrust of what has come immediately before Rom. 7:7–25 and what comes immediately thereafter. He puts it this way:

> Paul has taken great care to signal the transition from Romans 7 to Romans 8: first by contrasting the "fleshly then" and the "spiritual now" in 7.5–6, two verses which provide the structural foundation for the movement from 7.7ff. and 8.1ff., and second, by introducing the "spiritual now" in 8.1 with the emphatic "therefore now" (*ara nun*). Such structural indicators are strengthened further by the intentional inclusion of a thematic overlap in 7.25. . . . Since in Paul's day chain-link construction was not an uncommon transitional device in assisting an audience . . . the placement of 7.25 within its surrounding context would not have been unusual or confusing. It would not have been seen as a structural anomaly requiring either textual reconstruction . . . or psychological explanation. Instead it would have been seen as a transition marker used for the benefit of Paul's audience.[32]

As an aside, it is worth reminding that Origen offers this same sort of analysis on Rom 7 as "impersonation" back in hoary antiquity.

In short, if Paul can go to these sorts of lengths to use rhetorical conventions to convict and persuade a Roman audience that he has not even met, we may be sure that it is a mistake to underestimate what was rhetorically possible for Paul and other writers of the NT. Not all of them had Paul's skills and finesse. But almost all of them had some knowledge and made some use of not just micro-rhetoric but also macro-rhetoric, and it is high time we were in more agreement with Origen and Chrysostom and Jerome and Melanchthon and others on this score.

The upshot of this is straightforward—Rom 7 is not a description of the Christian life; it is a Christian description of the pre-Christian condition of all those in Adam, and not yet in Christ. *This means much of the Reformation, and particularly the Lutheran, discussions of Rom 7 and the concomitant implications for human anthropology are wrong. The failure to take into account the rhetorical way Paul tells these stories leads to bad theology.* We should have realized something was amiss when we read Paul's brief biography in Phil 3—"If someone else thinks they have reasons to put confidence in the flesh, I have more: circumcised on the eighth day, of the people of Israel, of the tribe of Benjamin, a Hebrew of Hebrews; in regard to

---

32. Longenecker, *Rhetoric at the Boundaries*, 92. On the frequency of use and popularity of this rhetorical device, see *Rhetoric at the Boundaries*, 11–42.

the law, a Pharisee; as for zeal, persecuting the church; as for righteousness based on the law, faultless." Faultless means blameless from the legal point of view, not a lawbreaker. It does not mean sinless, but nevertheless, this text surely rules out that Rom 7 is Pauline auto-biography.

Neither Biblical theology nor systematic theology should be done while ignoring detailed *contextual* exegesis, including the exegesis that takes into account rhetoric where appropriate. It's time to bury the notion that Rom 7 is somehow a description of the life of a Christian. It will be helpful if we now consider whether Jerusalem had more to do with Athens than just the use of Greco-Roman rhetoric.

Chapter Six

# The Imports
## The Promise and Problems of Greek Philosophy vis-à-vis Jewish Ideas and Stories

What indeed has Athens to do with Jerusalem? What concord is there between the Academy and the Church? What between heretics and Christians? Our instruction comes from "the porch of Solomon," who had himself taught that "the Lord should be sought in simplicity of heart."

Away with all attempts to produce a mottled Christianity of Stoic, Platonic, and dialectic composition! We want no curious disputation after possessing Christ Jesus, no inquisition after enjoying the gospel! With our faith, we desire no further belief. For this is our faith which deserves the palm, that there is nothing which we ought to believe besides.

—Tertullian, *Prescription Against Heretics* (AD 197ff.)[1]

Classical Christian theology dealt with the personal character of God in the doctrine of the Trinity. The Christian faith does not speak of God as one person but rather as three persons. The divine essence as such was not conceived as person.

—W. Pannenberg, *Introduction to Systematic Theology*[2]

---

1. See now the really excellent study of G. Bray chronicling the whole troubled history of the relationship between Greek philosophy and Christian theology, entitled *Athens and Jerusalem: Philosophy, Theology and the Mind of Christ*.

2. What this in turn means is that from a Trinitarian point of view, the term "God"

The sort of Protestant and Catholic attempts at Systematics that we have examined thus far are frankly not really attempts of what most systematicians would call Systematics. Rather they are systematized forms of Biblical theology or later historical theology (e.g., about Mary or the Lord's Supper), with little or no attention to philosophical theology, and as a result they almost entirely ignore the work of various of the early church and medieval Church Fathers who had detailed interaction with Aristotelian and Platonic philosophy.

Whether we are dealing with someone like Origen, or the Cappadocian fathers, or even as late as Aquinas, there is indeed a detailed interaction with Greek philosophy. But there was as well an allergic reaction to such mixing of the teachings of the NT with or analyzing of the NT by Greek philosophy, most notably by Tertullian, who has been called the first great Christian theologian in the West (i.e., in Carthage).

And among the contemporary Christian theologians, the former approach is also true of Wolfhart Pannenberg. Furthermore, he offers detailed interaction with modern philosophers of relevance ranging from Heidegger to Tillich and numerous others. If this sort of careful and detailed interaction with both ancient and modern philosophy of relevance to theology is supposed to be an integral part of Systematics, then Sproul and Grudem and their disciples are not doing Systematic theology—it's at best systematized Biblical theology, and of a particular Reformed sort.[3] Of course one of the reasons for the latter approach is the belief that Scripture is not only the final authority in matters of faith and practice, but *de facto*, the only real authority for faith and practice. This is a problem if we look at the origins of the phrase *sola Scriptura*, as a Catholic critique of the idea that the pope was the final authority, and then later among some Protestants it came to mean the *only* authority, or at least the authority by which reason and tradition and experience should be normed.[4]

We have already in this study intimated some of the problems caused by trying to integrate Biblical theology into a Greek philosophical framework, namely when it came to the discussions about Christ's two natures at Chalcedon in AD 450, an idea not found in Scripture, and it is questionable whether it is the best amplification or implication of what the NT does say about Christ.

---

does not refer to A Person; it refers to the essence shared by three persons who are part of the divine identity.

3. His three-volume masterwork is simply titled *Systematic Theology*.
4. See my *Sola Scriptura*.

That is an example of the problems of thinking of Biblical theology from a more philosophical point of view, but on the other hand there is considerable promise and help in clarifying things if we listen to the Christian philosophers. For example, consider what Pannenberg says about the Trinity:

> In Jesus' teaching and prayer, the word "Father" came to function as a name, not a mere symbol. It was the only name for God Jesus used. And only in that way of addressing God and of relating to him did the unspeakable mystery acquire personal quality. Thus, the personal character of God of the Christian faith is bound up with the word "Father" as Jesus used it. The word "Son" as indicating a second person in the Trinity is derived from "Father" as a personal name for God, and it is only in relation to the Father and the Son that the Spirit could be considered as personal too. Hence the personal concreteness of God, at least in the Christian tradition, depends on the name "Father." Therefore, the exchange of this name inevitably results in turning to another God.[5]

To this Pannenberg adds, "Because as Father he is related to the Son in all eternity, he is personal in eternity in the unity of Father, Son, and Spirit."[6] And it should be clear from the above that the use of Father language in the context of Jesus talking about God, who Jesus also says is spirit (John 4), has nothing to do with it being a manifestation of patriarchal culture or a reflection on the gender of the first person of the Trinity. Rather, it is a manifestation of God being personal, and in a particular kind of personal relationship with the Son.[7]

And here is a place where philosophical theology in tune with Biblical theology and also Systematic theology can be helpful in spelling out Christian doctrine *because* we do *not* have an elaboration on or full explanation of the Trinity in the NT. Instead, what we have is the raw data and ideas for a Trinitarian theology, found in NT benedictions, in the baptismal formula in Matt 28, in various Christological statements and Christological hymns and the Aramaic prayer phrase *marana tha*, not to mention the divine and personal language applied to the Spirit—the Spirit can be blasphemed or grieved.

---

5. Pannenberg, *Introduction to Systematic Theology*, 32.
6. Pannenberg, *Introduction to Systematic Theology*, 35.
7. And one may rightly ask if the Son had a gendered identity, before He took on flesh and became a male human being. My take on that would be probably not.

All this data needed further reflection, elaboration, and explanation, which is in part what the Council of Nicaea attempted to do. I am thankful most churches still regularly recite the Nicene Creed from time to time, but not the Chalcedonian formula. The Nicene Creed provides something of a blueprint for how to go beyond just what the Bible says about the Trinity in helpful ways, without going against it. Depending on how one interprets the language of Christ being the only begotten Son who existed before the creation of the universe, there are not merely personal implications of the language of Father and Son applied to God but also ontological implications.[8]

But in all such discussions, we must allow for a certain amount of uncertainty as to exactly what was meant. There is a place for dogma in regard to things that are not really debatable, like Christ as sole redeemer of humankind, but there is also a place for openness and a willingness to explore possibilities in regard to things that are less clear. This is another reason philosophical theology and Systematics can be helpful, making clear the logical and rational implications of this or that view, for instance on the idea of the two natures of Christ.[9]

But there are other ideas about God that come from Greek philosophy and do not appear to comport with what the Bible says about God. Let's consider the notion of God's impassability and immutability. There are some Biblical texts thought to suggest these ideas—chiefly Num 23:19; 1 Sam 15:29; Mal 3:6; and Jas 1:17. Let us look briefly at each in turn, but before doing so, there is an immediate problem from a Christian doctrinal point of view. If the incarnation or taking on of flesh by the Son of God does not count as *some kind of change*, or addition to the Godhead, it is hard to know how to talk about it. And this is all the more the case when we

---

8. *Monogenes* (John 1:14), however, could mean something like unique, one of a kind, only one, without implications about "begetting" or how Christ became the Son. Then there is the term πρωτότοκος, sometimes translated "first born" in Col 1:15, but it is a word that doesn't even occur in ancient Greek. The problem in that text is what would "first born" from the dead mean? So, some commentators have suggested the term simply means "first" before creation, and first in terms of experiencing a resurrection body immune to disease, decay, and death.

9. Notice that in Phil 2:5–11 we are indeed told that the Son is by very nature or in his essence (the term *morphe* is used) God. It then goes on to say He emptied himself of something, and took on the very essence or nature of a human being. The text does not say He has two natures; it says He is truly in the very form or nature of God (not merely divine) and then it says He is truly a human being as well. While it is understandable that some have seen a two-natures idea here, it is not at all clear that is what Paul means. More likely, as Richard Bauckham suggests, it is claiming that the Son is part of the identity of God. See Bauckham, *Jesus and the God of Israel*. Nothing in the Gospels suggests Jesus had two natures. Rather, He was truly God (an identity statement, not a description of His makeup), and also truly a human being.

learn that Christ took His resurrection body with Him into heaven at the ascension. To be sure, this does not need to mean a change in God's *moral character*, but still it is some kind of change, and as such brings into question the idea of immutability in general.

Speaking of Yahweh, Num 23:19 says, "God is not human, that he should lie, not a human being, that he should change his mind. Does he speak and then not act? Does he promise and not fulfill?" This, however, is talking about God's moral character, which does not change over time. God always tells the truth, and He always does what He promises to do. There is nothing here that would suggest God is impassable, namely not subject to emotions. Indeed, there are plenty of Biblical texts that suggest that God has deep emotions—e.g., anger against sin. Exodus 34 says God is slow to anger, but this clearly doesn't mean He never reaches the point of being angry. Indeed, the Hebrew metaphor used to describe this is "God's nose burned"—He got red in the face (Deut 29:27–28). And equally there are places which talk about God's love for humankind, for instance John 3:16; indeed in 1 John 4:7–8, God is said to be love!

One of the better and more accessible introductions to the OT prophets is Abraham Joshua Heschel's *The Prophets*, in which he emphasizes the passion and pathos of God shown in text after text. So whatever immutability might mean, it is impossible that it means impassable. Indeed, a text like Acts 9:4—"Saul, Saul, why are you persecuting me?"—suggests not only that Christ suffered on the cross, but as one spiritually linked to His people, the body of Christ, He suffers when they suffer. Jurgen Moltmann's classic and very influential book, *The Crucified God*, explores this subject in a profound way.

First Samuel 15:29 says much the same about God's moral character and that He does not change His mind as the previously cited text from Numbers stresses. Malalchi 3:6 likewise quotes God as saying, "I, the Lord, do not change," but again this does not require the Greek idea of absolute immutability to be imported into the discussion.

James 1:17 is another verse cited: "the Father . . . who does not change like shifting shadows." But again, this is a reference to God not changing in His *character*, and perhaps also implies God does not change His *mind*. What James is combatting here is the idea that God might at times tempt human beings to sin or do evil, which James flatly denies. To the contrary, says James, every good and perfect gift comes to human beings from God who Himself is good and perfect. This discussion should also come into play when we are talking about where sin and evil come from. God is not the cause of either.

Much the same can be said about Christ, who is said to be the same yesterday, today, and forever (Heb 13:8). Again, the issue is Christ's character, and that He does not change His mind about things like sin, or the love of God for humanity, or the plan of God for human salvation.

So, only in a limited way can we talk about the immutability of God, and frankly the pagan idea of God's impassability should not be brought into the discussion. As R. Jenson rightly stresses, "Mediterranean antiquity defined deity by immunity to time, by impassibility; offensively to this definition, the gospel identifies its God by temporal events of Exodus and Resurrection."[10] Of course, God is not subject to *irrational* emotions like some of the Greek or Roman deities, and if that is all one means by impassable, then the term is alright as a description of God's character.[11] Indeed, God's emotions reflect both His very rational deep anger over sin which destroys human lives and human community and leads to hatred and violence, and at the same time God's salvific actions reflect His very rational deep love for humankind and His plan to rescue them from themselves. These things reflect God's unchanging holiness and His unchanging compassion and mercy. As it turns out, there were some Church Fathers who were wary of simply taking over Greek philosophical notions as a way to explain God and God's character.

As Pannenberg points out, "Ever since Gregory of Nyssa the Christian doctrine of God conceived of God's nature as infinite. In this way, in contrast to Aristotelian and Platonic metaphysics, it accounts for the biblical intuition of a radical otherness of God, unattainable to all creatures, an otherness expressed primarily through the idea of holiness.[12] In his transcendence beyond everything finite, God is holy, and it is precisely because of such transcendence that he is not bound to any place 'up there' or 'out there,' but can also be present within the world of finite realities. The infinite God is transcendent in the midst of our lives."[13] How then to express this in

---

10. Jenson, *Systematic Theology*, 1:16. It is remarkable in the Christian philosophy realm how often the pagan notion of impassability is simply taken as a given. See Pelikan, *Christian Tradition*, 172–277.

11. In light of all this it is rather surprising that The Gospel Coalition, a Reformed group of theologians, would be advocates for a more extensive view of God's immutability and impassability than is articulated above. See The Gospel Coalition website at www.thegospelcoalition.com, and on this matter, Barrett, "Immutability and Impassibility of God," a reflection based on the Westminster Confession of Faith. On the other hand, in view of the Reformed belief that God has predetermined all things by his eternal decrees, it is not entirely surprising that there would be an objection to the idea that God suffers or is subject to any kind of change.

12. On which see now Ayars et al., *Holiness*.

13. Pannenberg, *Introduction to Systematic Theology*, 30.

understandable terms? One way was to say things like "Christ in you, the hope of glory" (Col 1:27). Christ could *not only* be an incorporative being; He could *also* indwell the believer as could the Holy Spirit. Both things were true.

Some scholars have suggested that the author of Hebrews was influenced by some form of Platonism, such as Plato's attempt to suggest that this world is the world of shadows and pale copies of the eternal realities to be found in the eternal realm. The analogy with shadows cast on the wall of a cave while the real light source is elsewhere has been suggested as a source for statements in Hebrews like Heb 8:5: "The place where they serve is a sketch and a shadow of the heavenly sanctuary, just as Moses was warned by God as he was about to complete the tabernacle." But the problem with over-pressing this sort of language is that the writer also believes Christ brought about salvation in space and time. He talks at length about Christ's role in this in Heb 12:1–3 and mentions the cross. Not only so but Christ is portrayed as the historical paradigm—the trailblazer and finisher of faithfulness. What is happening on earth is not a mere copy or sketch of what is happening in heaven; it is the place where salvation was wrought in the first place.

Finally, there is the case of Origen, who did accept some Platonic ideas, which were at odds with Biblical ways of thinking; for example, he accepted not only the Greek idea of the human soul, he also accepted that these souls pre-existed, a notion the writers of the NT would have rejected out of hand.[14]

We have barely scratched the surface of the possible influences and uses of Greek philosophy by the NT writers, and we will say more shortly, but this is sufficient to make clear that we should critically analyze such possible influences and see what their real nature and import are. But I would stress that this sort of philosophical analysis of the NT can be overdone, especially since the character of the content of the NT is profoundly Jewish, so that at most, the Greek influence comes through because these Jews themselves were somewhat Hellenized in their thinking and writing. We will attend to a different aspect of this subject in our subsequent chapter on logic and rhetoric, including dealing with "the logic of God Incarnate."[15]

14. See the discussion by Morris, *Logic of God Incarnate*.

15. It is of course also true that there are many problems with applying various forms of modern philosophy to the analysis of Biblical Theology. For example, the unhelpful attempt to read Biblical Theology through a Kantian epistemological lens when it comes to the issue of what Kant says about reality and our perception of it, but see Lampe, *New Testament Theology in a Secular World*, e.g., 28: "Reality is a construct of the brain." Is there really nothing beyond what we can perceive with our five senses? Even Sextus Empiricus thought there might be (*Pyr.* 1.97).

Chapter Seven

# The Exports
Where Did the Ethics Go? What If They Are Theological Ethics?

> *Ethics in the Bible* refers to the system(s) or theory(ies) produced by the study, interpretation, and evaluation of biblical morals (including moral code, standards, principles, behaviors, conscience, values, rules of conduct, or *beliefs* concerned with good and evil and right and wrong), that are found in the Hebrew and Christian Bibles. It comprises a narrow part of the larger fields of Jewish and Christian ethics, which are themselves parts of the larger field of philosophical ethics. Ethics in the Bible is unlike other western ethical theories in that it is seldom overtly philosophical. It presents neither a systematic nor a formal deductive ethical argument. Instead, the Bible provides patterns of moral reasoning that focus on conduct and character in what is sometimes referred to as virtue ethics. This moral reasoning is part of a broad, normative covenantal tradition where duty and virtue are inextricably tied together in a mutually reinforcing manner.[1]

English is a strange language. Take for example the word *oversight*. On the one hand, it can mean to properly supervise some project that needs to be done, usually by someone else. On the other hand, it can mean having overlooked something that needed to be done. When it comes to ethics, it's

---

1. This is the helpful summary in Wikipedia, "Ethics in the Bible," para. 1; emphasis added.

mostly the latter meaning regarding some forms of Biblical and Systematic theology.

In the attempt to avoid the notion that works, even the good works of believers, might have something to do with human salvation, some Protestant theologies hardly mention ethics, even in a volume entitled *Systematic Theology*. One of the victims of such an approach is Biblical ethics, and it causes a failure to ask the right questions about the relationship of theology to ethics in the Bible, and in Christian theology in general. This should have struck the student of the Bible as passing strange, because so much of the Bible, especially the OT, but also a large portion of the NT, is about ethics.

Early Judaism, like the ancient Israelite religion, was more about orthopraxy than orthodoxy, and by orthopraxy I mean both ethical behavior and what came to be called religious practices such as sacrifices, food laws, Sabbath observance, issues of clean and unclean. These things were not at the periphery of Jewish religion; they were at the heart of it. While the theological statement called the *Shema* ("hear O Israel, the Lord our God, the Lord is One") was crucial, it focused on just one thing, but compare this to the Ten Commandments, all of which, with the possible exception of the first two commandments, were about behavior—ethics.

Indeed, there are some 613 commandments in the Mosaic covenant alone, and by my count several hundred more in the new covenant. It behooves us then to ask once more the question of the relationship between theology and ethics in the Bible, a question that is marginalized by sequestering theology away from ethics, or creating a Systematic Biblical theology that does not sufficiently take into account Biblical ethics.

## The Implications of the Image of God

To ask the question what is the relationship between theology and ethics in the Bible is in part to ask the question what is the relationship of belief and behavior. Does behavior have anything at all to do with belief, and anyway, isn't active believing a form of behavior? For instance, believing involves loving and worshiping the one true God of the Bible. We must also ask— What does God most want from us? Just a confession of faith, or a confession that entails obedience to God's commands, including loving God and neighbor with one's whole heart, something that doesn't just involve how one feels about God and neighbor?

I would argue that the relationship between theology and ethics is not abstract but rather organic. It is not theoretical. It has to do with real people, all of whom are created in the image of God. It is not sufficient to say, "if all theology involves grace, then all ethics involves gratitude." This is true but inadequate. Biblical ethics requires active love and respect of all those created in God's image, both the born and the unborn, and also those who have passed away, including those who have gone to be with the Lord.

The language of being in God's image is first applied in Genesis to Adam and Eve before they sinned. In the NT it is directly applied to Jesus Himself and then to His followers who are being conformed to the image of Christ. One way of putting this is that all human beings bear the image of the first Adam, and the NT insists that we also need to bear the image of the last Adam—Christ.

But what does it actually mean to "be created in the image and according to the likeness of God"? Some have suggested it means we have been created as human representatives of God on earth, meant to be fruitful, multiply, fill the earth, and rule over it. In other words, we are miniature versions of our Creator with the capacity to make and to govern. But as we will have occasion to mention in another part of this study, only God truly creates out of nothing; we are simply makers, refashioning what exists.

Others have suggested we, of all God's creatures, have been created with the capacity to have a personal relationship with God. This is partially true (but what about the angels?), but it doesn't really explain what the image itself amounts to, and why Christ is said to be the image bearer in the NT.

Perhaps then we should study the meaning of the Hebrew word *tselem* and see what light that shines on the matter. It turns out the word has as a basic meaning: "idol." Humans are God's "idols" on earth, the beings which represent God and are supposed to bear the closest likeness to God of all God's creatures. This is why God's people are forbidden to build idols of lesser creatures, lesser parts of creation. This is idolatry. Humans should be worshiping the creator they are created in the image of, not something less than human or other than human (e.g., angels, powers and principalities, forces of nature, animals). For that matter they are not to worship mere humans either.

It is interesting that extra-biblical ANE literature suggests that kings were the first to whom "image of God" language was applied.[2] By contrast, the Bible applies it to all human beings. While all of this is in the neighborhood of a right answer, we need to pay closer attention to the full Hebrew phrase *created* in God's image, AND after God's likeness. This is surely *not* just two ways of saying the same thing. To be after God's likeness surely

---

2. This is in part why kings were said to be some god's son in some special sense, anointed with that god's power and authority.

means in part to reflect God's moral character. As image bearers, humans are supposed to be capable of representing the true God and His character in the world.

Now a moment's reflection will tell us that from a Biblical point of view, we are created beings, NOT inherently a part of the ultimate Creator, and this Creator/creature distinction is fundamental to Biblical thinking about the relationship of God and humankind. Humans cannot reflect the *ontological* character of an all-powerful, all-knowing, omni-present eternal God. Human beings have been created with limitations of time, space, knowledge, and power, and they have been created mortal.[3]

If we reflect for a moment on the positive attributes that are supposed to be reflected in humans who are "after the likeness of God," various of God's attributes come to mind:

God is holy, and we should be holy.

God is love, and we should be love.

God is just, and we should be just.

God is good, and we should be good.

God is merciful, and we should be merciful.

In short, we should be like God in our moral character, which is at least part of what it means to be "after His likeness." When we consider the effects of the Fall, we remember that while God's image has been effaced, it has not been erased in humankind. It has been distorted but not destroyed. In short, human beings are not as bad as they could be, and indeed they can be redeemed and restored to being human and kind, humankind. Salvation is a reclamation project to restore the image of God in us so we can be image bearers and likeness reflectors. So, when the world looks at a believer, they should get a partial glimpse of the character of God.

Let's be clear that human beings cannot save themselves. They've fallen and cannot get up by means of mere human will, power, or effort. Salvation is not a five-step self-help program. A savior is needed to correct our warped and wicked ideas and straighten out our bent wills so we can not only think God's thoughts after Him, but also model God's character to the world, bearing in mind what the author of 2 Pet 1:3 says: "God's divine power has

---

3. There has always been a debate about whether Adam and Eve were created mortal or not. In my view they were. They were created very good, but mortal, which is why there was also the tree of (everlasting) life in the garden of Eden, and why they had to be evacuated from the garden after they sinned. They did not physically die because of their sin; they spiritually died and became self-centered, narcissistic beings.

given us everything we need for a godly life through our knowledge of Him who called us by his own glory and goodness."

The very next verse, 2 Pet 1:4, says emphatically, "Through these things he has given us his great and precious promises, so that through them we may become *partakers of the divine nature, having escaped the corruption in the world caused by evil desires*." It is perfectly clear from the context that the inspired author is talking about human beings partaking of or modeling the moral character of God, *not* participating in His ontological attributes. This verse is not about the divinizing of human beings or *theosis* despite what some Orthodox theologians have said. Note the clear reference to escaping evil desires, which points in the ethical not the ontological direction.

This passage is telling Christians they should live without excuses. God has given us all we need to live a good and godly life. Notice the word *epignosis*. This doesn't merely mean "information"; it refers to "understanding" on the basis of crucial knowledge which leads to acknowledging God. The corollary to this is if one does not understand, it is not surprising one will not model a good and godly life. In short, a certain amount of saving knowledge is required as a guidance which shapes the character of the recipient. Knowledge is the key.

Put another way:

- *Without knowledge of God, manifesting God's character is impossible.*
- *What does that tell us about ourselves in an age of biblical illiteracy even in the church?*
- *Ignorance is not bliss when it comes to salvation or exhibiting the moral character of God on earth.*
- *One of the causes for rampant sin even in the church is ignorance of God. You cannot imitate what or whom you do not know!*

It is no wonder at all that the following are some of the problems we face in the church today:

1. Pastors without a deep knowledge of God's Word.
2. Anti-intellectual attitudes by believing Christians.
3. Assumptions that knowledge gets in the way of piety.
4. Purely affective approaches to our relationship with God.
5. False assumptions about the nature of salvation.

The key to reforming the church in regard to these things is not just realizing the importance of nurturing and modeling godly character. Yes indeed, the connection point between theology and ethics is this reality called "the image of God." But the Christian is not called to just have the renewal of the image originally borne by Adam. The Christian is called to be conformed to the image of Christ Himself, the last Adam. Consider for a moment what Heb 1:1–4 says about Christ. He is:

1. the heir of all things;
2. the co-creator of all things;
3. the perfect reflection of God's glory (divine presence);
4. the bearer of the imprint (*charakter*) of God;
5. the sustainer of all things by His Word;
6. the purifier of sin; and
7. the ruler over all angels and people.

As it turns out, salvation is not just a matter of knowing God as He revealed Himself to His OT people, or the moral reform of character that knowing can bring about, but rather salvation hinges on being saved by grace through faith in Christ and being conformed to His image, not merely in what we believe about God, but also *in how we behave*, with the knowledge that the finish line comes at the resurrection when we are conformed to Christ even in the flesh, by means of a bodily resurrection. Full salvation involves justification and sanctification in which we work out what God works in us with the goal of real holiness, and finally the work of salvation is complete at the resurrection.

Consider for a moment what Paul says in Rom 3:22–24, part of which reads, "This righteousness is given through the faithfulness of Jesus Christ to all who believe, . . . for all have sinned and lack the glory of God, and all are set right freely by his grace through the redemption that came by Christ Jesus."

This righteousness doesn't just involve being given right standing with God. It also involves the renovation work done by being born again, born from above. It is not just a status; it is the beginning of moral renewal—sanctification. Paul promises in 2 Cor 3:17–18 as we contemplate the glorious character of Christ we are being transformed into His image, but the actual work involved is done by the indwelling Spirit, not by human effort. We become what we admire. Paul goes on to add in Rom 5 the following: "Consequently, just as one trespass resulted in condemnation for all people, so also one righteous act resulted in righteousness and life for all people

. . . so that, just as sin reigned in death, so also grace might reign through righteousness to bring everlasting life through Jesus Christ our Lord."

Notice the close association of righteousness and life "for all people." The death of Christ on the cross is the one righteous act that changed the world, and that death was for all people, which does not simply mean all sorts of people.[4] When we realize the integral connection of theology and ethics through the concept of the image of God, certain conclusions follow, which we can sum up here:

- Theology describes the character and action of God to transform humanity back into the image of God so that we can fulfill the great commandment and the Great Commission.
- Christ is the means by which this transformation happens through the power of the Spirit.
- Our imitation of Christ and working out our salvation is also part of the sanctification process.
- From an ethical point of view, this also means that each person has value regardless of class, race, gender, or disability.
- The *imago Dei* is in every individual who is therefore able to be evangelized and thus redeemed.
- Theology and ethics work together in evangelism, the outflow of the Great Commission.
- The goal is not only the salvation of humankind but also the restoration of creation so it can participate in the true worship of God as Rom 8 suggests.
- Salvation is the means of restoration. The goal of the restoration is a proper relationship with God, so that all creatures may love and worship God with their whole beings, so when Christ returns there can be a new creation, not merely new creatures raised from the dead. In short, both Biblical and systematic theology need to involve both theology and the ethics entailed by that theology because these are theological ethics, not just any kind of ethics. Theological ethics are the kind Jesus taught in the Sermon on the Mount, or Paul taught in his letters.

---

4. An important distinction to be made is between eternal life, which only God has and has always had, and everlasting life, which is a gift to human beings that begins at a particular point in time and continues on into eternity. God is not giving humans his unique eternal life that only God has. He is giving us everlasting life by means of salvation by grace through faith in Christ.

## Holiness

The subject of holiness could be placed in the theology or the ethics category, because it has to do with both sanctification and also with human behavior in response to the work of the Holy Spirit in a person's life. And very clearly, holiness in the NT is taken to another whole level, because of the indwelling of the Spirit in the believer since Pentecost. Holiness does not just mean being set apart for God in the NT, though it does involve that; it also involves a heart full of love for God and neighbor, which generates heart-felt behaviors of loving self-sacrifice for others, patterned on the self-sacrificial behavior of Jesus.

It is striking that when Paul sums up *the will of God for the believer* he says this: "It is God's will that you should be sanctified: that you should avoid sexual immorality; that each of you should learn to control your own body in a way that is holy and honorable" (1 Thess 4:3–4). Holiness, or sanctification, is absolutely about using the inspiration and power of the Spirit to live a life of moral rectitude. Sanctification is not just about an experience; it's about empowerment to behave, to model one's self on Christ's life and teachings.

In the Wesleyan tradition this involves not only the concept of progressive sanctification and working out one's salvation with fear and trembling. It also involves entire sanctification, but what actually that means is much debated. We will be engaging with the recent work by M. Ayars, C. T. Bounds, and C. T. Friedman simply entitled *Holiness: A Biblical, Historical, and Systematic Theology*, mainly just the last hundred pages of it where the Systematic theology discussion transpires.

Before we get to that interaction, let it be said that the phrase "Christian Perfection" was not the preferred way John Wesley referred to what he was talking about. He preferred the phrase "entire sanctification," and with good reason. If he used the term *perfection*, or was talking about something more than having a peak experience of the perfect love of God which cleansed the heart and cast out fear (1 John 4), he knew he would have to qualify the term *perfection* again and again and again. For instance, he would always say he was not talking about "sinless" perfection, and sometimes he added that he was referring to the empowerment to avoid conscious willful sinful actions or intentional sin.[5] This went hand in hand with his exegesis of 1 Cor

---

5. But even with a moment's reflection on the Biblical witness there are also sins of omission, things one fails to do, which one ought to do; there are sins of passion without forethought being involved; and there are accidental sins, for instance when your car slips on some ice despite your effort to prevent it, and you run into another car, and someone is killed. This is still vehicular homicide whether one intended it or not, and

10 where Paul reassured his Corinthians that God could provide a means of resisting temptation, and not giving in to it.

But Wesley knew perfectly well that intentional sinful actions were by no means all there was to sin. He knew that defining sin too narrowly to allow for the use of the term *perfection* was not in accord with scriptural teaching, which not only refers to sins of thought, word, and deed, but even discusses sins of omission at points, and accidental sins, and unintended sinful consequences of an action that was not sin in itself. No one who reads Wesley's *A Plain Account of Christian Perfection* could ever be under the impression that Wesley was a naïve optimist about holiness, or did not know the problems with defining sin too narrowly, or for that matter perfection too narrowly. Bearing all this in mind, let us consider some of the discussion in the recent book on holiness.

In the first place the authors are to be commended for making this a comprehensive approach to the subject, looking at all the books of the Bible and what they say about holiness, but then studying the subject through church history by examining the discussions of the theologians of the church over the course of the last almost two thousand years. Finally, after all that they turn to Systematic theology, which is our concern here.

There is no compromise in the way they describe God's absolute and immutable perfection, and how human "perfection" is something far less than God's, even when the subject is the final perfecting of a human being and full conformity to the image of Christ by means of the resurrection when Christ returns. The focus of the Wesleyan discussion of perfection is on the *experience of God's perfect love* which results in holiness of heart and life of the believer.

To say that God is holy means He is wholly other from His creatures, and there is a permanent ontological distinction between God and humans or angels. God is the Creator, and we are His creation. Among other things, this means that 2 Pet 1:4 does not mean *"theosis"* or the divinizing of human beings.[6] We become partakers of Christ, and so of the moral character of God.

But to discuss God's holiness also means the following: "God is morally good, righteous, and just which applies to his values, his actions, and his requirements of us. God is ethically pure, incapable of sin.[7] He is the

---

it is still a violation of "thou shalt not kill." But so are intentional acts like deliberately choosing an abortion of convenience when there is no medical reason to do so, so the life of the mother can be saved, or when it does not involve rape or incest.

6. On which see chapter 1 above.

7. Not least because God cannot be tempted, as Jas 1 says.

standard of every moral excellence.... God strengthens and empowers the good, while negatively he opposes and judges all unrighteousness and evil."[8]

Furthermore, holy love demands moral purity for true union with God. "Holiness is what enables the full expression of love for which we have been created. It makes possible true human flourishing."[9] Lest we think that holiness simply has to do with moral purity, we must reflect on Heb 12:14, which says, "Without holiness, no one shall see God." This surely implies that holiness is necessary if we are to have a truly intimate relationship with God. It appears to be a prerequisite, which requires the grace of God, or the Spirit of God working in the believer to make them morally fit to come into the presence of the holiest Being in the universe.

It is interesting that in the original creation narrative, everything God creates is said to be good, or even very good (*tov m'ov*). It is not said to be perfect; that is perhaps because humans were not immune to temptation and sin and so being corrupted, unlike God who is perfect, and not subject to temptation, nor can God be corrupted.[10] While Adam and Eve bore the image of God, they are not yet all they could be. That in fact doesn't happen until the resurrection when we are fully conformed to the image of Christ, even in our bodies. Here I must part company with these authors when they say, "God must bring humanity to a place where they are made incorruptibly holy, no longer subject to sin, evil, and death. God does this in the end by bringing humanity into full union with Himself in heaven, the new creation."[11]

Heaven is not the new creation. Heaven is the interim state for the believer before they become their complete selves by means of resurrection, having a body immune to disease, decay, and death. And this *doesn't* happen in heaven; it happens on earth when the dead in Christ are raised. Indeed, as Paul says in 2 Cor 5:8, in heaven we will be away from "the body" and present with the Lord. We do not receive that resurrection body upon arrival in heaven. That would be a rather profound misreading of 2 Cor 5:1–8.

Nor do we get the impression that the saints in heaven think they have arrived in their final state or perfection. See Rev 6:9–11: "When he opened the fifth seal, I saw under the altar the souls of those who had been slain because of the word of God and the testimony they had maintained. They called out in a loud voice, 'How long, Sovereign Lord, holy and true, until

---

8. Ayars et al., *Holiness*, 270.

9. Ayars et al., *Holiness*, 271.

10. I am very wary of the way this book uses the word "perfect." Can we really talk about Adam before the Fall as perfect? Why not just use the proper Biblical terms and say he was created "good."

11. Ayars et al., *Holiness*, 277.

you judge the inhabitants of the earth and avenge our blood?' Then each of them was given a white robe, and they were told to wait a little longer, until the full number of their fellow servants, their brothers and sisters, were killed just as they had been." Perfection for them has not come in heaven; they must look to the future of God's people on earth at the resurrection. The saints under the altar are given temporary clothing, robes, and told to be patient. That hardly sounds like they are in a state of perfection. More like they are in a state of irritation.

There is the further problem with this *Holiness* book's presentation that we keep hearing about the idea that we are embodied souls. Embodied spirits maybe, but not embodied souls—a very un-Jewish way of putting things. When Paul contrasts the natural condition of humans as involving a *psuchikon soma* now with a *pneumatikon soma* later at the return of Christ in 1 Cor 15, he is not contrasting a body made of "soul" with a body made of "spirit." The former, which is what Adam had and we have, is a body animated by life breath, as the Genesis story says, while a *pneumatikon soma* is a body animated by the Spirit, a permanent form of life, everlasting life. Notice that Jesus says He is commending His spirit, not soul, into God's hands in Luke 23 at the end of His earthly life. We would do well to drop the whole use of the term *soul*, not least because the Greco-Roman notion of the immortal soul is not at all what *psuche* means in the hands of Jewish Christian writers in the first century AD.

They believed humans had a spirit, which would go to be with God, like Abraham did (see Luke 18), and humans had a body, to which was necessarily added an animating principle—life breath. First Thessalonians 5:23 does not suggest we have both souls and spirits. Yes, the term *psuche* can be used holistically to refer to a whole person, a life, but in tandem with the term *body* it simply refers to the animating principle of life breath, just as the story of the original Adam indicates, using the term *nephesh*, the Hebrew equivalent of *psuche*. It is also not helpful to suggest "we are created to become fully like God."[12] No we aren't. We are created to be like God in some respects only. "Fully" is saying way too much. We do not cease to be creatures either in heaven or in the resurrection.

I could go on critiquing this approach to holiness and perfection, for instance drawing on the Sermon on the Mount when Jesus says, "Be perfect, as your heavenly father is perfect." In context what this means is be just as loving as your heavenly father is loving, as the context in Matt 5:45–46 makes quite clear, even loving those who don't love you, even your enemies

---

12. Ayars et al., *Holiness*, 279.

as Jesus stresses. *Jesus is not talking about an experience of perfection; He is talking about loving behavior like the Father's loving behavior.*

Having said the above, I have no problem with any of the following: (1) dynamic spiritual experiences subsequent to conversion, call them the second or third or fourth blessing; (2) the idea that the Holy Spirit can cleanse a person inwardly of their sense of guilt and shame for sin. This also has Biblical precedent; (3) the idea one can experience the perfect love of God which makes one a better person who no longer suffers from fear-based thinking. But experiencing the perfect love of God which casts out fear is one thing, having an experience that makes a human being perfect in some ultimate sense is another; (4) the idea that one can receive new spiritual gifts subsequent to conversion that one did not have before, or new callings; (5) what I do have issues with is calling any of this perfection in any sort of ultimate sense. Truly sanctified or holy perhaps, but perfect, no, not so long as we have foibles, errors, short-comings, and lack of fully knowing God, etc.; (6) further, I have issues with Pentecostal theology about a baptism in the Spirit subsequent to conversion, when that phrase is only used once in the NT in 1 Cor 12 to refer to being joined by the Spirit to the body of Christ; (7) likewise, I have issues not with the authenticity of the gift of speaking in tongues as a gift still available to Christians today, but with the idea that it is somehow the litmus test or initial evidence that one is a born-again Christian. This is false. Indeed, 1 Cor 14 makes quite clear it is a gift that only some genuine Christians have, like the gift of interpreting tongues or the gift of prophecy.

In the holiness tradition, a variety of overly optimistic interpretations of key Biblical texts about holiness and sanctification can happen, with negative and unbiblical results. I will give two illustrations. I once had a Nazarene couple come to me who were having marital problems, only they *couldn't* be having marital problems because they had been taught that their sin natures had been eradicated and they were perfected in love. What's wrong with this picture? They were still manifesting selfish, sinful tendencies. The fact that they had had peak spiritual experiences which had been interpreted as some kind of perfection had misled them into thinking of themselves in much too optimistic kinds of terms.

It is perfectly possible to have genuine experiences in and of the Spirit, but to theologically misinterpret the *significance* of them. Consider for a minute St. Paul, reflecting on his life late in his career. He says this in Phil 4:

> I want to know Christ—yes, to know the power of his resurrection and participation in his sufferings, becoming like him in his death, and so, somehow, attaining to the resurrection from the

> dead. Not that I have already obtained all this, or have already arrived at my goal, but I press on to take hold of that for which Christ Jesus took hold of me. Brothers and sisters, I do not consider myself yet to have taken hold of it. But one thing I do: Forgetting what is behind and straining toward what is ahead, I press on toward the goal to win the prize for which God has called me heavenward in Christ Jesus. (vv. 10–14)

If Paul, after all he had experienced and gone through, can say late in life, "Not that I have already obtained all this or have already arrived at my goal, but I press on to take hold of [the goal]. . . . I do not consider myself yet to have taken hold of it," then this should be the humble attitude of every Christian whatever their progress in sanctification. They are not yet perfect, nor have they already attained to the resurrection. They are still Christians living in bodies subject to disease, decay, and death, and yes, subject to temptation, though God can help them overcome that. But it's an ongoing battle.

The second illustration comes from a former colleague of mine who grew up in the Wesleyan tradition in a church in Indiana. Every summer as a teen his parents would take him to the revivals and evangelistic meetings, hoping God would take hold of him. And every summer he would go to the altar to be "born again." Now, again, he may have had a series of real spiritual experiences, but clearly he wasn't born again in the Biblical sense multiple times. That's a one-off initiatory experience. Later on, he was able to joke about this, saying, "I was born again so many times in those meetings I had stretch marks on my soul!" Well, at some point he was born again, and became a real servant of Christ and a fine minister and preacher, and more. But the interpretation of all that was not quite Biblically accurate.

On the other side of the coin is the recent revival at Asbury University.[13] This was entirely a student-led event over sixteen days, and God did some serious "soul" work with many of those students. Some really were born again, and gave up all kinds of sinful things—like addiction to computer pornography. Some reached a new stage of Christian maturity and heard their call to ministry. Some gave up drugs and fell in love with Jesus. And so many had an encounter with the Holy Spirit that was palpable and they were caught up in love, and wonder, and praise of God, which according to some theologians is the chief aim of the Christian life—to worship God with all that you have and are. Thank God for genuine revival when the Spirit falls on those who sing and pray and worship day and night for days

---

13. See now Baldwin, *Generation Awakened*; and Nicholson, *Cooperating with the Spirit*.

at a time. Even skeptics who came into Hughes Auditorium said, "The sense of the presence of the Spirit in that place was just palpable. The building was spiritually alive and people were being swept up in it."

It is the job of Wesleyan theologians not to quench or stifle the Spirit or the enthusiasm of those caught up in revival, but to help them to interpret it properly and in a Biblically accurate manner, without being overcome with the exuberance of the moment. God can indeed do exceedingly, abundantly more than we could ever ask or imagine, but He has already given us His Word so we can rightly interpret what has happened in such genuine spiritual experiences. And as my old church history professor Richard Lovelace used to say, "The Word without the Spirit is like wineskins without vivifying wine, but the Spirit without the Word to contain, shape, define, preserve it is like wine without wineskins."

# Chapter Eight

# Human Logic or the Logic of God?

It is not logical, Captain.
>—Spock to Captain Kirk

The Bible . . . is less like a compass or a chart than a guide for finding the Pilot.
>—C. F. D. Moule, *Christ Alive and at Large*

Within the scope of God's revelation, there is an inherent logic to the revelation if and only if one accepts a whole series of presuppositions, for instance: (1) that there is a God, and *that* God is as revealed in the Bible; (2) God was able to adequately and accurately reveal His nature, will, and salvation plan in human language; (3) the all-powerful God is capable of performing what came to be called miracles; and (4) God most fully revealed Himself in His Son who took on flesh and became human in order to save the world of humanity from its sinful self. And that's all just for starters.

We will say more about the logic of God in a bit, but first it is in order to note that ordinary human logic is also used in the NT especially, in the form of syllogisms and enthymemes. We will explore these first. What underlies these is the assumption that human reason, properly used, can aid in our understanding of God and His Word.

## Human Logic in the Service of God

In 1 Cor 15:12–19 we read the following:

> But if it is preached that Christ has been raised from the dead, how can some of you say that there is no resurrection of the dead? If there is no resurrection of the dead, then not even Christ has been raised. And if Christ has not been raised, our preaching is useless and so is your faith. More than that, we are then found to be false witnesses about God, for we have testified about God that he raised Christ from the dead. But he did not raise him if in fact the dead are not raised. For if the dead are not raised, then Christ has not been raised either. And if Christ has not been raised, your faith is futile; you are still in your sins. Then those also who have fallen asleep in Christ are lost. If only for this life we have hope in Christ, we are of all people most to be pitied.

This is a classic case of using a syllogism to refute a false assumption by some Corinthians, namely that dead persons do not rise from the dead. The way that this sort of logic works is that if you can't accept the *necessary consequences* of your belief that dead persons don't ever rise, then there has to be something wrong with your dogmatic statement that they don't, and the logic behind it. A syllogism is a form of deductive logic. The form of the syllogism, which can have multiple parts, is "if a then b then c," or in this case, "if not a, then not b, and if not b, then not c as well."

The Greeks were well familiar with this sort of logic; indeed it was part of Greek elementary education. Children were taught how to think logically by learning to create simple syllogisms. We may thank Aristotle's *Organon* for helping get this educational ball rolling, because teaching Aristotle's rhetoric and logic was fundamental to ancient education in Greek, and teaching how to form syllogisms and enthymemes was one way of getting a person to think logically about something.

In this case the unacceptable consequences which Paul outlines is that a person's faith is in vain, and there is no hope of everlasting life, and by the way, there was no point in Corinthians doing proxy baptisms for their dead relatives. Worse still Paul's listeners were all still in their sins, had not been redeemed, and were not in right relationship with God, *if Christ is not raised from the dead*. The denial of resurrection of the dead as a possibility leads not only to the conclusion that Christ was not raised, but also that all this missionary work of Paul has been in vain. All his hard work was pointless if Christ was not raised.

Since syllogisms like the one in 1 Corinthians are already quite familiar, I'm going to spend more time here on enthymemes in the NT. "An enthymeme is an argument with a hidden premise. Enthymemes are usually developed from premises that *accord* with the audience's view of the world and what is taken to be common sense."[1] One of the main reasons for misinterpretation of various statements in the Pastoral Epistles is because the scholar or lay person reading the Pastoral did not recognize the plentiful use of enthymemes in these three documents. Besides the missing premise in an enthymeme, what makes it different from a straight syllogism is that syllogisms are dealing with an argument where something is deemed *logically necessary* as a conclusion, whereas with enthymemes the conclusion is simply deemed probable (see Aristotle, *Rhetoric* 1.3.11). Let us consider some of enthymemes in the Pastorals.

Enthymemes, or incomplete syllogisms, required some thinking and logic of the audience. The audience needed to supply the missing premise! Aristotle tells us that the reason to suppress a premise is because it is odious to state the obvious, or better said it's an insult to the audience's intelligence (*Rhetoric* 1356b4–6). Things are stated in a certain way so the audience will reason its way to a conclusion. In other words, the original audience is expected to use logic and reasoning to understand the message of the enthymeme, and so must we, which requires we know something about ancient Greek rhetoric, otherwise Paul will be misunderstood.

Enthymemes will often include familiar maxims, and the first one in Titus does so citing a maxim by a Cretan writer about Cretans, saying, "All Cretans are liars" (Titus 1:12).[2] Maxims that are already part of conventional wisdom help convince an audience of something because it is already familiar to them and accepted, even though this maxim is deliberately ironic, since it is formed by a Cretan and raises the question, is this an example of a Cretan telling a lie or telling the truth?

Please note that the ill-informed have mistakenly thought that we have in the Pastorals a random collection of traditions with no logical or evident connection. This is false. Furthermore, these enthymemes are about both theology and ethics and their interconnections. Most of them take the form, if you do A, then B will happen. The subject matter is about God, or things that lead to salvation because God's plan works a particular way, or things God wants or demands, or appeals to the proper character of religious life (mentioning vices and virtues and character traits), or appeals to sacred tradition or prophecies and other prescriptions of Scripture.

Let us turn to Titus 2:1–15 for some excellent examples of syllogisms, with a suppressed premise in parentheses:

1. Younger women should submit themselves to their own husbands

---

1. Wikipedia, "Enthymeme," para. 1; emphasis added.
2. An ironic saying to include in an enthymeme since it also implies the author of the maxim, who was a native of Crete, was a liar or at least a big exaggerator.

2. (For outsiders will judge our faith based on their behavior)
3. So the Word of God will not be discredited by observers.

Or consider the following:

1. Titus must set a good moral example offering teaching with integrity
2. (For opponents are looking for inconsistencies in our leaders)
3. So that the opponents have nothing to criticize.

Or again

1. Slaves must subject themselves and give evidence of complete reliability
2. (So that they will be a good witness to their masters)
3. For by doing so, they will add honor and luster to teachings of our Savior.

What we learn from the many enthymemes in the Pastorals is that the audience is assumed to be rational and able to recognize the form of discourse offered to them, and even fill in the blanks, at least collectively when they gather as a group. Logic, and logical argument, was expected. Recognizing rhetorical forms was expected. Now it is true that here Paul can expect more since he is writing to two of his coworkers whom he has discipled in the past. But since we have also seen the use of rhetoric and logic in Rom 7, it is fair to say Paul also expected reasoning and an understanding of rhetoric of his fledgling converts as well.[3] A good understanding of the theology of the NT in particular needs to have at least a basic understanding of ancient logic, reasoning, and rhetoric. Let us turn now to an attempt by Thomas V. Morris, a Christian philosopher, to approach the mystery of the incarnation, critiquing philosophical objections to it by using philosophical logic.

## The Logic of God Incarnate

One of the major concerns of Tom Morris in his book, the title of which is seen above as the title of this chapter section, is with the philosophical discussion of identity statements. As Morris points out, the identity statement made about Christ is not "Jesus is God" *simpliciter*, but rather "Jesus

---

3. For the myriad of enthymemes in the Pastorals and their detailed analysis, see my *Letters and Homilies for Hellenized Christians*, 1:1–390.

is the Son of God."[4] And this comports with the presentation of Jesus in the Gospels. Jesus does not run around Galilee or Judaea saying, "Hi, I'm God," because what that would mean to His fellow Jews is "Hi, I'm Yahweh," something Jesus was not claiming. Even when we have statements like "I and the Father are One," as the verb *are* indicates, we are talking about two persons who are in some intimate way related. The Son is not claiming to be the Father. The text does not say, "I and the Father am One (and the same)."

And as Morris stresses, identity statements are not the same as predications. The claim the Son *is* God is what philosophers call a predication, not an identity statement. Confusion of these two types of statements using the verb *to be* leads to mistaken claims of logical inconsistency. Morris presents a series of logically inconsistent arguments against the reality of the incarnation and is able to show the flaws in the reasoning involved, one of which is a regular mistaking of identity statements for mere predications.

Another helpful insight of Morris is his advocacy of the philosophical distinction he makes between being merely human and being fully human. While ordinary mortals like you and me are merely human, subject to all kinds of errors, not to mention being sinners, Jesus was fully human in the non-fallen sense of what that would mean. He always resisted temptation, even when it was a struggle. He was never merely selfish or self-centered. In short, He never manifested the effects of human fallenness, the heart turned in upon itself, also called narcissism.

Jesus' love was always a holy love, an other-centered love. He was generous and self-giving, not self-absorbed. He was sad when the rich young ruler could not give up his material possessions and become His disciple. Jesus wept at the grave of a friend, and His heart went out to Jairus who was desperately trying to get help for his dying daughter. He also stopped a funeral procession and raised a young man, due to His compassion for the widow who had likely lost her only means of support in Nain.

Jesus was truly human, truly what a human being at their best should be, and in a very real sense we can see an indirect portrait of who Jesus was by studying not only His actions, but also His teaching, such as the Sermon on the Mount. Like His Father, He loved the world and knew He was sent to save it from itself. He was Adam gone right, the eschatological Adam, as Paul suggests in Rom 5:12–21 and 1 Cor 15, and as Luke's genealogy in Luke 3 intimates. It took a God-Man, the Son of Man of Dan 7:13–14, to rescue humanity from its sinful and self-destructive death spiral.

Despite all the helpful deconstruction of arguments against the possibility of the incarnation, what Morris ends up defending is the two natures

---

4. Morris, *Logic of God Incarnate*, 20–21.

doctrine hammered out in 450 at Chalcedon, even to the extent that he affirms the notion of Christ having both a human and a divine mind. We have already had reason to question the Biblical basis for that idea.

Nevertheless, the important takeaway from examining *The Logic of God Incarnate* is that there are no *compelling* logical arguments against the plausibility of the Son of God taking on flesh and dwelling among the human race for a time. There is nothing unreasonable or illogical about this idea, which in the end is not just an idea or thought experiment, but rather *an event* that happened in space and time.

John Wesley and others of his era used the phrase "right reason," and what was meant by this phrase was that human reason was needed, in tandem with revelation from God, to understand the world and God's will in it. Reasoning was a faculty God gave human beings so they could learn things both from close examination of and logical deductions based on nature, human nature, and careful, detailed study of God's Word as well. Thomas Aquinas suggested that prudence is right reason in action, the moral virtue that leads us to live good, ethical, godly lives. Prudence is necessary for correct judgments, and it forms and informs our character and helps us more easily make wise choices and act on them.

Neither Wesley nor Aquinas were suggesting "let your conscience be your guide" apart from revelation and careful reflection on God's Word as well as on the world. Reason, or right reason, was not seen as an authority equal to that of Scripture, any more than tradition was seen to be just as much of an authority as Scripture according to Wesley, but both were considered secondary guides and authorities for the Christian life. But what happens when certain *genuine* Biblical ideas or teachings get emphasized at the expense of more important ones? We will examine this problem in the next chapter.

## Chapter Nine

# Putting the Emphasis on the *Wrong* Syllable
## Adjectives at the Expense of Nouns

I must have been in the right place
But it must have been the wrong time
I'd have said the right thing
But must have used the wrong rhyme.
    —Dr. John

Sometimes it is a matter of a wrong emphasis, not a matter of a wrong idea or wrong deduction. In my book *Who God Is*, I've pointed out at length the problem with analyzing God's character by focusing almost exclusively on the adjectives applied to God in the Bible at the expense of the nouns. This is, as well, a major problem with systematized Biblical theology and some forms of Systematics, particularly of the Reformed and also Augustinian sort. On any fair showing as much if not more emphasis should be placed on the nouns applied to God as on the adjectives, and they include the following major ones—God is love, life, light, spirit, and one.

Of course, adjectives like almighty, holy, sovereign are important, but they are not *more* important than those nouns. So, my goal in that small book was to put the *emphasis* back on the right *syllable* starting with the startling remark in 1 John 4 that God IS love.

Here, my concern is to provide a pointer as to where we might start a proper discussion about the most fundamental things one should know and say about God. Here are some clues to how to conceive and articulate a more robust and accurate systematized Biblical theology, or even an attempt at Systematics when it comes to discussing the God of the Bible.

## God Is Love

Sometimes it is true that where one starts a journey determines where one is going to end up. If I start out in the direction of Louisville from here in Lexington, there is no chance I will be ending up at Myrtle Beach, South Carolina. I'm going in entirely the opposite direction—heading west rather than heading east. And it is fair to say that if one starts with "God is love" and fully embraces the meaning and implications of that pronouncement, there are simply places you cannot end up in thinking about God and His plan of salvation for humankind.

Most of us are quite familiar with that brief but rich sermon we call 1 John, and one of its major themes is the following: "Whoever does not love, does not know God, because God is love. . . . Whoever lives in love, lives in God, and God in them." Now of course the author is not talking about just any kind of love. He's talking about holy love, and we are being prompted to reflect on the fact that God's holiness is not without love, nor is God's the kind of love that does not involve holiness. God's love is a self-giving love, not a self-indulgent one. And it should not be confused with lust or *eros*, unlike the tales about the Greco-Roman gods.

The thing about love as an action is that it must be freely given, freely received, and freely responded to. It can be neither coerced nor predetermined. In short, inherent to love is at least a measure of freedom. One can be wooed, or persuaded, or led to love, but one cannot be forced to do it. Among other things what saying God is love means is that God is a free agent. God is not compelled even by His own nature to love. No, God chooses to love because it is consistent with His nature and character. God could have let the world of fallen humanity quite literally go to Hell with no injustice involved, but it would have been totally out of character for Him to do so.

One of the more shocking things 1 John 4 says is not merely that God lives in believers, but that His love *comes to completion* in us. What the author means is that when we respond in love to God's love and love God back, we've created the intended perfect circle of love. As the old saying goes you can only keep love in your life by giving it away. Whoever does not love their brother or sister they have seen must not love God. In fact, love drives out all fear of judgment by God, because God's love is perfect.

It seems clear that the Beloved Disciple who wrote this sermon did not think there was anything more fundamental about God's character than *agape*, nor anything more fundamental about the way He related to His people, pouring His love into them, nor anything more fundamental about how they should respond to God and to each other than love, holy love.[1]

This sort of love does not occur on its own in a fallen world full of sinners who lack the glory of God. But the good news is "anyone who enters into a real relationship with a loving God can be transformed into a loving person."[2] Not only so, but even more astounding is the claim that when one is transformed by God's love, a person *comes to know God as God actually is!* We may use the cliché "to know you is to love you" about people we care about, but our author is saying the reverse: "having been transformed by God's love, and beginning to love God in turn, a person comes to love God *as He actually is*—for 'God is love.'"

And the reverse is also true—those who do not manifest *agape* do NOT know God. There is a reason the great commandment is about loving God and neighbor with one's whole heart. There is equally a reason why Paul stresses the greatest member of the triad faith, hope, and love is love. And if one ponders that claim from the poem in 1 Cor 13, one can understand why Paul says this. One day, when Christ returns, faith will turn to sight. One day when Christ returns, our deepest hopes and longings will be realized. The one quality in this life that carries over into the next life unchanged (though enhanced or amplified) is *agape*.

Just how strange this claim is in the Greco-Roman world is that the noun *agape* hardly occurs in ancient or Hellenistic Greek, and never of a deity, and when it does occur, C. H. Dodd calls it a cool and colorless word meaning something like "esteem," not at all how the NT writer uses the word.[3] And if that dramatic repurposing of the word was not enough, consider how odd the *proof* of God's love is said to be!

By God giving His Son to die for an undeserving world, atoning for their sins, God demonstrated His character and His desire to be reconciled to lost humanity. The pagan world would rightly have thought—what sort of god comes and dies for selfish, self-centered, ungrateful human beings? And

---

1. If, as I have argued at length in *What Have They Done with Jesus?*, the Beloved Disciple is one and the same with the one identified in John 11 as "the one whom Jesus loved," then the author of this sermon in 1 John knew personally what the character of Christ was as one who revealed the very character of God.

2. Smalley, *1, 2, 3 John*, 238.

3. See Dodd, *Johannine Epistles*, 111–12.

the answer is the kind of God who loves the world of humanity so much that He was literally dying to pour His love into them and erase their debt of sin. Not only so, but God desired to give those very redeemed persons the gift of everlasting life (1 John 4:9–10). In other words, this God who is love wanted an everlasting relationship with those He redeemed and reconciled. As the ancient Christmas hymn asks—"What wondrous love is this, oh my soul?"

James Denney helps us understand why the cross of Christ reveals the depth of a holy God's love. "If the propitiatory death of Jesus is eliminated from the love of God, it might be unfair to say the love of God is robbed of all meaning, but it is certainly robbed of its apostolic meaning. It no longer has that meaning which goes deeper than sin, sorrow, and death, and which recreates life in the adoring joy, wonder and purity of the first Epistle of John."[4]

We might have expected the writer to conclude that since God loves believers like this, we in turn should love God that way, but instead he insists that since we have received such love from God, we should love other believers this way. If we are surprised by this conclusion, then we have forgotten how integrally theology and ethics are interwoven in the Bible, as we have emphasized earlier in this study.

And we are reminded here that when God's love fills up a believer's inner being, it casts out fear. It is sad and tragic to see a Christian person live in fear, and do fear-based thinking and decision making in life, rather than faith-based thinking and decision making. It is the latter to which the Beloved Disciple calls believers in this sermon. And lastly, as Hos 11 rightly portrays God, God is a like a loving parent who does not give up on His wayward children. God's love for us does not change, even when it is not returned, even when it is rejected. As Shakespeare once wrote in "Sonnet 116," "Love is not love which alters when it alteration finds . . . O no! It is an ever-fixed mark." Or as the British poet Geoffrey Studdert Kennedy once said:

> I bet my life on Beauty, Truth,
> And Love, not abstract but incarnate Truth,
> Not Beauty's passing shadow but its Self.
> Its very self made flesh, Love, realised.
> I bet my life on Christ—Christ Crucified.
> Behold your God! My soul cries out. He hangs,
> Serenely patient in His agony,
> And turns the soul of darkness into light.[5]

---

4. Denney, *Death of Christ*, 152.
5. This is from his poem entitled "Faith," in Studdert Kennedy, *Unutterable Beauty*, 5.

And in his most powerful poem, "The Sorrow of God," done in dialect, he has a soldier in the WWI trenches (where Studdert Kennedy had been a chaplain during that war) who has been meditating on why God allows humans to slaughter one another instead of just putting a stop to the whole human experiment finally come to a conclusion.

And strangely enough the answer the soldier comes to is it is because God is love, and so God must allow humans a modicum of freedom, for love cannot be predetermined or compelled, and God wants His creatures to love Him. He wants this so much that God in Christ suffers for us, and then He suffers with us, as the Damascus Road episode shows. So the soldier concludes the following:

> Well, maybe that's 'ow it is wi' God,
>   'Is sons 'ave got to be free;
> Their wills are their own, and their lives their own,
>   And that's 'ow it 'as to be.
> So the Father God goes sorrowing still
>   For 'Is world what 'as gone to sea,
> But 'E runs up a light on Calvary's 'eight
>   That beckons to you and me.
> The beacon light of the sorrow of God
>   'As been shinin' down the years,
> A-flashin' its light through the darkest night
>   O' our 'uman blood and tears.
> There's a sight o' things what I thought was strange,
>   As I'm just beginnin' to see
> "Inasmuch as ye did it to one of these
>   Ye 'ave done it unto Me."[6]

Sadly in this day and age, the term *agape* has been used to justify kinds of feelings that are anything but holy. Joseph Dongell was right to be concerned when he said, "I had worries about how an emphasis on love would sweep us into strange and destructive theological waters. Over the last century and a half it has been clear that love-oriented theologies have generally been moving away (in varying degrees and in varying ways) from classical orthodoxy. In this connection one thinks of Universalism, liberalism, pluralism, open theism, process theology, and pansexual affirmation among others. These should not be confused with each other, are not necessarily 'birds of a feather,' and do not rise or fall together when being assessed. Yet within each, love stands at or near the center of thought."[7] Just so. Thus, it is all the

---

6. Studdert Kennedy, *Unutterable Beauty*, 137.
7. Dongell, *Most Excellent Way*, 21–22.

more important that one distinguish the holy love of God, which if poured into a person cleanses them of sin, from various other sorts of love or feelings which in fact are inherently sinful according to the Biblical witness.[8] It is thus critical to carefully explain what one means when one says things like we read about in 1 John 4.[9]

## God Is One

There are actually not that many dramatic theological statements about Yahweh in the OT, but Deut 6:4–5 is one of them, and it makes perfect sense to talk about this now because it is combined with the command to love God. This "confession of faith" comes right after the Ten Commandments, and just at the beginning of Moses' attempt to instruct God's people and prepare them to receive the ordinances and statues that begin in Deut 12. It should be remembered that Jesus Himself, in Matt 22:40, says that all the commandments of God hang on, depend on the "Shema"—the "hear, O Israel" statement.

One could argue that the Shema distills the essence of the Ten Words, as they are actually called in the Hebrew text. The Shema starts by dealing with the identical issue raised by the first two of the Ten Commandments, and then, in essence, summarizes the other eight commandments in the command to love one's neighbor. The phrase that introduces the Shema is the same as the one that introduces the Ten Commandments, namely "attention, or listen up Israel." Obviously, something crucial and to be never forgotten is about to be said. The problem, however, is that there has been no little debate on how to properly translate the Hebrew of the Shema.

A proper translation of the Masoretic text reads,

> Hear O Israel: The Lord our God, the Lord is One. Love the Lord your God with all your heart, and all your "nephesh" [i.e., life breath or life force, sometimes translated "soul," but spirit would be a better rendering[10]], and with all your strength. These commandments I give you today are to be on your hearts.

A proper translation of the LXX version of Deut 6:4–6 reads,

> The Lord our God, the Lord is One. Love the Lord your God with the whole of your mind and with the whole of your soul

---

8. On which see appendix 1 below.

9. See the fuller discussion in my *Who God Is*.

10. I say this because Hebrews did not embrace the Greek idea of the immortal soul when this was written.

and with the whole of your power. And these words that I command you today shall be in your heart and in your soul.

But what exactly does the Hebrew term *echad*, translated "one" here, mean? Does it stress God's unity or His uniqueness? The former seems unlikely, because why would the unity of Yahweh be an issue? Here we must take into consideration the polytheistic environment in which the Hebrews lived, and clearly this is a statement making evident to Israel that whatever other beings might be out there, Yahweh alone is the God of Israel. If indeed, the statement means that Yahweh is the only real God, the only living and true God, then interestingly it is not a statement about the internal nature of God (like, say, the statement "God is spirit"[11]) but about the reality and uniqueness of Israel's God.

This would also seem to imply that God is consistent and unchangeable in character and in God's actions. God does not change His mind, and has no need to do so. In any case, it is clear from both the Shema and the first two commandments that Yahweh will brook no rivals, and Israel should have and does have no other god. Period. And because Yahweh is not merely the greatest of deities, but the only genuine and real deity, all others being pretenders, not contenders, this is why Yahweh requires exclusive allegiance and singularly whole-hearted worship focused on Yahweh alone. Idolatry is by definition an idea that presupposes a monotheistic context. But it also presupposes that there are other supernatural beings out there, which one could, but should not, worship. Paul in 1 Cor 10:21 calls them *daimons* or demons.

If we ask what love means in this passage, clearly enough it is not just about one's feelings, not least because feelings cannot be commanded, and yet love here is commanded. Among other things, love here means total commitment, affecting one's thoughts, words, deeds, behaviors, relationships, work habits, worship, giving, and much else besides. One can certainly say that love is law-shaped, for if you love God, you will keep His commandments (cf. Deut 10:12–13; 11:1, 3; 19:9; 30:16, 20). By contrast the discussions about other deities in the ANE does not stress loving the deity. The uniqueness of Yahweh, who loves people as the real living God, calls for a unique and complete response.[12]

---

11. On which see below.

12. In the Greco-Roman world, the gods mostly did not make large ethical demands, not least because they did not behave ethically by Biblical standards themselves. What they demanded was attention rather than neglect, sacrifice according to specific rituals, and the avoidance of sacrilege.

If we ask the implications of the Shema, I would stress that there is nothing here that rules out the idea that the one God could reveal Himself as three persons, or put another way, that three persons were all part of the one divine identity. Nothing here explains the internal or personal make-up of the one God, and it is even possible to argue that the Shema is simply about the one Christians call the Father, and in the OT is called Yahweh. And what is being said is Yahweh is unique, singular, incomparable, the one real living God that Israel was introduced to through Moses. Nothing here rules out future revelations that God was more internally complex than just talking about Yahweh. There is, however, another characteristic that Jesus Himself uses of God which does speak to what we would call the divine being or nature, namely God is spirit, and we will turn to that in a moment, but let us briefly consider another revelatory moment in the life of Moses—when he is called and commissioned at the burning bush to go liberate the Hebrew slaves in Egypt.

אֶהְיֶה אֲשֶׁר אֶהְיֶה in Exod 3:14 is an enigmatic phrase in Hebrew with several possible translations, the most obvious of which is NOT "I Am that I Am." The tense or aspect of the verb *hayah* here, which is imperfect, signals an incomplete action and so not likely a statement of being. It could be rendered "I will be what I will be," the point being God's actions in Egypt on behalf of His people will reveal who the real God is. Moses had asked for a name or identity marker to tell the Israelites who had sent him to liberate them.

Naming in the ANE was not about just putting a label on something or someone. Names often connoted something about the one named, and names were assumed to have power—for example compare the story of Jesus requiring the demon in the Gerasene demoniac story to reveal its name. Once one knew the name, one could have power over the one named. Or consider how Jacob literally means "heel snatcher" and refers to his actions in relation to his brother as they were coming forth from the womb, but it also tells us something about his later personality—stealing his brother's birthright. So, Yahweh may not reveal His personal name here, although the term *Yahweh* itself seems to also be a derivative of the verb *hayah*, meaning "to be," which means this God is indeed the great I Am, the eternally existing one, the living one in the full sense of the word.

Victor Hamilton shows the full spectrum of how the key phrase in Exod 3:14 could be translated—(1) "I am who I am"; (2) "I am who I was"; (3) "I am who I shall be"; (4) "I was who I am"; (5) "I was who I was"; (6) "I was who I shall be"; (7) "I shall be who I am"; (8) "I shall be who I was"; (9) "I shall be who I shall be."[13]

I favor the last because Moses is being sent to Egypt where God will take action on behalf of His people, and obviously that's what those people will need to know—if their God Yahweh is going to act, then they need to pack. What the name *Yahweh* suggests is that unlike human beings, and unlike pagan dying and rising gods, Yahweh is eternal, and so unlike any other being, all of whom are created beings, created by Yahweh the creator. A further revelation of the *nature* of the Biblical God comes in the characterization Jesus reveals—God is spirit.

## God Is Spirit

On any showing the conversation between a Jewish man and a Samaritan woman as recorded in John 4 was not merely groundbreaking; it was revolutionary. The Samaritans were strict monotheists, and their sacred scriptures was simply the Pentateuch, and not just any version of the Pentateuch, but the Samaritan version. They did not affirm the historical books, and did not recognize Jerusalem or Mt. Zion as the center of religious life or the temple on Mt. Zion as the focus of true worship. Instead, they worshiped on Mt. Gerizim near modern-day Nablus, which is still where they hold Passover today, being the only sect of Judaism that still has a literal sacrificial ritual on Passover. While the Samaritans were accused of not being true Jews, but some combination of Jews and Assyrians or other foreigners, the latter doesn't appear to be true for most of them, and their Pentateuch does not reflect pagan ANE religion. Probably, they were simply the remnant of some parts of the northern tribes after the disaster of the Assyrian invasion and partial exile of some northern tribe leaders in about 721 BC.

Jesus did not consider Samaritans or the land of Samaria out of bounds, despite the polemics by Judeans against them suggesting their whole land was like a graveyard, unclean, and their refusal to worship in Jerusalem proof they weren't Jews. And in the context of going through Samaria and stopping at Jacob's well for some water, Jesus had the following remarkable conversation with a Samaritan woman, probably of questionable moral character, as recorded in John 4.

> "Sir," the woman said, "I can see that you are a prophet. Our ancestors worshiped on this mountain, but you Jews claim that the place where we must worship is in Jerusalem."

---

13. Hamilton, *Exodus*, 64.

> "Woman," Jesus replied, "believe me, a time is coming when you will worship the Father neither on this mountain nor in Jerusalem. You Samaritans worship what you do not know; we worship what we do know, for salvation is from the Jews. Yet a time is coming and has now come when the true worshipers will worship the Father in the Spirit and in truth, for they are the kind of worshipers the Father seeks. God is spirit, and his worshipers must worship in the Spirit and in truth."
>
> The woman said, "I know that Messiah" (called Christ) "is coming. When he comes, he will explain everything to us."
>
> Then Jesus declared, "I, the one speaking to you—I am he."

Our concern here is with what is said about true worship, and the true nature of the one being worshiped, namely that true worship should comport with the one being worshiped, who is spirit. Not a spirit, but simply "spirit."

When Jesus says God is spirit, He is talking about the heavenly Father and His very nature. He is denying God's nature involves materiality or flesh. In other words, this God should not be envisioned as a larger version of a human being, and He should not be anthropomorphized.

A moment's reflection reminds us that this truth leads to a big question—Why would God the Son, who was not made up of material stuff or flesh, take on flesh? Why would He allow Himself to become mortal, vulnerable, subject even to temptation and death? The short answer is for us and for our salvation.

God absolutely does not need physicality to be who He is, or to be complete as God.[14] Unlike some pagan religions, the God of the Bible does not need sacrifices to provide Him with something He lacks—sustenance, life, breath, etc. God is not missing anything essential by not having a physical form or nature. One reason the NT stresses resurrection for human beings is while humans have a spirit (cf. even the human Jesus can say to the Father, "into your hands I commend my spirit"—Luke 23:46), they are not by "nature" spirit as God is.

Human beings need a body to be complete—hence resurrection is the final condition humans must experience to be all they can be, including to be like Christ the Risen One. Bodies are not only our means of self-expression but one of our means of distinction one from another. Mortal bodies change and fail, and can die. With God who is spirit, it is another story, unless of course God takes on flesh and allows Himself to be mortal in some way that we have trouble comprehending. God who is spirit does not change in character or nature. We have already explored, with the help of my old

---

14. And this is where Mormon theology goes very wrong indeed. God has no need of a body to be who He is.

friend and classmate Tom Morris, the logic of God incarnate, which, as it turns out is not a logical impossibility or an incoherent idea.

Here we need to ask—Why is Jesus saying that worship is *about to change*, in a way that better comports with God's nature? It's not going to be about a holy location, or about priests, temples, and sacrifices. No, worship is going to be wherever and whenever in spirit and in truth as Jesus brings in the Dominion of God. What has happened is that believers both corporately as the body of Christ but also individually are the place where God dwells—we are the temple, because we are in Christ who is the temple, the living presence of God.

But then too we are the priesthood of all believers with only Christ as the heavenly high priest. There is no intermediary priesthood, called clergy, because we don't need anyone offering sacrifices for us because: (1) Christ has already offered the one all-sufficient sacrifice to atone for all sins past, present, or future; and (2) each one of us is to present ourselves to God as living sacrifices, holy and acceptable to God (which by the way requires our holiness for it to be acceptable), whenever and wherever we can. We do not need a sacred space or even a sacred time to do that. Since the earth is the Lord's and God is everywhere, anywhere can be a place of worship, even in a graveyard, even underground.

It was one of the real privileges I had at the end of a tour of Italy, that I and my tour group had worship on a Sunday morning in Rome in the catacombs, where Christians centuries before had worshiped, and where many of them had been buried. Now the bodies were gone, but there were all the carved niches in this barrel-vaulted space where they had been buried, and with all the candles lit, and the great hymns echoing through that space, there was a strong sense of the presence of those saints worshiping with us from heaven, like the worship in Rev 4–5 that involved saints above and those below.

And when we sang that great hymn—"For all the saints, who from their labors rest, who thee by faith before the world confessed, thy name O Jesus, be forever blessed, Hallelujah"—I felt like all of Christ's people were worshiping together. This was all the more so when we took holy communion there and then as we sang, "Let us break bread together." We worshiped in spirit, whole-heartedly, and in truth, for God is both spirit, and as Jesus said, He is the Truth with a capital *T*. Notice that Jesus says that God is *seeking* precisely these kinds of worshipers, not merely those who go through the liturgical motions, or those who only sit and watch the performances on the platform.

God is not calling us to be couch potatoes for Jesus in the pews. Worship is not a performance by the few for the many, and we should not approach it as consumers of worship, but rather as producers of true worship. Worship should be theocentric, not people focused. It is not about giving the people what they desire and crave; it is about giving God what He desires and requires of us. True devotion is loving God in all we are with all we have, and in all we do. Worship is about adoration, celebration, jubilation, coronation, and destination all in one. It completes the life cycle of all creatures great and small. Notice that we are told in Dan 7:13–14 that this worship involves the Son of Man being worshiped by all human beings, as Phil 2:5–11 also suggests. Worship is a reaffirmation of the intended creation order. Our worship is eschatological in character—no longer does it involve priests, temples, and sacrifices, but not yet does it involve us joined together with all the saints physically when Christ returns and the new creation commences. There is so much more that could be said along these lines, but this must suffice to provide some clues of a better way God might be talked about in a truly Biblical systematic theology.[15]

---

15. See my study *We Have Seen His Glory*.

Chapter Ten

# Anachronism at the Expense of History
## The Problem Revisited

An *anachronism* is a chronological inconsistency that occurs when objects, language, or people from different historical periods are mixed together. Anachronisms can manifest in various forms:

- Objects misplaced in time (e.g., a pair of sneakers in an eighteenth century period drama).
- Characters using language from a different era (e.g., using modern slang in a movie set in ancient Rome).
- Technology or practices shown in a time period they did not yet exist in or would have become outdated in (e.g., teenagers using a rotary phone instead of smartphones in 2023).[1]

We have been dealing with anachronisms at various points in this study, and by now it should be apparent that it comes in many forms. Let's review briefly. One form of anachronism is taking a particular Biblical translation not merely as a translation, but as THE English translation which itself is inspired and without error. Unfortunately, this happens most often with the KJV or the New King James. Neither of these translations are the best one can do when we are talking about accurate rendering of the Hebrew

---

1. As helpfully defined at Nikolopoulou, "What Is Anachronism?," para. 2. Even people, by cultural choice, can be glorious anachronisms—for instance the old order Amish who refuse to use electricity, dress like eighteenth-century farmers, and still ride around in buggies drawn by horses.

and Greek texts, not least because, in the case of the 1611 King James, it is not based at all on our earliest and best manuscript copies of the originals in the original language because they weren't available then. And there are inherent problems with English when it comes to certain words and phrases difficult to render into English.[2]

A second form of anachronism comes from imposing a later theological system on the Biblical text, with Dispensationalism being a particularly egregious modern offender. Not only did this type of analysis of the Bible not really exist at all before about the 1600s, but it did not become a prominent theological approach before the nineteenth century, and it introduced into the discussion some theological ideas, like a rapture of the believers into heaven when tribulation comes on earth, that has no Biblical basis at all.

This escapist theology is grounded not only in a dubious theology about Biblical prophecy but also involves a hermeneutic that suggests that the Biblical text can be coordinated with current events, which are frankly not mentioned in the Bible. Revelation becomes the playground for all sorts of amateur theologians wanting to say "this is that" which John spoke of, or the "time is near at hand" despite Christ telling us He'll come like a thief in the night at an unknown and unannounced time. Even the earthly Jesus said He doesn't know when it will happen (Mark 13:32).

A third problematic example of anachronism is the reading of later Catholic theology back into the Bible as we have already seen, for instance about the immaculate conception of Mary, or the bodily ascension of Mary, or Mary's sinlessness or her perpetual virginity. And it is not just that these ideas are not in the Bible and come from later Catholic tradition. In some cases, they frankly contradict what the Bible says. For example, the evidence as we have it is that Mary, a good Jewish woman, went on to have a goodly number of more children with Joseph. They are not Jesus' cousins (they are always called His brothers and sisters), and they are not the children of Joseph by previous marriage.[3]

Of late, there have been a variety of Catholic and Protestant scholars (Brian Daley being a good example of the former), who have argued that the church should largely abandon modern historical original context exegesis in favor of following the methodology of the Fathers and their pre-modern approach to exegesis, which neglects the original historical contexts and meanings of the text in favor of later readings of the text in light of the interpretations of the Cappadocian and Antiochian and Alexandrian Church

---

2. See Alistair McGrath's wonderful history of the KJV in *In the Beginning*.
3. See, e.g., Shanks and Witherington, *Brother of Jesus*.

Fathers. The problem with this is not merely one of interpretation but the ignoring of the fact that the NT documents had individual inspired writers producing inspired individual documents, and they were *words on target having specific meanings* for their original audiences, *and the meanings did not change just because these documents were placed into a canonical collection.*

A particularly strident insistence on this anachronistic approach can be seen in the recent work of Craig Carter. Clifton Black, in reviewing his work lays out the various problems with this sort of approach. In a recent *RBL* review,[4] Black has rightly rejected a caricature of historical criticism by Carter in his recent monograph *Interpreting Scripture with the Great Tradition: Recovering the Genius of Premodern Exegesis* (Baker, 2018), which in fact argues historical criticism "suffers a . . . radical, even toxic, difficulty": it is a child of "so-called Enlightenment" modernity, whose repudiation of the Bible's divine authorship (42–44, 98), textual inspiration (44–45), worship of human reason (88–89), and "irrational rejection of Christianity as the true religion" (85) are symptomatic of its character as "a cultural pathology caused by the breakdown of the Great Tradition and the rise of neopaganism in Western civilization" (85). "Christianity"—specifically, "Christian Platonism"—"and modernity cannot be reconciled and cannot coexist permanently; they must inevitably clash in the struggle for cultural supremacy"—and for three centuries that battle has been waged on the field of biblical interpretation (91, 107; see also 109–10, 123–25, 153). "The liberal project," inaugurated by Spinoza and perpetuated by Schleiermacher (114–24), "needs to be abandoned because it is dead." Instead of a historical reading of the text in light of its original contexts and intent, we are instructed to read the text anachronistically in light of later orthodox readings of the Bible. As we have already seen in this study, this approach is seriously problematic, and it is not helped by caricatures of the historical study of the Bible in its original contexts. As we used to say in North Carolina, "this dog will not hunt"—it puts the dog back in dogmatics.

Sometimes anachronism takes the form of reading the text as if the writers of the Bible shared our way of looking at human anthropology, or for instance, time. On the latter point, the phrase "after three days" can mean the very same thing as "on the third day," and the Greek adverb *euthus*, while often translated "immediately," actually turns out to simply mean "next."

Or consider the use of the language of the heart. In the world of various Biblical writers, the heart was not merely a blood pump. Rather it was the

---

4. Black, Review of *Interpreting Scripture with the Great Tradition*, is the source for all the quotes that follow.

control center of the personality, where thoughts, feelings, will all resided. When the psalmist says, "cleanse the thoughts of my heart," he is simply reflecting this ancient way of viewing human nature in that era. Fortunately for us, the Bible doesn't try to teach a biologically accurate view of various body parts.

Consider for a moment the remarkable ancient Egyptian practice of mumification. The Egyptians, like other nearby peoples, believed the heart was the control center of the personality—the center of thought, will, and feelings. So, in their paintings in the tombs of the Pharaohs they depicted the final judgment as a scene where the human heart of a person is weighed on a scale. And in the practice of mumification, they would take out the internal organs including the heart and place them in canopic jars with preservatives in them. But as for the brain, they took that to be unimportant, and so they would suck that out of the skull and throw it away, like a person blowing the mucus out of their nose. One could say the Egyptian view of what one needed in the afterlife was a "no brainer"!

But this theology of the heart as the control center of the personality was typical of many ancient cultures, including Israelite culture. The psalmist says, "create in me a clean heart" (Ps 51:10), instead of a clean mind. The subject matters that the Bible teaches us about are not cosmology, or biology, or the age of the earth, but rather salvation history, theology, ethics, and spiritual formation. Unhelpful theologies sometimes involve pseudo-science of various sorts.

Of course there are even more deliberate and malignant forms of anachronism, like the idea that the Gospels are presenting us with an Aryan and anti-Semitic Jesus, who is just the opposite of a Jesus who loved His fellow Jews and wanted to lead them into a deeper relationship with God. Or if we think of the early Christian movement itself it was deliberately ethnically inclusive. The Gospel was indeed for the Jew first, but it was also for all the other ethnic groups which we have come to call Gentiles. Galatians 3:28 is emphatic—in Christ there is neither Jew nor Gentile. All are one in Christ.

This makes modern attempts to suggest Christianity or particular churches should be favoring one ethnicity over another, or worse, suggesting that Americans or more particularly Caucasians are God's new chosen people, not merely a heresy; it is the opposite of what the NT teaches. It's yet another form of racism cropping up in the one place where it should be most anathematized.

Not long ago, the Museum of the Bible had an exhibit of the "Slave" Bible. This was a Bible produced in the UK in 1807, intended for the British colonies of commonwealth countries in the British West Indies, or as we know it today, the Caribbean. It was intended for the use of and with slaves in these countries, and this Bible only included excerpts from fourteen OT books and eighteen NT books, and had deliberately left out any material that might suggest that: (1) slaves were equal human beings with their masters; (2) God liberates slaves (think Exodus); (3) rebellion against oppressive overlords is not against God's Word, and much more. In other words, it was meant to keep slaves in line and tell them to be content with their situation. Note the date this Bible came out. It came out while the Parliament at the instigation of William Wilberforce was abolishing slavery in the UK in 1807!

Slavery was not abolished in the British colonies until 1834, and again it was because of the constant efforts of Wilberforce and his coworkers and successors in the Clapham Sect. Again, Gal 3:28 says plainly, in Christ there is neither slave nor free, but all are one—all created in God's image, all renewed in the image of Christ. Apparently, Paul and others took seriously the message of Jesus' inaugural sermon in Nazareth in Luke 4:18–19, where, quoting Isa 61:1–2 combined with Isa 58:6, He said,

> The Spirit of the Lord is on me,
> because he has anointed me
> to proclaim good news to the poor.
> He has sent me to proclaim freedom for the prisoners
> and recovery of sight for the blind,
> to set the oppressed free,
> to proclaim the year of the Lord's favor.

Of what relevance is this to the task of Biblical or Systematic theology, you may ask? Much in every way, for the Gospel is not just about liberation from spiritual ills, or sin; it is also about exactly what Jesus said it is about in the quote above. As my forebear John Wesley said, there is no spiritual holiness without social holiness, and vice versa. It is not an accident that Paul in Philemon tells his friend and convert Philemon he needs to manumit his slave Onesimus and treat him no longer as a slave, but rather as a brother in Christ. And it is no accident that we have evidence of early Christians buying people out of slavery. As John Wesley once told William Wilberforce, "slavery is the most execrable sum of all villainies," and in his last letter in 1791 he insisted that Wilberforce not give up hope but keep on pressing the issue in Parliament.[5]

Jesus was not only about the liberation of slaves and the demon possessed and ill; He was also about the liberation of women, as is clear from His being either the first or one of the first to have women disciples, women He was not related to, who traveled with Him and the male disciples (Luke 8:1–3). And Jesus' teaching was radical in that regard as well because He

---

5. Wesley, "Last Writing."

told His male disciples that His followers had two options—heterosexual monogamy without divorce, or celibacy in singleness (Matt 19).

This last notion, that one did not need to be married to be His follower and help spread the Gospel, was itself revolutionary especially for women, for it meant they were not limited to the roles of wives and mothers and runners of the domestic sphere—the household. No, they could be many things—businesswomen like Lydia (Acts 16:13–15), teachers like Priscilla (Acts 18:26–28), deacons like Phoebe (Rom 16:1–2), and even apostles like Junia (Rom 16:7). Paul took this dual possibility for disciples seriously in his advice about marriage; he even said candidly that one would have more time for ministry if one remained single (see 1 Cor 7)![6]

In a recent publication entitled *Holiness: A Biblical, Historical, and Systematic Theology*, three scholars in the Wesleyan tradition have explored just what I've been talking about above in some detail and its relevance for the discussion of Biblical and Systematic theology, and in the rest of this chapter we will be interacting with that work.[7] Here we are dealing not just with the problem of modern anachronisms, which are bad enough, but with the neglect of a huge portion of the theological thrust of the Bible, and sometimes this has been a deliberate, one might even say systematic, neglect of the message of the Scriptures. We have dealt with some of the problems raised by the book in regard to spiritual holiness, but here it is relevant to mention social holiness.

It is not an accident that the Salvation Army, Goodwill Industries, Hull House in Chicago, and orphanages in England all arose out of the Methodist movement. Social holiness meant a real attempt to remedy some of society's ills, including the practice of slavery, as we have already mentioned. John Wesley quite rightly did not accept the idea that Christians should be so heavenly minded that they are no earthly good. He said about the Bible,

> Solitary religion is not to be found there. "Holy Solitaries" is a phrase no more consistent with the gospel than Holy Adulterers. The gospel of Christ knows of no religion, but social; no holiness but social holiness. Faith working by love, is the length and breadth and depth and height of Christian perfection.[8]

A Biblical or Systematic theology that doesn't deal with social holiness is not a fully Biblical much less a Systematic theology, especially since the latter is supposed to engage the modern discussion on crucial issues. Social

---

6. Besides my relevant commentaries, see also my *Women in the Earliest Churches*.
7. And see chapter 7 for more on this work.
8. Wesley, *Hymns and Sacred Poems*, pref., viii.

holiness includes ministry to the poor, to the homeless, to the abused, to the drug addicts, to the orphans, to those suffering disasters, and much more. I would include concern not merely for the born, but also for the unborn.

John Wesley would rightly say that the Bible does not endorse the idea that the unborn in the woman's womb is not yet a human being created in God's image, nor would he be happy with the idea that women have an inalienable right to have an abortion when it doesn't involve a medical emergency or a woman being a victim of rape or incest. A baby is not just a portion of a woman's body to do with as she pleases. A baby is a human being. Calling an abortion a form of health care when there is not some sort of health emergency is a misuse of the term *health care*. Certainly, it is not health care for the unborn.

And while we are at it, being pro-birth is not the same as being pro-life. The mother and baby may well need extra help after the birth, especially if this is a young or poor or unwed mother. Christians have an obligation to help in such situations, which is why Christian day care centers and mom and baby centers like we have here in Lexington are critical.

Many streams of Christian tradition have taken the Sermon on the Mount and the prophecies about beating swords into plowshares to mean that social holiness involves both peace-making and also personal pacifism, the refusal to do harm to other human beings if at all possible. Some have taken this to mean that while they could be chaplains or medics in an army, they could not carry or use weapons (see, e.g., the movie *Hacksaw Ridge*). Others have suggested that the use of lethal force is the lesser of two evils in a war against some wicked powers or nations, but that it must be used according to the rules of war—not targeting non-combatants. But that has to do with the decisions of nations and their legitimate governments, as Paul himself suggests in Rom 13, not the personal decisions of followers of Christ.

Equally, devout Christians will disagree on what the implications of social holiness require of us in some cases, but the principle that Christians must live out their faith in their personal and social relationships and stand up for the Biblical values, being people of love and virtue, is non-negotiable. These issues should be attended to especially in Systematic theology since we are talking about theological ethics in the Bible. Theology and ethics should not be divided from each other, and yes, of course, some types of ethical actions and principles have political implications. The attempt to over-spiritualize the Gospel at the expense of calling our world to live a more human, a more humane, a more loving existence is a mistake, and no Biblical or Systematic theology should endorse such a thing. But what role *should tradition* in the form of historical theology play in Biblical or Systematic theology? We must address that in the next chapter.

## Chapter Eleven

# Tradition at the Expense of Scripture or in the Service of Scripture?

> And how do we keep our balance? That I can tell you in one word: tradition!
> —Teyve in *Fiddler on the Roof*

While sometimes Protestants have been rightly accused of bibliolatry, a very rigid adherence to a "sola Scriptura" theology while anathematizing Christian traditions of all sorts, as I have shown in my last book, *Sola Scriptura*, what the phrase actually meant in Christian history for the vast majority of Catholics and Protestants who used the phrase was that Scripture was the final authority, not the only authority for faith and practice.

In an attempt to partially correct this error, Tom Oden spent no little time toward the end of his career appropriating lots of historical theology from the Church Fathers for use by Protestants so they would have a better informed and fuller approach to Biblical and Systematic theology. In fact, he did more than that. He attempted to produce a Systematic theology that was both ecumenical and comprehensive of the full scope of Christian theological teaching ancient and modern.[1] But the real strength of his work was in the recovery of the teaching of the early Church Fathers, including especially the Greek Church Fathers like the Cappadocian fathers and John Chrysostom whose native language was Greek, unlike for instance Augustine or Aquinas. It will be useful for us to interact with his classic study here a bit, now available in a single volume entitled *Classic Christianity: A*

---

1. It is interesting to compare Oden's work to that of Robert Jenson who also says he is trying to offer an ecumenical approach to Systematic theology.

*Systematic Theology*, which is a condensed version of the three previous volumes which emerged in 1987, 1989, and 1992. The good news is that often, but not always, the Church Fathers interpreted the Bible in a way that comports with the original inspired text, or simply spins out the implications of the Biblical teaching in helpful ways. Having pointed out the problems with simply following the Church Fathers' interpretations of the Bible without carefully comparing them to the Biblical texts themselves seen in their historical contexts, we can now turn around and show how in many case the fathers got many things right, and often developed further in a helpful way key theological ideas in the Bible.

Before we go further, I would simply remind the reader that we've already dealt with some examples of Christian traditions that not only went beyond but went against what the Bible actually says on a subject, for example about Mary the mother of Jesus, or about John son of Zebedee as the John who wrote the Fourth Gospel. It was John of Patmos who collected and edited the memoirs of the Beloved Disciple, and these were two different persons.

Here instead we want to more fully consider tradition as an *aid* to the interpretation of Scripture, and offer a reminder that the early Jewish Christians all affirmed the important role of tradition in their own faith (see, e.g., Jude citing Enoch and the Assumption of Moses), so there is a precedent in earliest Christianity for treating tradition with respect and as a helpful source for constructing a Biblical or a Systematic theology.

## The Discussion of God's Foreknowledge and Will

One thing that is quite clear from studying the early Church Fathers, particularly those from before the time of Augustine, and those who were the Church Fathers writing in Greek, is that they did not affirm the later Augustinian and then Reformation notions about God's foreknowledge and will.[2] Here is how the discussion is summed up in Oden's presentation of the consensus of the early period of theological discussion. Note as well that the Greek speaking fathers are not where these discussions really blossomed, but in those who spoke and wrote in Latin—Augustine and later Aquinas and especially those who followed in the tradition of Augustine.

> God foreknows the use of free will, yet this foreknowledge does not determine events. Rather what God foreknows is determined by what happens, part of which is affected by free will. God

---

2. The only real possible exception would be some passages in Origen, but alas, we only have a portion of his important John commentary.

knows what will happen, but does not unilaterally determine each and every event immediately—that would dishonor human freedom and the reliability of secondary causes. God fully understands and knows all these specific secondary determining causes that are at work in the natural order, but that does not imply that merely by fiat God constantly acts so as to overrule or circumvent these causes. God's merely knowing them does not negate or undermine their causal reality (Athanasius, *On the Incarnation of the Word*, 1-6; Hilary, *Trin.* 9.61-75). Hence God's foreknowledge does not imply God's omni-causality or absolute determination so as to eliminate all other creaturely wills. God knows what other wills are doing by divine permission (Justin Martyr, *First Apol.* 45-53). God's foreknowledge is precisely of free choice, of human and creaturely willing (Athanasius, *Four Discourses Ag. Arians* 3.30; Augustine, *CG* 5.9; Luis de Molina, *Scientia Media*, RPR: 424-26). God not only grasps and understands what actually will happen, but also what could happen under varied possible contingencies. If God's knowing is infinite, God knows even the potential effects of hypothetical but unactualized possibilities . . . God knows what would have been had things been otherwise and had different historical decisions been made (Augustine, *On the Spirit and Letter*, 58; Augustine, *Against Two Letters of Pelagians* 3.25-4.4). . . . It is God's knowledge of the middle or hypothetical ground between freedom and necessity which is neither the necessary knowledge that God has of himself . . . nor the knowledge that God has of the freedom of his creatures (Thom. Aqu., *ST*1 Q14).[3]

There is much more along these lines, and as an exegete I would say the language of "free will" goes too far in a Pelagian direction, but we can talk about the grace enabled power of contrary choice. If this ability is given universally like Wesley says with his prevenient grace idea, at least this grace restores a measure of meaningful choosing, which is precisely the reason God can hold sinning humans accountable for their bad behavior, including the rejection of the Gospel.

As we have already seen, God even takes into account when bad things are done on the basis of human ignorance, including the crucifixion of Jesus—"Father forgive them, for they don't know what they are doing!" The most important part of this consensus is the recognition that there are viable secondary causes at work in the human sphere, which should not be attributed to God.[4] There are, furthermore, various things that happen in

3. Oden, *Classic Christianity*, 49-50.
4. See pp. 20ff. above about the difference in presentation about David's decision to

nature (earthquakes, fires, devastating winds) that should not be called "acts of God" as 1 Kgs 19 makes clear—"for God was not in the earthquake."[5] God's will could not be discovered by examining "natural" disasters.

## God Is Love

The Church Fathers had much to say about God's love, and God being love, but not just any kind of love. Holy love is what characterizes God, both His nature and His actions. The Church Fathers had plenty to say on this subject as Oden makes clear:

> Nowhere is God defined more concisely than in the first epistle of John "God is love" (1 John 4.16; Hilary *Trin.* 9.61). . . . Consequently love is of all terms the one most directly attributable to God as *essential* to God's very being. God's holiness does not remain trapped within itself, but reaches out for others. When Scripture tells the story of how God reaches out, it does not merely use objective, descriptive, scientific language, but rather the warmest, most intimate, most involving, engaging, and powerfully moving metaphor in human experience—love (Clement of Rome, *Corinth*, 48–56).[6]

There are very precise statements about the relationship between God being holy and God being love.

> It was the love of God that sent God's only Son into the world (John 3.16). It was the holiness of God that required the satisfaction of divine justice through the sacrifice of the Son. These two themes are brought together powerfully in the first Johannine letter: "The love I speak of is not our love for God, but the love he showed to us in sending his Son as the remedy for the defilement of our sins" (1 John 4.10; Chrysostom, *Comm. on John* 27–28; Augustine, *Enchiridion* 32). . . . Neither holiness nor love alone could have sufficed, a love that lacked holiness could not have sufficed for the salvation of sinners (Anselm, *Cur Deus Homo*, 1). . . . Love is the way holiness communicates itself

---

have a census in the discussion in Samuel and in the parallel passage in Chronicles. This is yet another sign of the need to recognize the developing understanding of the Biblical writers when it comes to God's will, and how it relates to human willing.

5. Which is not to say that God never uses nature to reveal his will or execute his judgments on humankind. The point in 1 Kgs 19, however, is that human beings cannot discern the will of God by analyzing nature. It is the Word of God, rather than the world of God, that by and large must be relied on to reveal God's will.

6. Oden, *Classic Christianity*, 70; emphasis added.

under the conditions of sin (Clement of Alex. *Instr.* I.9). God's holiness detests sin; the motive for reconciliation is God's love for the sinner, which is so great that it is willing to pay the costliest price to set it aright.[7]

We have already had much to say about the nature and implications of God being love earlier in chapter 8 on the major nouns predicated of God in the Bible. Certainly, various of the Church Fathers thought one of the implications of texts like John 3:16 or 1 John 4 is that one must not limit the scope of the atoning death of Christ. Gregory of Nazianzus puts it this way: "For there is one God and also one mediator between God and men, Christ Jesus, himself man who sacrificed himself to win freedom for all humankind" (*Theological Oration* 4.30.14; and see also his *Second Oration on Easter*, seeing 1 Tim 2:6 as a declaration that the sins of all humanity have been forgiven).[8] In short, God did not limit the scope of the atonement, and the Cappadocian fathers were clear enough on that. Why is it that that didn't produce universal salvation? The answer was clear enough—the sinner must appropriate the existing benefits of the atoning death of Christ by grace through faith in Christ. If they choose not to do so, they have limited the atonement themselves in regard to receiving the benefits of Christ's death. But of course, Calvin and other Reformed scholars (e.g., Beza, Knox) found this inconsistent with their affirmation that God had predestined only some to be saved before the foundation of the universe. We have already shown that this view involves a serious misreading of Rom 8 and Eph 1, among other texts.

Even from a cursory examination of Oden's *magnum opus*, it becomes very clear that whether one calls it historical theology, or simply early Christian theological tradition, it is valuable because it involves a myriad of sorts of amplifications and implications of what the Bible actually teaches about all sorts of theological subjects. These Church Fathers knew they were extending the discussion in Scripture in various ways, and they knew as well that various of their expansions were open to discussion and debate.

In short, they understood that while Scripture was the primary authority, tradition including tradition-laden exegesis could be invaluable to a church that was growing and needed to better understand their foundational documents. Like the Nicene Creed, some of the most valuable discussions were on Christology, like Anselm's *Cur Deus Homo*, or many of Chrysostom's homilies on the Christological substance of Paul's letters.

---

7. Oden, *Classic Christianity*, 72–73.
8. See Oden, *Classic Christianity*, 109 and 414.

Certainly, for all these Church Fathers, had they used the Latin phrase *sola Scriptura*, what they would have taken it to mean is that Scripture is the final authority, the norm of other norms, not the sole authority. And this approach was necessary, not only because we do not have a full elaboration of the theology of the Trinity in the Bible, nor do we have a full elaboration on the sacraments of water baptism, and its relationship to the reception of the Holy Spirit, nor of the Lord's Supper either, though we have a little more help from texts like 1 Cor 11 on the latter.

## The Issue of Christ's Death and Human Freedom

The more one reads the Church Fathers, the more clear it becomes that the later period of theological reflection by Augustine, after he had changed his thinking about God's sovereignty and how it worked, made him the odd man out among the great theologians of the early church, whether we are thinking of the Latin fathers like Tertullian, perhaps the first great theologian after Paul himself, or the Greek fathers. And their views that human beings had a modicum of freedom of choice, or at least the power of contrary choice such that they could reject the will of God and sin, has been helpfully summed up in Oden's volume. This affirmation of human freedom affected the fathers' views on all kinds of things, including crucially Christ's death on the cross.

> If God were merely saving rocks or plants, the plan would have been different—for they do not have the freedom to respond or resist. The plan of salvation had to be worthy of *the character of the holy and loving God* and fitting to *the conditions of human freedom* so radically fallen into distortion and self-alienation. The plan had to be consistent with the extraordinary gifts the Creator had already bestowed upon humanity: reason, imagination, language, the capacity for justice and love, and self-determining intelligence. Any design short of all these conditions would have displayed less than the incomparable wisdom of God and would have been inconsistent with all that is known of the divine character (Baxter, *PW* 9.35, 20, pref.). . . . Therefore three options have been consistently rejected in the attempt of classic Christianity to make sense out of the biblical wisdom that leads to the cross: The first is to avoid divine coercion. The God who created freedom would not act simply by fiat. If human freedom is to be honored and transformed it cannot merely be coerced

by decree but rather must be reshaped by persuasion and drawn by a convincing demonstration of unconditional love.⁹

The Church Fathers were rarely unanimous on key theological points, but some of them received a wide consensus, for example on the notion that Christ's death was substitutionary in nature, that it was a sacrifice for the sins of others (Athanasius, *On the Incarnation of the Word*, 20; Cyril of Jerusalem, *Catechetical Lectures* 13.33; Cyril of Alexandria, *Against Nestorius*, 3.2; and all three of the Cappadocian fathers, Basil and the two Gregorys). These fathers were equally adamant that "it is not the atonement that is limited, but our receptivity to it. Our unwillingness to allow the Spirit to apply it to us is the limiting factor. The atonement is addressed to all humanity, intended for all, sufficient for all, yet it is effectively received by those who respond to it in faith (Hilary of Arles, *Introductory Commentary on 1 John* . . . Cyril of Alex., *Comm. on John* 4.2)."¹⁰

## Theodicy: The Problem of Evil and Suffering

> Theodicy is the attempt to speak rightly of God's justice . . . under conditions of suffering and evil. . . . No theological question is more difficult or recurrent than why bad things happen to good people. But there is one even deeper perplexity for Christians—why the Just One has suffered so absolutely.¹¹

On the one hand, theodicy is a problem for monotheism. If there are multiple gods, some good, some bad, then human suffering and evil in the world can be explained, and the problem of evil and suffering is neither solved nor alleviated. But what humankind most needs is not an explanation of where evil and suffering come from, but rather a solution to the problems such things cause.

On the other hand, theodicy in a monotheistic theology is often discussed in an abstract way such as—If God is almighty, He can't be all good,

---

9. Oden, *Classic Christianity*, 416–17; emphasis added. It is interesting that Jonathan Edwards in his most important theological work, entitled *The Freedom of the Will*, knew that these views were part of the Biblical witness, so, unlike Luther's *The Bondage of the Will*, where Luther talks about sin riding herd on the sinner, who has not even a little freedom left so that God has to completely override the human will to save the person, Edwards, by contrast, who is just as much a predeterminist as Calvin, insists that the sinner doesn't feel compulsed either to sin or to accept the Gospel, but in fact his feelings have betrayed him—only irresistible grace can save him.

10. Oden, *Classic Christianity*, 422–23.

11. Oden, *Classic Christianity*, 436.

or else where does evil come from, or why does He allow it? This sort of question becomes especially difficult for those in the Augustinian and Calvinist tradition who want to argue that God has predetermined all things, either actively or passively, from before the foundation of the universe. It is hard to see how on this showing God escapes being the author of evil and suffering and being complicit in sin. On the other hand, in a non-Augustinian framework, it is hard to see how the claim of God's almightiness and goodness can be upheld unless God has given to angels and humans a measure of freedom of choice, and even though that helps explain the origin of evil, sin, and suffering, it doesn't explain why God has not overruled such activity that is clearly against His will. And this brings us to the realization that the Church Fathers did not want to debate this issue in a purely philosophical way.

> For classic Christian teaching, the wisest theodicy flows out of a deep reflection upon the cross (Bede, *On 1 Pet.* 2.19–20). There the profound mystery of human suffering becomes transmuted by the even deeper mystery of God's suffering for humanity (Ambrosiaster, *Comm. on Paul*, 2 Cor. 1.5–7). There can be little persuasive talk of the goodness and power of God if the evil of the world is never in any way decisively overcome sooner or later. The allegedly almightiness of God would be thrown into question if evil were never conceivably overcome. . . . The gospel is good news precisely about evil's defeat (Chrysostom, *Catena*, 1 John 3, 8, CEC 123).[12]

Evil is not defeated, if the Gospel of salvation is merely about escape from the realm of evil and suffering—dying and going to heaven. It is no accident that in the NT the afterlife emphasis is *not* on dying and going to heaven *at all*. It is rarely and barely mentioned in our earliest NT documents, the letters of Paul. And while it is mentioned in the Gospels, and Revelation, the emphasis is on justice and final redemption being accomplished on earth, through Christ's return, His judgment on evil and the oppressors, and His rescue of those who have been faithful, even unto death, by means of resurrection, and its sequel, the new heaven and the new earth. This eschatological answer is inaugurated by Jesus Himself with His announcement that God's final reign on earth has broken into the sad and sinful suffering realm of human history.

And we are told clearly enough in places like Revelation and 2 Peter that the reason the End has not come sooner is that God's preliminary judgments on sin and wickedness are meant to bring people to repentance and back to God. The three sets of seven judgments in Rev 6–19 are not final

---

12. Oden, *Classic Christianity*, 436.

judgment, but the activity of a just and loving God trying to give humanity more chances to repent, having been chastised. As 2 Peter says, God desires that none should perish but all should come to a knowledge of God, and it also adds that God's timing for the end of the human dilemma is in God's hands, and He doesn't count time as humans do, for a thousand years can be as one day, on God's clock.

But there is in fact a further factor to be considered. If the saved already have the gift of everlasting life, which will take them into heaven, and beyond that into the resurrection, there is no absolute or divine necessity to prolong human life in a fallen sphere in a fallen body. Indeed, suffering and death can draw one closer to God and Christ, and indeed it can be said to be a form of sharing in the sufferings of Christ if it comes at the hands of persecutors and executors. As Jim Elliot, who was martyred by South American indigenous people, once said, he is no fool, who gives up what he cannot keep (this mortal life), to gain what he cannot lose (everlasting life in heaven and beyond). But that is only true for those who model their lives on Christ's and are faithful even unto death.

Unfortunately, ever since the early Middle Ages the emphasis has been put on the wrong eschatological syllable, namely dying and going to heaven, rather than looking forward to the return of Christ, the resurrection of the dead, final judgment and the new heaven and the new earth. And herein lies a major problem. Systematic theologies, including Oden's who places eschatology at the end of the study, are not in tune with the writers of the NT and their worldview, who were convinced the end times had already been inaugurated by the coming of Jesus, not by the second coming. And if the end only comes by future resurrection and a new creation, this emphasis, coupled with the doctrine of creation in Genesis insisting on the goodness of creation, means that Adam and all his descendants should be very concerned about creation care, not contributing to creation destruction.[13]

And unless one thinks that the writers of the NT, bless their hearts, were wrong about matters eschatological and thought Jesus was coming back next week (and there are plenty of Biblical scholars who still, wrongly, think this), placing such matters at the end of a systematic study is a mistake. The eschatology and Christology of the NT are so interwoven that they should not be radically separated in the discussion either. Even Gospel writers like Matthew and Luke begin with the conception and birth of Jesus, which is to say, the beginning of the coming of the Dominion of God on earth.

---

13. See, e.g., Sleeth, *Serving God, Saving the Planet*; Richter, *Stewards of Eden*.

What did the Church Fathers think of the teaching so often associated with Luther and the Reformation, namely justification by faith? Theodoret of Cyrus (*Eranistes* 3 FC 106:248–9) stresses that justification is the declaration of God that a person, however sinful, who trusts in Christ's atoning work is treated or accounted as righteous. "This is not a legal fiction but a merciful divine action historically offered on the cross."[14]

Justification reveals the reversal of God's judgment against the sinner, in that he or she is no longer exposed to the legal penalty, which is ultimately spiritual death. Rather they are restored to God's favor (Aquinas, *Summa Theologica* II-I Q113). The verdict of not guilty is rendered solely due to the sinner's new relationship with God, for he is hidden "in Christ" (Chrysostom, *Hom. Rom.* 10). "Justification's nature is pardon, its condition is faith, its ground is the righteousness of God and its fruits are good works" (Wesley, *Works of John Wesley* 5:55, 56).[15] Interestingly, Justin Martyr distinguished between justification under the old covenant by means of just deeds, but under the new covenant by grace through faith in Jesus (*Dialogue with Trypho* 90–95). Under the OT law, Yahweh doesn't justify the sinner, only the righteous or the just ("I will not acquit the guilty," Exod 23:7).

This is just a taste of the rich ore that Oden mined from the Church Fathers, and by and large it shows their desire to extend and amplify the Biblical teaching in ways that were helpful to their churches, without contradicting what they took to be the essential teachings of Scripture. Sometimes, they erred in this attempt, but more often than not they very helpfully enhanced our understanding of the Trinity, of the atonement, of God's foreknowledge, of theodicy, and much, much more. I agree entirely with Pannenberg that this material must not be overlooked or neglected if a person's systematic theology is going to be worth its salt.

---

14. See Oden, *Classic Christianity*, 583.
15. Oden, *Classic Christianity*, 584.

# Chapter Twelve

# Intertextuality and Dubious Theories of Meaning

Any text is constructed as a mosaic of quotations; any text is the absorption and transformation of another.
   —Julia Kristeva

One of the major trends in the Biblical scholarship over the last twenty plus years has been a focus on the issue of intertextuality. Usually, this term is used in Biblical circles to mean the use of the OT and extra-Biblical traditions in the NT, but sometimes the discussions at the Society of Biblical Literature and the Study of the New Testament (in Translation) have ranged more widely. One of the aspects of the discussion has been the assumption, sometimes without discussion or articulation, of theories of meaning that seem to be at odds with the very nature of Scripture—namely an inspired message from God that has a specific but also timeless meaning for believers in all ages.

I have taken the time to do three detailed studies on intertextuality, one on Isaiah, one on the Psalms, and one on material from the Pentateuch. These foci were not chosen randomly but rather were chosen because those OT books were the ones that provide the vast majority of citations, allusions, and echoes of the OT we find in the NT. So, let's consider some of the things to be learned from these discussions that are of relevance for the discussion of both Biblical and Systematic theology. One of the ironic things one discovers is that the varied and often creative use of the OT we find in the NT is at variance with the rather wooden and questionable attempts to read the NT wholescale back into the OT (e.g., the angel of the Lord in the OT must have been Christ, and Yahweh's living presence called *ruach*/spirit/wind/breath must be a reference to the Holy Spirit).

Furthermore, the writers of the NT are perfectly capable of using the OT in a creative way, indeed in an allegorizing way, to get their current point across. I call this a homiletical use of the OT. Yes, they were capable of doing a literal contextual exegesis of a text, but they also showed the ability to approach the OT in other and more creative ways. A good example is what is going on in Gal 4, where Paul knows he is allegorizing a non-allegorical historical story. Here's the remarkable tale he tells:

> Tell me, you who want to be under the law, are you not aware of what the law says? For it is written that Abraham had two sons, one by the slave woman and the other by the free woman. His son by the slave woman was born according to the flesh, but his son by the free woman was born as the result of a divine promise.
>
> These things are being taken figuratively: The women represent two covenants. One covenant is from Mount Sinai and bears children who are to be slaves: This is Hagar. Now Hagar stands for Mount Sinai in Arabia and corresponds to the present city of Jerusalem, because she is in slavery with her children. But the Jerusalem that is above is free, and she is our mother. For it is written:
>
>> "Be glad, barren woman,
>> you who never bore a child;
>> shout for joy and cry aloud,
>> you who were never in labor;
>> because more are the children of the desolate woman
>> than of her who has a husband."
>
> Now you, brothers and sisters, like Isaac, are children of promise. At that time the son born according to the flesh persecuted the son born by the power of the Spirit. It is the same now. But what does Scripture say? "Get rid of the slave woman and her son, for the slave woman's son will never share in the inheritance with the free woman's son." Therefore, brothers and sisters, we are not children of the slave woman, but of the free woman.
>
> It is for freedom that Christ has set us free. Stand firm, then, and do not let yourselves be burdened again by a yoke of slavery.

Paul lets his audience know he is taking this text figuratively, not literally. I'm quite sure the Jews in Paul's audience would have been shocked at Paul associating Hagar, the slave girl, with Mt. Sinai, which is said to correspond to the current Jerusalem! Especially the Judaizers who were trying to persuade the Galatian Gentiles to get circumcised and keep the Mosaic law would have been shocked and outraged at this creative use of that story from Gen 21 with help from a quote from Isa 54. The point, however, is that Paul is making a creative use of a text, while knowing perfectly well that the historical story itself has its own contextual meaning, but he is not referring to that at this point. I could give other examples, but this will have to do.

This example of "intertextuality" has raised all sorts of questions about the use of the OT in the NT, and in general the proper interpretation of the OT, especially in light of the fact that in early Judaism there was a world-class allegorizer of the OT called Philo of Alexandria, who interpreted the OT with the help of Greek philosophy in a major way. And he helped spawn Christian interpreters like Clement of Alexandria, and then Origen who followed this lead, and were responded to by the more historical and literal readers of the OT in Antioch, such as John Chrysostom.

## Intertextuality and Theories of Meaning

Whatever else one might say of both the Church Fathers and the vast majority of modern Christian systematicians, they both assume that there is indeed a given meaning in the written texts of Scripture, not least because these are God-inspired texts. Rightly so.

In my study *Isaiah Old and New* I have critiqued at length modern theories of meaning which lead some scholars of intertextuality to say things like the following:

> Texts have no meaning but rather enable the production of meaning in the act of reading. The generation of meaning is always codetermined—intended or not, consciously or unconsciously—through the actualization of potential relationships of the text in question to other texts.[1]

There are numerous problems with this theory of meaning, when it comes to Biblical texts. While it is certainly true that there are active readers who bring their own ideas to the reading of Biblical texts, there was already a meaning encoded into those Biblical texts, and the first task of the good exegete was to figure out what that original meaning was and is. The meaning in the text has not changed over the centuries, and it is not true that modern readers get to tell the text what it means or ought to mean, certainly

---

1. Alkier, "Intertextuality and the Semiotics of Biblical Texts," 3–4.

not when the book in question is the Holy Scriptures. Anachronism in the form of reading things into the text that aren't there is to be discouraged, not encouraged.

The Biblical text is not an ink blot into which one can read whatever comes to one's mind, or one prefers. As B. Childs rightly says, a Biblical text (and other great texts) has a coercive effect on the reader if the text is at all interesting or compelling.[2] Certainly, in Systematics, modern theories of semiotics and theories of meanings being in the eye of the beholder (or in the reading of the text and its interaction with the beholder) are not assumed to be true or helpful in the interpretation of the Biblical text.[3] As I say at the end of my critique of such approaches, "Whether the Scripture can speak to new generations is *not* dependent on its meaning being malleable, like a shape-shifter in a science fiction movie. It is dependent on whether it is telling us some fundamental enduring truths from and about God, ourselves, and the interaction between God and ourselves. In other words, it is dependent on whether it has a stable meaning in all generations which can be helpful to address the human dilemma in all ages, because at root our problems are basically the same—'we have all sinned and lack the glory of God.'"[4]

Much more helpful than some of these recent forays by some Biblical scholars into the meaning and intertextuality of Biblical texts is the work of E. D. Hirsch on meaning, who in his landmark study, *Validity in Interpretation* (1967), argued that the sensible belief is that the text means what the author meant. He adds that at least in some cases it is possible to recover the author's intended meaning and that readers should set that as their intended goal. He distinguishes between the meaning of a text, which doesn't change over time, and the significance of a text, which can and does change over time. Finally, he urges that objectivity is possible in the interpretation of important and classic texts.

We should also listen to the critique of reader-response and postmodern readings offered by Francis Watson:

> A Christian faith concerned to retain its own coherence cannot for a moment accept that the biblical texts (individually and as a whole) lack a single determinant meaning, that their meanings

2. See most helpfully his study *Biblical Theology of the Old and New Testaments*.

3. See my detailed critique of such approaches in *Isaiah Old and New*, 467–75.

4. See Witherington, *Isaiah Old and New*, 474–75. One hilarious example of what can go wrong is when Stanley Fish, very much an advocate of meaning is in the eye of the beholder or in one's interaction with a text, had published a book on meaning, and it received some very critical reviews, and he then said, "That's not what I meant"! Alas, his own theory of meaning did not allow him that out!

are created by their readers, or that theological interpretations [*sic*—surely he means interpreters] must see themselves as non-privileged participants in an open-ended, pluralistic conversation. Such a hermeneutic assumes that these texts are like any other "classic" texts: self-contained artifacts, handed down to us through the somewhat haphazard process of tradition, bearing with them a cultural authority that has now lost much of its normative force, yet challenging the interpreter to help ensure that they will at least remain readable, and continue to be read.[5]

There are, however, even more problems with some of the assumptions brought to the Biblical text by Biblical scholars themselves. One of the things that is assumed, as I have said in my review of Richard Hays's *Echoes of Scripture in the Gospels*, is "an audience (or at least members in an audience) that has an encyclopedia of reception large enough to recognize echoes of OT texts in the Gospels, and even places where phrases in a quoted text are (deliberately) omitted such that they know to go back and search the Scriptures to appreciate the larger context and resonances of the quoted portions of, say, Isaiah."[6] He is talking about what is called metalepsis (not to be confused with mental lapses). Metalepsis is the practice of leaving something out in a quotation but expecting the audience to go back to the source and find the fuller, richer meaning of the quoted text, filling in the blanks.

But I am doubtful that we can assume what Hays assumes about the audiences of the Gospels. First of all, the audience is overwhelmingly hearers, not readers, of the Gospels. The general level of literacy in Jesus and Paul's age and world was not such that most people could read these texts. Literacy of the sort Hays is talking about was the privilege of the socially elite, and the evidence that *most* early Christians were among the socially elite is entirely lacking. The movement was led by such folk, but their audiences were mostly not at that level.

Secondly, precisely because the last paragraph is historically accurate, we need to treat these texts as oral texts—that is, texts meant to be heard, with a skilled reader, a lector reading to them. We see this very practice at the beginning of the book of Revelation, where we read in Rev 1:3, Blessed is the one who reads aloud the words of this prophecy, and blessed are those who hear it and take to heart what is written in it." There is a practiced reader (and he would have to be skilled to read a manuscript in *scriptum continuum*—a continuous flow of Greek letters with no separation between

---

5. Watson, *Texts and Truths*, 9. Watson would strongly reject, as do I, Dale Martin's attempt to say the opposite of this in his *Biblical Truths*.

6. Witherington, *Isaiah Old and New*, 456.

words, between sentences, between paragraphs, and no chapters and verses) who reads the text out loud, and then there are hearers.

Thirdly, so far as we can tell, there were not a lot of OT scrolls lying around in the house churches in the first century of early Christianity, nor were there a sufficient number of actual Jewish scribes who were converts to Christianity who knew the Scriptures so well that they could catch the nuances of OT allusions and echoes, and even "metalepses"[7] in the text that was being read out.

Florian Wilk in his helpful discussion about Paul's use of Isaiah says this:

> With regard to the connections between Paul's letter and the book of Isaiah, however the perspective of the author is more important and fruitful than that of the addressees. The difficulty of a reader-oriented perspective in this case consists in the fact that we know nothing about the degree of knowledge of Scripture that the Christians to whom Paul wrote had.... The extent to which they would identify inexplicit connections with Isaiah [i.e., allusions or echoes] must remain completely open.... One can hardly imagine, however, that ... such a learning process led the addressees to the point where they would track down unmarked references to Isaiah to a significant degree. *This would require scriptural knowledge available only to specially trained persons.*[8]

This leaves us with a conundrum—were the NT documents written for literate elite readers, say like a Theophilus that Luke mentions in the introduction to his two volumes? And were they expected to have OT scrolls lying around, or a sufficiently Scripture-saturated memory to be able to explain not only the scriptural quotations but the allusions and echoes as well? This seems to be assuming far too much about early Christians and their social situation, and as Wilk suggests this definitely calls into question a reader-oriented approach to these texts. No, we need to focus on the author and what he intended to convey to those audiences who HEARD these documents, and were not necessarily able to study them at length and look up cross references!

Then there is the fact that first-century Christian writers and readers believed in predictive prophecy, which is to say, they believed that one didn't need to create meaning through a process of intertextuality, rather there was

---

7. I.e., the practice of deliberately alluding to OT texts and trusting the audience could fill in the blanks of the context or parts of the content.

8. Wilk, "Paul as User," 85; emphasis added.

already a surplus of meaning in the inspired OT texts such that one found out what they meant when they came to fulfillment in Christ or in early Christianity. Peter puts it this way:

> Concerning this salvation, the prophets, who spoke of the grace that was to come to you, searched intently and with the greatest care, trying to find out the time and circumstances to which the Spirit of Christ in them was pointing when he predicted the sufferings of the Messiah and the glories that would follow. It was revealed to them that they were not serving themselves but you, when they spoke of the things that have now been told you by those who have preached the gospel to you by the Holy Spirit sent from heaven. Even angels long to look into these things. (1 Pet 1:10–12)

And in 2 Pet 1 we read, "Above all, you must understand that no prophecy of Scripture came about by the prophet's own interpretation of things. For prophecy never had its origin in the human will, but prophets, though human, spoke from God as they were carried along by the Holy Spirit."

In other words, these NT writers understood they were dealing with inspired texts, not cleverly devised fables, or the products of an overheated human imagination.

Perhaps the biggest flaw in this whole modern intertextual approach to NT texts is that the writers of the NT are not urging their audience to look backward to the OT to find meaning and understanding, but rather to look forward to the continued fulfillment and consummation of what the inspired OT writers were looking and longing for. The authors believed they lived already in the eschatological age of fulfillment, and so the major point of these NT documents is to get the audience to embrace what God is doing now and will do in Christ and by the Spirit.

At the end of the day, I do not think that the NT documents were simply written for the sake of the literate, or those with a good font of knowledge of the OT, as the texts themselves and the intertextual study of them might suggest. I think they were tools for the literate to read out and use with the larger Christian audiences as they made disciples of all sorts of persons. I think Edwin Judge was right all along that the early Christian movement was led by socially more elite persons like Paul and his coworkers, or Peter working with the more literate Silvanus/Silas.[9]

---

9. See his seminal essays collected and edited by my old mentor David Scholer: Judge, *Social Distinctives of the Christians in the First Century*.

## Systematics and Semiotics?

It is perhaps fortunate that most Biblical and Systematic theologies in the modern era are quite innocent of the current detailed discussions about intertextuality, meaning being created between the reader and the text, metalepsis, and related matters. The place where some Biblical theologians tend to go wrong is in assuming it's all about prediction and fulfillment in the NT, while ignoring the more creative ways the OT is used from time to time in the NT (see above on Gal 4). Indeed, most of the time the OT is being used in a homiletical way, and the writers are not doing detailed contextual exegesis of the OT, any more than they are constructing clever allusions to the OT texts trusting that their audiences can fill in the gaps. These texts tell us much about their authors, but it is questionable how much they tell us about their audiences.

The normal way most Biblical theologians approach intertextuality is by simply asking about the clear use of the OT in the NT, such as we find in G. K. Beale and D. A. Carson's massive edited volume *Commentary on the New Testament Use of the Old Testament*. The mistake that is sometimes made in this kind of approach is the assumption that one can then simply read the NT back into the OT.

The problem is that, as we saw in Gal 4, Paul is simply making use of historical narrative to make another and more contemporary point to his audience. He is not doing exegesis of the story of Hagar, any more than the author of Hebrews is assuming that Christ was actually Melchizedek in disguise in OT times, or that the three visitors to Abraham in the OT were the Holy Trinity.

Such approaches do not allow for the progressive nature of God's revelation nor for the creative use of the OT in the NT in numerous places. Was the instruction in the OT about allowing oxen to eat some of the grain they were threshing out really an allusion to the fact that missionaries like Paul were worthy of being paid for their Gospel labors (cf. Deut 25:4 to 1 Cor 9:9 and again in 1 Tim 5:18)? No. This is simply another homiletical use of the OT to make a NT point, though the principle that a worker should be able to benefit from his work is similar in the case of animals or humans.

What Paul and the other writers of the NT are likely assuming is that there are enough persons in the audience who were literate, including Biblically literate, to be able to understand the drift and point of the things the text is teaching the audience, and can help the others understand it. But still a good deal of it would have been over their heads (as for instance 2 Pet 3:16 suggests). Perhaps the preaching was a word on target for any listeners, but the documents were intended for the literate and more mature Christians to use to help develop disciples who were more Biblically knowledgeable.

But what does one do with clear evidence that Jewish Christian writers used Jewish traditions not found anywhere in the OT? Did this mean that that material was scriptural as well? Did they have a larger OT canon or approach to Jewish tradition than a Biblical theologian might be comfortable with?

For instance, what about the little document called Jude?

In v. 9 it says, "But even the archangel Michael, when he was disputing with the devil about the body of Moses, did not himself dare to condemn him for slander but said, 'The Lord rebuke you!'" And then in vv. 14–15 we read, "Enoch, the seventh from Adam, prophesied about them: 'See, the Lord is coming with thousands upon thousands of his holy ones to judge everyone, and to convict all of them of all the ungodly acts they have committed in their ungodliness, and of all the defiant words ungodly sinners have spoken against him.'"

Neither of these texts come from the OT; rather we are talking about material from the Assumption of Moses (a tradition about Moses being taken up bodily into heaven) and from 1 Enoch. While the author of Jude doesn't mention either book, and simply calls Enoch a prophet, he assumes what is said in these traditions are true. And we could also point to the use of traditions from Sirach and Wisdom of Solomon in various places in the Gospels and Paul's letters. How does this material fit into a schema of Biblical or Systematic theology, or should it simply be ignored? At a minimum, Jude and 2 Pet 2 and probably 1 Pet 3 assume a tradition of bad angels being incarcerated in Tartarus, like the even later story about the Devil being put in a holding tank in Rev 20.[10] One of the subjects chronically neglected or mishandled in Biblical and systematic theologies is the roles of angels, good and bad, in the salvation history drama. But certainly, the writers of the Bible believed in such beings and their influence on the human drama.[11]

This neglect is not entirely a surprise because it is part and parcel of the neglect of the eschatological orientation of the NT in general, and books like Revelation in particular. What happened when the church became overwhelmingly Gentile in character is that vertical afterlife thinking began to dominate horizontal afterlife thinking, and there were Church Fathers like Eusebius who were dubious that Revelation should be in the canon because

---

10. Tracing the trajectory of this tradition from the OT through the material we've just mentioned is fascinating. See the discussion in my *Jesus the Seer*.

11. A neglect that still plagues the church today. See the stimulating book by our departed brother and colleague Mike Heiser, *Unseen Realm*, as well as his books on angels and demons.

they had lost the understanding of Jewish apocalyptic prophecy, or found it far-fetched.

By the time you get to the Reformation, there were scholars like Calvin who did not do a commentary on Revelation because he simply didn't understand it. Not surprisingly what has happened with apocalyptic prophecy in the OT and NT (Daniel, Zechariah, Ezekiel, Revelation) is it became in the nineteenth and twentieth centuries (due to its neglect by most churches and forms of scholarship) the provenance and playground of those who would contemporize these texts, taking them to be about current events and current history, and about how God will help the believers escape the Tribulation to come by means of a Rapture.

In an overreaction to this misleading school of thought, another whole tradition took an a-millennial approach to church history, as if Satan has been in a holding tank not bothering the nations for the last two thousand years (cf. Rev 20). It is not a surprise that systematicians have steered clear of the Dispensational approach to these texts, but at the same time were not always doing justice to what the book of Revelation teaches, which in fact involves telling Christians to be prepared to suffer, to be faithful to the end, even to die for their faith, which is called overcoming or even victory!

The church in Rev 12 is said to be spiritually protected on earth from Satan, but remains on earth through all the trials and tribulations. Spiritual warfare is going on, but it is being waged by angels in Revelation, and the most Paul can urge is for Christians to be prepared to stand and withstand the evil onslaught (Eph 6). There is nothing in that text that encourages Christians to go on the offensive against the powers of darkness, though deliverance by exorcisms is still seen as a viable ministry of the church. Nevertheless, the basic advice is to not dabble with darkness or the dark lords. The undercurrent is clear enough—Satan is alive and well on planet Earth and is dangerous. As 1 Pet 5:8 warns, "Be alert and of sober mind. Your enemy the devil prowls around like a roaring lion looking for someone to devour." But there is also the reassurance that we should leave the crushing of Satan to God as God is active against his influence (Rom 16:20). Notice the "under *your* feet" phrase, in other words the Lord is prepared to battle when the Devil is bewitching, bothering, and bewildering believers.

In other words, both Biblical theologians and systematicians should have done a better job of recognizing the overall eschatological orientation of the NT, and not relegated eschatology to the end of the book, as if it only had to do with the future. Further, they should have done a better job of dealing with what the NT actually says about the powers and principalities and the ongoing spiritual battles being fought mainly by angels and the Lord on behalf of the church. And at the same time the message of spiritual protection for the church from evil found in Revelation should have been highlighted, without making the mistake of assuming that this means individual Christians can't possibly commit apostasy. The gates of Hades will not prevail against Christ's community. It will not ever die out.

We've been discussing this because the discussion of OT prophecy, and for that matter NT prophecy, has not always been done well in Biblical theology and in Systematics, not least because of a lack of clear understanding of apocalyptic prophecy in particular.

Though it does come at the end of Oden's discussions, because he is compiling the wisdom of various Church Fathers, there are some helpful reminders in his catenae of quoted or paraphrased materials. The fathers do not neglect to warn that Lucifer is the supreme embodiment of evil, the super-personal adversary of humanity (Lactantius, *Inst.* 3.29; Tertullian, *On the Soul*, 20; Jerome, *Against Rufinus*). Satan is a deceiver who seeks to destroy truth while seeming to defend it (Athanasius, *Life of Anthony*; Tertullian, *Against Praxeas*, 1). Irenaeus repeats the NT phrase that Satan, by means of deception, has become the god of this world (Irenaeus, *Fragments* 46). Because fallen angels are viewed as rational creatures they are destined to be judged (Matt 8:29; 1 Cor 6:3; 2 Pet 2:4; Chrysostom, *Hom. 1 Cor.* 16.5). "God does not primordially desire that any creature [human or angelic] should be lost, but consequent to their own choice, God gives creatures the freedom that has the consequence of complete separation from the joy of the presence of God (1 Thess 1:9; Rom 1:10; 1 John 2:17; 1 Tim: 6:9; Augustine, *Ag. Julian*, 2.9.32)."[12]

These same Church Fathers had a good deal to say about Hell, namely that it involved eternal fire, and so eternal punishment, but at the same time "there is no ecumenically received Scriptural authority for the view that God arbitrarily or pre-temporally predestined people to Hell without their own choosing or cooperation or without the benefit of conscience and common grace."[13]

Oden goes on to point out the fathers wrestled with the question about those who have never heard the Gospel, either before the time of Christ or later, and the conclusion is that they will be judged according to the light they have received, and how they have responded to it (Rom 1:18–32 and

---

12. Oden, *Classic Christianity*, the quote is from 833, but the whole discussion on 831–33 should be consulted. This is much too brief an account of these eschatological matters, but at least it shows that the Church Fathers were concerned about and discoursed on these things.

13. Oden, *Classic Christianity*, 828, but the whole discussion on 826–29 should be consulted.

2:6–16).[14] So, for instance, Abraham is taken as an example of pre-Christian true faith in Rom 4 and Gal 3 (see also the parable of the rich man and Lazarus—Luke 16:19–31). But how does this fit into the declaration that all have sinned and lack or have fallen short of the glory of God?

I have always thought that since Rom 11 suggests that when Christ returns, non-Christian Jews will have the chance to respond positively to Christ Himself, so maybe Gentiles will as well? I do not know any scriptural warrant for this, and I'm well aware that there are various texts that make clear some angels and humans are going to Hell, but perhaps there is a wideness in God's mercy to give everyone a fair chance to respond positively to the Gospel? That would comport with the fact that God is Love (1 John 4). But we have said enough for now about these matters.

---

14. Oden, *Classic Christianity*, 826.

Chapter Thirteen

# The Jenson Tonic
A Proper Approach to Systematics

A theologian who describes his or her own work as "Lutheran" or "Reformed," or whatever such, and meant by that label to identify the church the work was to serve, would either deny the name of church to all but his or her own allegiance or desecrate the theological enterprise.
—Robert Jenson, *Systematic Theology*

The alert reader will recognize by now that I have basically been critiquing attempts at Systematics by Evangelical Protestants, and to a much lesser degree Catholics, though in the case of the Reformed scholars I critiqued, what they are actually doing is not Systematics as classically defined but systematized Biblical theology. I would not want to leave the impression that there are no good attempts at Systematics as traditionally defined, such that it doesn't just amount to a systematizing of Biblical or historical or philosophical theology à la Grudem or Oden or Morris and others.

By way of reminder here is the clearest and most complete definition of Systematics: "With a methodological tradition that differs somewhat from biblical theology, systematic theology draws on the core sacred texts of Christianity, while simultaneously investigating the development of Christian doctrine over the course of history, particularly through philosophy, ethics, social sciences, and natural sciences. Using biblical texts, it attempts to compare and relate all of scripture which led to the creation of a systematized statement on what the whole Bible says about particular issues."[1] What this requires is a breadth of knowledge and a skill set that very few Biblical scholars possess, and I am not one who does.

None of the studies we have interacted with, with the possible exception of Pannenberg and Jenson, have sufficiently studied "the development of Christian doctrine over the course of history, particularly through philosophy, ethics, social sciences, and natural sciences." Oden did explore the development of doctrine in historical theology but did not attend to the modern disciplines mentioned at the end of that sentence. Robert Jenson on the other hand seems to have the knowledge and skill set to deal with all these areas, relating them to Biblical theology and its developments over time.

And the reviews of his two-volume Systematics are full of praise. Francis Watson calls Jenson America's theologian,[2] and even George Hunsinger, who has raised serious criticisms of Jenson's work, says the following of Jenson's work: "The twentieth century's most accomplished systematic theology written in English" and Jenson "has few peers in any language . . . for he has at his fingertips an astonishing fund of citations and quotations from every period of theological history and every ecumenical tradition . . . all are summoned it seems at just the right moment and for just the right effect. Besides being theologically deft, the work is also culturally, scientifically, and philosophically sophisticated."[3]

So, it will bear some good fruit to examine both evidence of his method and also some of his results. Here we are helped by Thomas McCall in his study *Which Trinity? Whose Monotheism?* We will make some general comments first before engaging with McCall's critique.

## Judging Jenson

At the very outset of his two volumes, Jenson makes clear that he is seeking to do systematics having benefited from Catholic, Protestant, and Orthodox exegesis; Biblical theology; and attempts at Systematics *within* those particular Christian traditions. He is quite clear in stating, "I have adopted a plan that diverges from both the Catholic and Protestant standard outline. The basic Scholastic division is taken up [by which he means that in the first place the proper subject of Systematics is God, and then secondly everything else], but Christology and pneumatology, together with discussions

---

1. Wikipedia, "Systematic Theology," para. 2.
2. Watson, "'America's Theologian,'" 215.
3. Hunsinger, "Robert Jenson's *Systematic Theology*," 161.

of the historical Jesus, of the doctrine of the atonement, and of the resurrection, are drawn back into the doctrine of God, swelling that doctrine to make half the total work."[4] This is the ground he covers in volume 1 of his Systematics, and volume 2, which is entitled *The Works of God*, treats everything else including everything to do with creation and all God's creatures. I find this division of material helpful, because it makes clear that theology proper is about God and what God "hath wrought." It is not an exercise in anthropology, for example. It is theocentric from start to finish. And herein lies an essential difference between Biblical theology, which discusses all the discreet topics which we have noted before, and Systematic theology.

Again, what we have been examining up to this point are exercises in systematizing either Biblical or historical theology in some particular way (e.g., according to Reformed theology, or for example creedal theology advocated and upheld by the Fathers), but this is not what Jenson is doing. Finally, it appears, we have gotten to a learned attempt to do Systematics pure and simple, with the term *theology* having its proper meaning—namely, the doctrine of God and God's work.

Relying in the first instance on the work of P. Stuhlmacher and W. Pannenberg, Jenson insists that the Good News about the resurrection of Jesus is the origin of Christian theology (so Stuhlmacher) and that within the context of early Judaism, Jews who believed in resurrection would have understood that this entailed God vindicating Jesus and His message, and what logically followed from this was Jesus was Lord of all (see Phil 2), and the creeds correctly saw this to imply that He was seated at God's right hand, and will in due course judge the world (so Pannenberg).[5]

As Jenson says, theology then is the "thinking internal to the task of speaking the gospel,"[6] which in turn means the Christ event, including especially the death and resurrection of Jesus and His appearances, changes the way the followers of Jesus viewed God, the Spirit, and frankly all the promises and prophecies of the OT.

Consider Jenson's emphatic statement about how Christians should approach the Systematic theological task: "To attend to the resurrection is to attend to God self-identified as 'the one who raised the Lord Jesus.' Whoever—and indeed whatever—did that, the church says, is the reality we mean by 'God.' To attend to the Resurrection and to attend to this particular putative God, to take either as the object of our reflection, are the same . . .

---

4. Jenson, *Systematic Theology*, 1:x.

5. Cf. Jenson, *Systematic Theology*, 1:4, and nn 1 and 2, where he cites the German articles by Stuhlmacher and Pannenberg.

6. Jenson, *Systematic Theology*, 1:5.

to attend to the gospel in its character as witness to a determinate reality is to worship in trinitarian specificity: in petition and praise to the Father with the Son in the Spirit."[7]

Jenson calls the doctrine of the Trinity the first deliberately defined dogma (presumably at Nicaea and Chalcedon). And herein the discerning reader will be able to tell the difference between Biblical theology, which at most can show how the raw data for Trinitarian thinking is found in the Bible, and Systematics, which draws out and draws together the implications of the Good News on this matter. He adds that Protestants are right that our assignment is to proclaim the Good News, and Catholics are right that when the catholic rule of prayer is not followed, theology slips from its object. In other words, properly done, Systematic theology should involve both cognitive reflection and discussion and at the same time worship of God. It is both "speculative" and practical if done properly. But Jenson adds the cautionary word: "*Theology is not the adding of proposition to proposition in the steady construction of a planned structure of knowledge. It is a discussion and debate that as it continues regularly confronts new questions. . . . It is the fate of every theological system to be dismembered and have fragments bandied about in an ongoing debate.*"[8]

At the end of this chapter on Prolegomena Jenson is able to say about Systematic theology: "Systematic theology is so called because it takes up questions posed not only by current urgency, but also by perceived inherent connections of the faith. Thus, systematic theology may raise problems that otherwise have not yet emerged in the church's life, and maintain discussions whose immediate ecclesial-pastoral challenge is in abeyance."[9] This enterprise should not be caricatured as some sort of trivial pursuit, like asking how many angels can dance on the head of a pin. It will be noted that the attempts at so-called Systematic theology reviewed before this chapter do not truly meet the challenge of dealing with issues of current urgency, or do so only in passing. Systematic theology helps us use the Gospel to address modern concerns, but also helps us to understand the inherent logic and implications of that Gospel. As such it adds to our basic understanding of what the Biblical text meant and means, as well as how it might be applied today in cultural situations very different from those of the Biblical writers.

What does Jenson think about the authority of Scripture? He cites the Reformation notion that Scripture is the final authority, the norm over which there are no higher norms. The Spirit, he says, creates the identity not

---

7. Jenson, *Systematic Theology*, 1:12–13.
8. Jenson, *Systematic Theology*, 1:17–18; emphasis added.
9. Jenson, *Systematic Theology*, 1:22.

only of the church but also of the Scripture so there is a sense in which the church did not make the canon; it received it under the Spirit's guidance. True, the church decision that these twenty-seven Christian documents plus no others in the fourth century is a dogmatic statement; however, it was made under the providential guidance of the Spirit and confirmed in three different regions of the church in the last third of the fourth century.[10]

What we have learned thus far is that Systematics not only has a viable function that involves more than what Biblical Theologies normally are focused on, and, as Jenson makes clear, we *need* the additional articulation of the Trinity, the atonement, and other key scriptural theological ideas and trajectories that we find in Systematic theology. It is not meant to merely be a systematizing of Biblical Theology of whatever denominational or historical approach. And it asks questions of the text that are not simply hot button issues for the church today.

We do need to understand better what the teaching of the atonement should look like, beyond the basic statements we find in Scripture, but at the same time the later amplifications of atonement theology should be normed by the Biblical statements, to the extent that is possible. For example, Systematics helps us rule out the ransom to Satan theory, or, to speak of eschatology, the rapture theology, as well as the notion that the early church got the timing of the second coming all wrong, and had to re-do its eschatology.

One of the major points that Jenson raises about God in the Bible clearly supports our earlier contention that one should not be doing theology in the abstract, but must pay close attention to how the theologizing arises out of the narrative thought world of the authors. Stressing that the God of the Bible is deeply involved in the messiness of human history, and so is involved in space and time, Jenson says this: "The biblical God can truly be identified by narrative, his hypostatic being, his self-identity, is constituted in *dramatic coherence*. . . . The proposition that God's self-identity lies in dramatic coherence is in any case mandatory for those who wish to worship the biblical God."[11] This is so because God identifies Himself in and by His historical actions. He tells Moses that "he will be who he will be," and His character, identity, power will be revealed by His actions in Egypt, or as the NT writers would say by His actions of sending Christ to the cross,

---

10. But see the way Jenson frames this, *Systematic Theology*, 1:26–27. I think it is better to simply say with Bruce Metzger that the church did not form the canon, it recognized it, than to say the church formed the canon. The books themselves were inspired and formed by apostles and their coworkers in the first century AD, not in the fourth century. See my *Sola Scriptura*.

11. Jenson, *Systematic Theology*, 1:64.

and then raising Him up from the dead. Jenson puts the matter eloquently as follows:

> Even Israel's ability to conceive a continuity of her own history through the discontinuities of her fate, and for centuries, to interpret and reinterpret the history theologically to produce the Scripture the church received, did not result from continuous ability to synthesize the religious and conceptual deposit to date, but depended on her antecedent and repeatedly rewon conviction that YHWH in his personal identity had been and would be the protagonist of her doings and sufferings, however apparently discontinuous; the scriptural narrative is thus itself Israel's sole construal of the Lord's self-identity.[12]

Jenson is also correct that a dramatic story is by and large constituted by the way it ends. It is only at the end of the salvation drama, in the new creation, that God is all in all, and fully revealed, as He dwells with His people forever (Rev 21–22). The resurrection of Jesus is a preview of coming attractions. To turn this salvation story, this Good News, into a series of abstract ideas that one then links together is absolutely not in accord with the Biblical witness.

In his second volume, Jenson focuses on God's works—His creation and His creatures. We have an excellent example in the very first chapter of how Systematic theology can not only ask the hard questions, but explore in depth ideas, narratives, puzzles, that goes well beyond simple exegesis of the text. For example, Jenson's discussion of the Biblical doctrine of creation exhibits fully the contribution Systematic theology can make.

In distinction from religions that assert that creation and creatures are just an *emanation* from, and so a part of, God, the Bible asserts that God is wholly other, distinct from the material creation and creatures, and that the latter came into existence by God speaking... "and God said." Furthermore, when it comes to the creation of human beings in God's image, He was creating a dialogue partner, or as Jenson puts it, a counterpart. The Genesis account has been rightly understood as involving *creatio ex nihilo*, and this is true of both Jewish and Christian exegesis of Gen 1 (see 2 Macc 7:28). The verb *bara* is only predicated of God, for God alone is the Creator of all things. Humans are not co-creators; they are "makers," using things that already existed to do their creating or to do their work.

Jenson rightly points out that Gen 1 is not meant to be seen as a mere etiological myth, but "taken realistically as a narrative of past events."[13] Jenson also shows how one can get to the point of doing either Biblical or

---

12. Jenson, *Systematic Theology*, 1:64.
13. Jenson, *Systematic Theology*, 2:8.

Systematic theology without neglecting or ignoring the narrative thought world of the Biblical writers. Even Gen 1 is a narrative, a theologically loaded narrative, not a myth. As Jenson says myths are not intended to narrate particular events, but what happens in all events. "The origin they are telling is logical and ontological, not temporal."[14] One clue that this is right is that creatures in the Genesis story have an absolute beginning, a beginning in space and time, and they have a purpose and a goal. The narrator intends to tell of a historical beginning: "It does not in fact tell us anything about what things were like when there were no things."[15]

What distinguishes humans from other creatures is that while God speaks *about* all the creatures, He only speaks *to* human beings created in God's image (and to angels). Only humans and angels can have what Martin Buber famously called an I–Thou relationship with God, and it is precisely that which was lost when Adam and Eve sinned. That intimacy with God, a personal relationship, became an I–It relationship with God, somewhat like the lesser creatures had, a relationship that was fear based, not faith based, for God is a holy God. There is so much more that could be said about the rich exploration of creation, of salvation history, and of the Good News by Jenson, but now it is time to take stock of Jenson's work, which indeed merits the title of Systematic theology, by definition.

It will be useful then to work through my colleague Tom McCall's critique of Jenson at this juncture, as he is a Systematics scholar as well. What we can say is that whatever errors or deficiencies in his work, and there are some,[16] Jenson demonstrates that Systematic theology is and should be something *more* and *other* than Biblical or historical theology systematized.

## A Critique of Robert Jenson's Systematics

Tom McCall's approach for his critique of Jenson's work is from the perspective of analytic philosophy and its detailed attention to the logical coherence of claims being made. From the outset McCall is concerned with Jenson's focus on God's identity as it is revealed in history. He puts it this way: "For Jenson, God's identity is determined by his history. And God's

---

14. Jenson, *Systematic Theology*, 2:10.
15. Jenson, *Systematic Theology*, 2:11.
16. For instance, his discussion of the Holy Spirit (Jenson, *Systematic Theology*, 1:146–61) spends too little time talking about the Spirit's relationship to the believer, while focusing almost entirely on the Spirit's relationship with the Father and Son, and yet it is precisely in the relationship to human beings that we hear about grieving or quenching the Spirit, or even blaspheming the Spirit. More needed to be said about the latter.

history is bound up with our own. God's history 'with us' says Jenson, is decisively shaped by our betrayal of the 'with us.' Creation, fall, redemption, and consummation are thus not only the crucial points of human history; somehow they are also the constitution of the divine identity."[17] McCall calls this revisionary metaphysics, and offers a helpful caution—it is one thing to say God's identity is *revealed* through His actions in history; it is another to say His identity is *determined* by those events, or even that God is identified "*as* those events." Probably McCall is correct that Jenson is deliberately being rhetorically provocative, and in so doing he is revealing his disdain for traditional metaphysics. He does not want to talk about the relationship and communion within the Trinity in eternity, but rather focuses on what transpired in human history between the man Jesus and His Father.[18]

McCall, following G. Hunsinger and others, is concerned that Jenson is much too indebted to G. W. F. Hegel, such that while God is not identical with the world, He cannot be fully actualized without it. God then is metaphysically conditioned and fully actualized by something other than Himself. In short, God cannot be fully God without the world![19] If this is really what Jenson is asserting, then indeed it is problematic even just on the basis of Biblical exegesis. The pre-existence of the Father and the Son and the occasional comments about their relationship prior to the incarnation are an important part of the Biblical witness.

The Biblical witness is that God the creator is one thing, and creation another, and that God is transcendent. There are indeed some problems, as we have mentioned, with the idea of the aseity of God, but it is not the notion that God's essence and existence are not dependent on anyone or anything outside Himself. The point, however, is that since Father, Son, and Spirit are all part of the divine identity, that essence includes the relationship between the three, even prior to the incarnation and Pentecost. And here is where I stress that the progressive *understanding* of God as God reveals Himself gradually in Scripture is one thing, and the essence of God's identity is another. This is a matter of progressive revelation of who God is, not a matter of God going through a process of self-fulfillment such that He only becomes who He is through historical events. Again, if the latter is Jenson's idea, then McCall's critique is warranted.

Ultimately McCall is saying that Jenson has made the mistake of confusing identity with identification. Yes, God is identified and revealed

---

17. McCall, *Which Trinity? Whose Monotheism?*, ch. 4 entitled "'Whoever Raised Jesus from the Dead': Robert Jenson on the Identity of the Triune God," 127–55, here 135.

18. McCall, *Which Trinity? Whose Monotheism?*, 135.

19. McCall, *Which Trinity? Whose Monotheism?*, 136; here he is following Hunsinger's critique.

through His actions. No, God's identity is not completed by His actions. His identity is revealed or manifested through what He does; it is not constituted by those actions.

In particular, Jenson's approach ignores the identity statements like God is love, God is light, God is one (i.e., unique), God is spirit, which we explored earlier in this study. True, humans only know this because of God's revelation to us, but those statements are about who God is in the very divine nature which existed prior to the revelation of these facts to Israel, and then to the followers of Christ. What would be helpful to explore is the relationship of these noun predications to the adjectival ones like "God is almighty." It seems to me a problem that metaphysics has too often focused on the adjectives, like saying "God is sovereign" at the expense of, or to the neglect of, the nouns.

Further, as McCall stresses there is a moral problem with Jenson's approach if he means to say God in some sense intends sin and evil.[20] Further, "If God's identity is constituted in his triumph over evil, then evil belongs eternally to his identity, and his goodness is not goodness as such but a reaction, an activity that requires the goad of evil to come into full being."[21]

McCall, in a balanced way, commends Jenson's endorsement of the "identification thesis," namely, that the Biblical picture of what is said about the divine life must be endorsed, not some prior metaphysical commitments. Yes, God can be identified by His revelatory speech and actions. I would just pause here and say that sometimes metaphysical notions like impassibility and immutability are interjected into the discussion of God by philosophers at the expense of the Biblical witness, and I think Jenson is right to protest such non-Biblical ideas, but he goes too far in expressing a sort of allergic reaction to metaphysics in general.

McCall goes on to rightly point out the inadequacies of Jenson's approach to Christ's pre-existence, especially in passages like Phil 2 and 1 Cor 8, and then drills down into the detailed problems with Jenson's affirmation of the "identity" thesis. Rightly so.[22]

What we learn from all this is even Systematics at its best is not without some flaws, and deserves again and again to be normed and critiqued on the basis of the Biblical witness and the witness of church theologians ancient and modern. This does not negate the positive contributions Jenson has made, nor the fact that he pursues the task of Systematic theology in

---

20. McCall, *Which Trinity? Whose Monotheism?*, 139; here he is following the critique of David Bentley Hart.

21. This is McCall, *Which Trinity? Whose Monotheism?*, 139, quoting Hart approvingly from *Beauty of the Infinite*, 164–65.

22. McCall, *Which Trinity? Whose Monotheism?*, 137–55.

the right way, such that it is clearly distinguishable from the systematized Biblical theology of Sproul or Grudem or the three authors of the recent Wesleyan attempt at presenting a thorough-going theology of holiness, or compendiums of historical theology like that of Oden. Here, I will simply add that Systematics scholars, as well as Biblical theologians, need to attend to the *various* problems I have discussed in the preceding chapters that have plagued such theologies in the past. In short, they need perfecting and need to hear and heed the cry of "always reforming."

Chapter Fourteen

# Concluding Unscientific Postscript

When I began as an author of *Either/Or*, I no doubt had a far more profound impression of the terror of Christianity than any clergyman in the country. I had a fear and trembling such as perhaps no one else had. Not that I therefore wanted to relinquish Christianity. No, I had another interpretation of it. For one thing I had in fact learned very early that there are men who seem to be selected for suffering, and, for another thing, I was conscious of having sinned much and therefore supposed that Christianity had to appear to me in the form of this terror. But how cruel and false of you, I thought, if you use it to terrify others, perhaps upset ever so many happy, loving lives that may very well be truly Christian.

—Søren Kierkegaard, *Either/Or Part II*

As should be all too apparent by now, this study has *not* tried to present the reader with a biblical or systematic theology,[1] or to scare them to death with the "terrors" of theology but rather to provide a discussion of how: *(1) an adequately biblically informed Biblical or Systematic theology should and should not use Scripture; (2) how anachronism could be avoided; (3) how the narrative thought world of the Biblical writers could be given its due instead of abstracting ideas from that thought world and then lining up ideas in a particular, consistent but too narrow way; (4) how Christian tradition can be helpful in the discussion of Biblical or Systematic theology but also how it can be at odds with the Biblical substance of the theology; (5) how ancient logic,*

---

1. For the former, see my *Biblical Theology*.

reasoning, and rhetoric can help the interpreter better make sense of the biblical text and better inform the way one does Biblical or Systematic theology; (6) how hermeneutics helps when it comes to recognizing how the OT is used in the NT; and (7) how knowing that what the Bible *teaches* is not identical with all the things it mentions or touches. It teaches theology, ethics, salvation history, and spiritual formation. It is not a scientific textbook about ever so many things downloaded on an ancient people long before they could grasp modern science. (8) The Bible has an inspired meaning, and it is our job to learn what it is and apply it to our lives and the lives of others. The Bible was not intended to be a resource by which individuals can find their own truths, their own meanings in it. No, it was intended to be a source of revelation of God's truth and meaning. (9) While it is certainly true that Reformed, Wesleyan, Catholic, and Orthodox theologies disagree with one another at various points, this in itself is not the main problem with them. The main problem is that at key points they also differ from what the fairest exegesis of the Biblical text teaches us on important theological subjects, and since the Bible itself is or should be the norm and standard by which we measure any kind of theology that we do, this is a serious shortcoming.[2]

And that brings me as to why the title for this final chapter, borrowed from Kierkegaard, has been chosen. While Systematic theology sometimes treats, as part of its field of focus, an interaction with modern science and its discussions about a whole series of subjects (think for instance of the modern discussion about mind/brain distinctions, or whether human minds survive physical extinction), such discussions are well beyond the area of expertise of most Christians and most Christian scholars, try as they might to get up to speed.

One wonders if it would not be better for Biblical and Systematic theologians to stay in their own lane, and leave the discussion of the relationship of the Bible to the modern cultural and scientific issues to the actual Systematics scholars and philosophers. The reason I raise this question is not because I favor obscurantism or a ceasing of discussions between theologians and scientists but because the Bible is absolutely not a scientific textbook, and the subjects it actually teaches are salvation history, theology, ethics, and spiritual formation. It does not teach the age of the earth, or geology, or cosmology, or most of anthropology, or physics, or medicine, or chemistry, or auto-mechanics, or modern technology, and I could go on.

Are there implications in the Bible and in Christian theology that could lead to meaningful discussions with modern secular science? Of course there are, as the BioLogos discussions have shown at length. But this

---

2. See now my *Sola Scriptura*.

is not, by and large, because the Bible has taught one thing, and modern science says something contrary to that.

The one area of possible exception is the discussion of creation theology vs. certain approaches to evolution, but perhaps not theistic evolution. Recent discussions by so conservative a philosopher as William Lane Craig and also by Professor Joshua Swamidass have shown that these discussions may yet provide some fertile soil for a non-secular approach to these issues in Biblical or Systematic theology. Note that most of the *so-called* Systematic theologies we have mentioned in the earlier chapters of this study (which really are only systematized Biblical or historical theologies), after we mentioned Pannenberg and before we discussed Robert Jenson, do not have any meaningful, lengthy interaction with contemporary scientific or sociological or psychological thought.[3]

If Systematic theology is supposed to do that, then the works I've dealt with in this study, with the exception of Jenson, are some kind of systematized Biblical theology, or in the case of Oden systematized historical theology, or in the case of Pannenberg some kind of systematic philosophical and apologetic theology. Perhaps Systematic theology in the past has been defined too narrowly *by Biblical scholars*.

But all the factors we have pointed out that should be taken into account when doing Systematic theology should be carefully considered, and all the pitfalls we have pointed out in Biblical interpretation should be avoided. The goal is not some narrow concept of theological consistency. The goal is understanding and teaching the truth of God, the truth about God and His salvation, and the sad truth about fallen human beings, desperately in need of rescue by the God of love.

One more thing. There is no substitute for good contextual exegesis of Biblical texts, which includes taking into account the historical context and the meaning those texts had when the inspired Biblical writers wrote them and they were received by the earliest followers of Christ. What the texts meant then is still what they meant when the NT canon was formed, or when we explore those texts today. This means there are inherent problems with various forms of "canonical" theology which operate with an a-historical or even an anti-historical bias. Here's how I would put it.

The problem with the canonical approach is that it ignores the historical contexts in which the NT books were originally given, and ignores the fact that those individual inspired documents had a meaning for their original audiences. These were audiences which did not exist in the fourth century when the NT canon was closed. Thus, a canonical approach involves a

---

3. Craig, *In Quest of the Historical Adam*; Swamidass, *Genealogical Adam and Eve*.

theological way of dealing with the material at the expense of the original historical contextual meaning of those texts, including an intertextual way of dealing with the books in the canon, as if their current juxtaposition determines their meaning. The latter may help us see the further significance of those texts for later periods of church history, but it does not help us figure out the original inspired meaning of those texts. Before finishing this study, an appendix is in order where I discuss a recent attempt to argue that God changes His mind on fundamental things like sexual ethics. In my view, this is not in accord with the Biblical witness, much less with Biblical or Systematic theology.

# Appendix One

# Is God Quixotic, and Changing His Mind About Sexual Ethics?

A Review of *The Widening of God's Mercy* (Yale University Press, 2024), by Christopher B. Hays and Richard B Hays, 272 pages

### PART ONE: Preliminary Thoughts

In the beginning of *The Widening of God's Mercy* we are given personal stories from both Chris and his father, Richard Hays, as to why there has been a change in mind about what we should think about the Scriptures' prohibitions of same-sex sexual activity (in both the OT and NT), as well as related matters, such as gay marriage, the ordination of LGBTQ+ persons, and the like.[1] The trajectory of their argument is to reach a conclusion that LGBTQ+ persons should be given full inclusion in the Christian church without asking them to change their sexual behavior, indeed without excluding them in any way from being clergy, being married in a Christian ceremony, and so on. And what led to this conclusion is participation in church communities where there is "full inclusion" of those folks. In short, *personal experience* has led to a reevaluation of how to deal with the Biblical data. And don't expect to find any treatment of the key texts in the OT and NT which prohibit same-sex sexual activity. They deliberately are omitting

---

1. This review first appeared on my blog The Bible and Culture, "The Widening of God's Mercy," parts 1–4, on the Patheos website.

any such discussion, presumably because as they say—the traditionalists are right about what those imperatives actually say. Richard is explicit in saying he hasn't changed his mind about what those texts say and mean.

Chris also shares his frustrations with the perceived inconsistent policies of Fuller Seminary as to what faith stand is required of members of the faculty when it comes to "the presenting issue" that this book seeks to address. Part of the argument, as we shall see, is that the Bible is full of "contradictions" or, put another way, full of evidence that God changes His mind from time to time on major issues partly in response to human requests or protests. We will deal with the "changes His mind" idea in the next part of this review.

In regard to full disclosure as to where I am coming from on this large issue, the two studies I published are (1) *Biblical Theology*, Cambridge University Press (2019), that won the Association of American Publishers (AAP) Prose Prize along with Tom Wright's *History and Eschatology*, as the book of the year in theology and philosophy, and (2) *Sola Scriptura: Scripture's Final Authority in the Modern World*, Baylor Press (2023). The latter concludes that what the phrase meant for the Catholics who first used it (William of Ockham or Marsilius of Padua or John Wycliffe) and then the Protestants is that God's Word, the Holy Scriptures, are *the final authority in matters of faith and practice*, not a human being, not even the pope, and not human experience. This, in turn, means that human experience, reason, or tradition, if they have some kind of authority, clearly have lesser authority when discerning what is true about God and His will for humankind.

A major problem with *The Widening of God's Mercy* is that it does not understand the nature of progressive revelation, which is not the same thing as saying God changed His mind, not least because progressive revelation means we gradually learn about God's will and the believer's ability to understand that will. Nor does the book recognize the Scriptures as the final authority for faith and practice unless, of course, using one's own judgment, one gets to pick and choose which Scriptures. This, in turn, sadly makes *the interpreter*, not God, and not the Scriptures, the final arbiter of the truth in these matters. And this is no small matter!

## PART TWO: God's Unchanging Nature

At the very outset of the book Chris presents us with an example from 1 Sam 15:11–35, Exhibit A that God does indeed change His mind, and that Samuel is telling a lie when in 1 Sam 15:29 the prophet says the following: "The Glory of Israel does not recant or change his mind! He is not mortal that he should change his mind!" Now this theme is not an isolated statement found only in 1 Sam 15:29.

For instance, Num 23:19 clearly says, "God is not a human being that he should lie nor the offspring of humans that he should change his mind." And there would be no need for God to do so since God is all-knowing. God knows all actualities and all possibilities. Indeed, the Scriptures are clear that He knows things in advance of their happening (see Rom 8), which means He knows how things will turn out in the human future. Malachi 3:6 says, "I the Lord do not change, therefore you oh children of Jacob are not consumed."

In other words, though human beings may change their mind and commit various acts that are sinful, God does not do that. Further, God does not go back on promises He has made to His people about not destroying them when they rebel or reject God's Word. Hosea 11:1–9 should be considered since it involves the clear statement at v. 9 that even though God is very angry with His people, He is not like human beings who are quixotic and go back on their word or change their minds. This last text is about God's compassion on sinful Israel, and clearly about how God does *not* change His mind.

The argument that because God is compassionate and merciful, then He *can* change His mind about whether something is sinful or not is a nonstarter. The concept of God NOT changing is clearly linked to God being the creator of all things. Psalm 102:25–27 reads, "In the beginning you laid the foundations of the earth, and the heavens are the works of your hands. They will perish but you remain, they will all wear out like a garment. Like clothing you will change them, and they will be discarded but you remain the same, and your years will never end." God is different from His creation and His creatures, especially in the fact that God does not change or change His mind.

The NT is equally clear on this matter. James 1:17 says God is the father of lights, and in Him is no variation, no shadow of turning, indeed no darkness at all. Furthermore, one cannot appeal to Christ Himself as a changeable part of the Godhead. Hebrews 13:8 clearly says Christ is the same yesterday, today, and forever. The eternality of Christ is the basis for saying He has an unchangeable priesthood.

But aren't the differences in the various covenants indications that God has changed His mind about some things over time? Absolutely not. Jesus explains in Matt 19 that many of the laws God gave Israel, before the time of Jesus, were given, not because God kept changing the rules but because of the *"hardness of the hearts of God's people."* For example, this is why God allowed divorce under the Mosaic law. It was God's fallen people, not God, that needed to change to receive the original plan God had in mind for marriage "from the beginning of creation."

Yes, there is such a thing as progressive revelation in the Bible. For instance, in the understanding of secondary causes. It was Satan, not God, that led David to take the census as a comparison of Samuel and the later Chronicles literature makes clear (cf. 2 Sam 24 to 1 Chr 21). Another example is an understanding of a positive afterlife in terms of resurrection, and a kingdom of God coming on earth, not merely in heaven (cf. Dan 7:13–14; Dan 12:1–3).

The reasons these things were not revealed to God's people during the time of the patriarchs but rather much later is not because God changed His mind but because God's people were not ready in the Mosaic era for such revelations. Over time they became more receptive to a broader understanding of the mysteries of life and the afterlife. And, of course, the ultimate illustration is that in the NT Christ is the fullest revelation of God's unchanging character, and the sending of the Spirit makes possible the believer's understanding of such mysteries of the faith. God didn't change His mind through these various covenants; rather He progressively revealed more and more of the truth about many things. It is human beings who by God's grace changed their minds about who God is and what His saving will involves, not just for Israel, but for the world.

It will be useful at this point to note that the Hebrew word *nacham* about which Chris says has as one of its major meanings "change of mind" *does not in fact mean that*. Here is the full list of what the Hebrew lexicon says is the spectrum of meaning of this verb in its various forms:

> *Nacham*: to be sorry, console oneself, repent, regret, comfort, be comforted
> 1. Niphal:
>    To be sorry, be moved to pity, have compassion
>    To be sorry, rue, suffer grief, repent
>    To comfort oneself, be comforted
>    To comfort oneself, ease oneself
> 2. Piel: to comfort, console
> 3. Pual: to be comforted, be consoled
> 4. Hithpael:
>    To be sorry, have compassion
>    To rue, repent of
>    To comfort oneself, be comforted[2]

---

2. Brown et al., *Brown–Driver–Briggs Hebrew English Lexicon*, "nacham."

Though older translations of the Hebrew sometimes translated the word *nacham* to mean "repent" even when applied to God, this is problematic. Repent refers to a response to a sin, indeed a sin against God, but the Bible is emphatic that God can't be tempted, tempts no one, and is holy and righteous and never sins. God doesn't violate God's own will! Unlike sinful human beings, God has no need to repent. What one can say is that this verb, when used of God, is an example of anthropomorphic language, and one must be careful about how one assesses its meaning.

I have no problem at all with the idea that God has compassion, sometimes regrets some things, can be moved to pity, can comfort and console His people, and that God, who loves His people, sometimes suffers because of and with His people. The Bible is not an advocate of the Greek philosophical idea of a God who is impassable and has no feelings. None of that, however, means that God changes His mind, and especially not about fundamental matters of theology or ethics. If 2 Tim 3:16 is true, and all Scriptures are God-breathed and profitable for training in *righteous conduct*, then we should not expect that God changes His mind about such things.

And while we are at it, since it is the Holy Spirit that is doing that inspiring, we should hardly think that when Jesus says the Spirit will lead His disciples into all truth, a further and deeper understanding of Biblical truth, that He will be leading them to endorse ideas that contradict what the Bible actually says repeatedly when it comes to ethical behavior. Certainly not.

## PART THREE: OT Teaching on Sexual Matters

Chris's presentation of the relevant OT evidence is well written and addresses an audience of clergy and laity. It is not meant to be a scholarly monograph, but it is to be taken seriously as written by two seasoned scholars who have read the academic discussion and reflected deeply on the relevant matter.

His treatment of Ezek 20:25-26 is another example of his suggestion that God changed His mind. Chris thinks this text suggests that God advocates His people offering child sacrifice, whereas most OT texts strongly oppose that practice. Let's look carefully at what the Hebrew text actually says. In the first place it is clear enough this is a *judgment oracle* from God. Here is what it says because of God's people being disobedient: "I gave them statutes that were not good and ordinances by which they could not live. I defiled them through their very gifts in their offering up all their first born, in order that I might horrify them, so that they might know that I am the Lord." God says in this very text that the statutes and ordinances did not reflect His good will. Then there is a statement of how God defiled them through their offering up all of their first born. Notice what it does not say. *It does not say God commanded them to offer up their children in sacrifice.* It says the recalcitrant Israelites were offering up their children to God, like we know some also did to Molech. In this regard this text differs from God's testing of Abraham by *commanding* him to offer up Isaac. What it does say is that God defiled them through their very gifts, in other words God sees such action as defiling and horrifying—but He wants His people to have the same sense of revulsion as He Himself has in regard to such actions.

Here is what two Jewish interpreters say about this difficult text. David Altschuler says, "The Israelites were forced to submit to oppressive laws and statutes in exile." David Kimchi says, "The Israelites were removed from God because of their sacrifices of firstborn sons to Molech."[3] Clearly this is a difficult text, but considering that it is part of a judgment oracle, in which God makes clear this is *not* His desire or good will for children to be sacrificed, and the text does not say He ordered the Israelites to do this. It only says they were doing it; thus we should not take this text as clear proof God changes His mind.

The discussion of the war passages in the OT and of the so-called *lex talionis* are again said to be examples of God changing His mind. What is never mentioned is that God is dealing with fallen and sinful people. What is never mentioned is that the *lex talionis* was intended to limit, not license, revenge taking which was already happening. Properly interpreted in context, this command meant "only an eye for an eye, only a hand for a hand, only a life for a life." As we have seen in the discussion of Jesus' teaching on what Moses says about divorce, there is a hermeneutical key given by Jesus when reading such OT laws, namely, they were given due to Israel's hardness of heart, to limit, not license, their sins.

It is surprising that there is no meaningful discussion of human fallenness and sin in these chapters, even though the Genesis story warns us about what's coming. Remember one of the curses on Eve was "your desire will be for your husband and he will lord it over you" (Gen 3:16). In other words, to love and to cherish will degenerate into "to desire and to dominate." This was the beginning of patriarchy, which plays itself out in living color in the rest of the Bible. Patriarchy, like slavery, was a result of human sin and human fallenness, and this downward slide began with Adam and Eve. No wonder Paul later say that Christ was born under the Mosaic law (which was given to limit sin) to redeem God's people out from under a law they could not fully keep as fallen sinful people (Gal 4).

---

3. Both cited in Maccoby, "Statutes That Were Not Good," 6–7.

There is also no discussion here of Michael Heiser's remarkable study, *The Unseen Realm*, in which he forcefully argues that the "harem" or holy war idea was meant to be an attempt to eliminate the Nephilim and their offspring who come on the scene originally due to sexual mixing of humans and fallen angels (Gen 6). In short, it was not about genocide perpetrated against all non-Jews in the land, or even a specific non-Jewish ethnic group; it was dealing with the problem that originally led to the flood in the first place. In short, there are various ways one can interpret the narrative in Joshua.

On the other hand, Chris is right that from as early as the story of Abraham, it is said to be God's intent to bless all the families and nations of the earth, indeed, to have His chosen people be a light to the Gentiles, as the idea was later called. This theme can be traced from Abraham right through the historical books and the prophets. This is all the more reason to take seriously and look carefully at what Michael Heiser says in *The Unseen Realm*. Something needs to be said here about the dialogical passages in the OT, including in the prophets like Amos, some of which are in the Pentateuch and some of which are in the prophets as discussed in chapter 6 of the Hays's book (see, e.g., Amos 7:2). In some of these discussions a prophet or a patriarch is often depicted as pleading for mercy or leniency on God's people when God could rightly judge them. And in the end God shows mercy or relents. But the question that should have been asked about all such passages is, Did God not know in advance where this conversation was going? Did He not know where Amos's heart was? Did He really not know these other persons depicted as negotiating with God?

Surely the answer is, since God is all knowing, He did know where the conversation was going. He did know what was on the heart of His patriarch or prophet and had already resolved to have mercy. He didn't change His mind, but He dialogued with an Abraham or an Amos so they would better understand God's will and be made to feel they were a part of the process of participating in what was God's will all along. In each of these cases it was to have mercy. In other words, Exod 34:6 was and is always true about God. God doesn't have to change His mind to be: "Yahweh, Yahweh—A God who is merciful and gracious, slow to anger, and abounding in steadfast love and faithfulness..."

## PART FOUR: The Treatment of the NT

Let it first be said that Richard's treatment of the Gospels does indeed place the emphasis in the right place in terms of God's mercy and compassion as expressed in Christ's various teachings and healings and acts of fellowship. The problem with these chapters is the important topics they *fail* to address. Examples are Christ's views on marriage, sexual sin, the eternal consequences for rejecting the Good News, and Christ's call of sinners to repentance in light of the coming Kingdom of God (see, e.g., Mark 1:15 as a summary of His message).

We must have a concept of progressive revelation, namely that Jesus and His teaching and actions and character are the clearest revelation of God's character. If so, there are points at which, when Jesus says something definitive on these relevant matters or even if one of His apostles like Paul does so, we must take these teachings very seriously as the clearest and furthest revelation of the character of God. God is righteous, and holy, and just. He is also called Love in 1 John 4, and is light, life, compassionate, merciful, and more. It is right to put an emphasis on the nouns like love, bearing in mind that we are not talking about *eros* but rather *agape*, God's holy and gracious love.

So, it is in order to point out that while the Hays's book basically does not address the issue of marriage (which is odd), Jesus has something very clear to say to His disciples about this matter when the question is asked about why Moses permitted divorce. The importance of this passage is so great that we must give it some detailed attention. Here is a translation of Matt 19, bearing in mind that the Mark-10 account of this same teaching says Jesus said "no divorce":

> Some Pharisees came to him to test him. They asked, "Is it lawful for a man to divorce his wife for any and every reason?"
>
> "Haven't you read," he replied, "that at the beginning the Creator 'made them male and female,' and said, 'For this reason a man will leave his father and mother and be united to his wife, and the two will become one flesh'? So they are no longer two, but one flesh. Therefore, what God has joined together, let no one separate."
>
> "Why then," they asked, "did Moses command that a man give his wife a certificate of divorce and send her away?"
>
> Jesus replied, "Moses permitted you to divorce your wives because your hearts were hard. But it was not this way from the beginning. I tell you that anyone who divorces his wife, except for sexual immorality, and marries another woman commits adultery."
>
> The disciples said to him, "If this is the situation between a husband and wife, it is better not to marry."

Jesus replied, "Not everyone can accept this word, but only those to whom it has been given. For there are eunuchs who were born that way, and there are eunuchs who have been made eunuchs by others—and there are those who choose to live like eunuchs for the sake of the kingdom of heaven. The one who can accept this should accept it." (vv. 3–12)

First of all, notice that Jesus only endorses heterosexual monogamy, and He does so on the basis of His understanding of the original creation order design of God. God made us male and female for each other. Only males and females could share a one flesh union that could lead to the fulfillment of God's plan that they be fruitful and multiply. Jesus is citing Gen 1:27 and then 2:24. The only alternative He offers His own disciples is celibacy in singleness, using the language of being like a eunuch.

What about the exception clause, found both here and in Matt 5:32? The word used in the exception clause is *porneia*. A *porne* was a prostitute (hence the English term *pornography*), and so the noun could mean except on grounds of prostitution. But the other singular meaning is incest—except on grounds of incest, like the case of Herod Antipas with his brother's wife. One could see Jesus commenting on that since John the Baptizer also did. The other meaning of *porneia* is any and all sorts of sexual immorality. But this is unlikely to be the meaning in this passage since the disciples rightly discern that Jesus is being *stricter* than Moses on this issue and throw up their hands, saying if this is the case, then better for a man not to marry.

What is equally important is to notice Jesus' comment on Moses' permission of divorce. We are told that God allowed divorce *due to the hardness of their hearts*. And here we have a window on Jesus' own hermeneutic. He thinks that various of the OT laws were given because of the spiritual state of God's people at that point. But now Jesus and the eschatological age have come, therefore new occasions can bring forth new teaching. This new teaching is not progressive in the modern sense of progressing beyond the OT teaching in ways that negate ethical rigor. To the contrary, Jesus is more demanding in His sexual ethic than the OT, not only basically ruling out divorce (and remarriage in Mark 10:11) for those "whom God has joined together," but also intensifying the demand in regard to adultery, to include adulterous thoughts (see Matt 5). Jesus is taking away the male privilege of divorce in His Jewish setting which, as a result, gave women more security in marriage. But He is also allowing that the command to be fruitful and multiply is not *required* of all His followers—they can be single for the sake of the kingdom. You will not find a discussion of this anywhere in *The Widening of God's Mercy*. What Jesus does *not* say is that His disciples should be allowed to find other sorts of marriage arrangements than the one God intended at creation of humankind as male and female.

Another subject that could have used a careful discussion in this book is covenants. Covenants in the OT, such as the Abrahamic and Mosaic covenants and then the new covenant announced by Jer 31 and enacted by Jesus and His followers, are arrangements set up by God between God and His people. That there are limits to who is included in the saved category should be clear from Jesus' sayings about people going to Gehenna, or His parable of the rich man and Lazarus, or His saying about the narrow gate, or His parable about the sheep and the goats. Neither Jesus nor His apostles and early followers thought that the Gospel was some form of universalism. As Paul says repeatedly, salvation is by grace through faith in Christ crucified and risen. While Christ has atoned for the sins of the world through His death and is the objective means of human salvation, the subjective means is by trusting in Christ, being born again, and being baptized by the Spirit into the new covenant community.

Thus, when we see that the new covenant doesn't require Sabbath observance of Jesus' followers, this is not a sign of a change of mind or incipient universalism. Rather, it's a sign that the covenant has changed, and includes some of the same commandments as found in the Mosaic law, but many new ones as well. Such is the nature of contracts between God and His people; they differ according to the point in time in salvation history they are covering. Jesus is not merely an advocate of a more enlightened reading of the OT, though that is true. He is also offering teachings that go well beyond and sometimes against some of the materials in the OT (e.g., Jesus' prohibitions of oaths). This is true because He perceives the eschatological saving reign of God is breaking in, and the new occasion require a new covenant, with many new commandments. This is not only for God's Jewish people, but also for non-Jews, as would become clearer later.

Understandably, the term *mercy* comes up again and again in Richard's treatment of Jesus' teaching. Jesus does emphasize mercy, but what is mercy? Mercy is what a sinner needs and gets when he or she is not punished according to strict justice. Mercy is not the same thing as grace.

It is interesting that Richard points to the word *hesed*, which he translates as steadfast love. It is interesting because that very word *hesed* is universally translated in the LXX as *mercy*, not as steadfast love, or loving kindness. Of course, the NT is in Greek, and its authors use the LXX more than any other version of the OT. Jesus is perfectly well aware that tax collectors and "sinners" are indeed in need of repentance (which E. P.

Sanders says means "notorious sinners").[4] Note the parable of the tax collector pleading for mercy, while the Pharisee lifts himself up by comparing himself to the IRS agent. In the story of Zaccheus, we see this need for and response of repentance clearly. It is no accident that Jesus says salvation has come to his house on that day.

Note that Richard follows Chris's lead and suggests that Hos 11 shows God changing His mind to have mercy instead of judging (p. 138). This is not an accurate reading of the whole passage. God is depicted as debating with Himself what He will do, and in the end concludes, because He is God and not quixotic likes humans, that He will *not* change His mind about His original love and mercy for His people. God will be faithful to His promises even when Israel is faithless. It is right to place the emphasis on Christ's compassion and mercy, but not at the expense of what He says about eternal consequences for rejecting His Good News message. Jesus says far more about people going to Gehenna or outer darkness than any other speaker in the NT with the exception of John of Patmos. It is important not to neglect the justice and righteousness of God, which is a theme throughout the Bible. Justice and righteousness ironically become an expression of love, through the substituting of God's Son to be the atonement for our sins. It should have been us on the cross but, as Paul says, the God of righteousness could not pass over sin forever and remain the person who God is—a God of holy love, not holiness without love, and not love without holiness.

In their dealing with the book of Acts, most of the exegesis is fine until one gets to the Decree of the Jerusalem Council, which is definitely not about a creative re-reading of Leviticus. For one thing there is no mention of the prohibition of "things strangled" in Leviticus at all. This is actually a clue to the social setting James has in mind, namely idol feasts in pagan temples. Pagans did indeed strangle birds so the life breath would enter into the statue of the god, and thereby invigorate or feed the deity. Furthermore, *eidolothuton* refers to meat sacrificed to an idol, which would be followed by a feast in which the idol or god would be the host. If one asks the right question as to where a Jew would assume one could find all four things prohibited in the decree (*eidolothuton*, blood, things strangled, and *porneia*) all in one place, including sexual immorality, it would be in a pagan idol feast in a temple's dining room. After too much wine there would regularly be sexually immoral behavior with the servers or slaves.

In short, the decree is about *venue*, not about a Levitical *menu*. Paul implements the decree in 1 Cor 8–10 where he prohibits attending idol feasts in temple dining rooms. Indeed, he says there is no problem with

---

4. See Sanders, *Paul and Palestinian Judaism*.

eating anything one finds in the meat market, including animals sacrificed in a pagan temple. Again, the issue is venue and where one finds those four prohibited things together, not menu. Finally, the reason James reminds the Gentiles about the heart of the Mosaic law, namely the Ten Commandments, is because at its core it is a prohibition of idolatry and immorality, including *porneia*.

So, if one wants to take the Jerusalem Council example as a paradigm for how to deal with the "presenting" issue in regard to same-sex sexual expression, James's answer would be God's Word prohibits it! And so does the teaching of the Apostle to the Gentiles in Romans and 1 Corinthians. One must reject the idea of an analogy between inclusion of various non-Jewish ethnic groups into the covenant community, something all along hinted at in the mission of the chosen people to be a light to the nations. This has nothing to do with accepting sexual practices which are clearly at odds with specific statements in both the Mosaic law and the new covenant teachings. Again, the Holy Spirit's leading us into a deeper understanding of the Scriptures does not include leading us to contradict the clear teaching of Scripture on some important theological or ethical matter. If the decree of James suggests anything, it suggests that in the new covenant community the sexual ethical standards will still be as demanding as in the Mosaic law, if not more so. There is no trajectory of change on that issue in Scripture. Indeed, Jesus and Paul call us to a higher standard of ethical rectitude, including in regard to the form of marriage they endorse.

Richard's treatment of the Pauline letters rightly emphasizes the theme of mercy and love, while deliberately avoiding saying anything about the Pauline texts (e.g., Rom 1:18–32; 1 Cor 6:9) that clearly enough condemn same-sex relationships. As it turns out, and we learn in the final chapter about "Moral Re-Envisioning," this was part of the deliberate strategy of this whole book. The strategy was to NOT deal with the OT and NT texts that do indeed teach that the various behaviors being touted as normal by the LGBTQ+ community are either explicitly or implicitly ruled out by these texts and also the ones that say that God's intent is for heterosexual monogamy when it comes to marriage, a teaching Jesus Himself insists on. And once more with feeling, it is quite false to say that what was being condemned in the Bible is NOT same-sex relations between consenting adults. There are various ancient examples of that from Jesus and Paul's world, so that claim needs to be dropped, as Preston Sprinkle and others have shown.[5]

---

5. See the blog post of Oct. 12, 2024, on my blog The Bible and Culture on Patheos: Sprinkle, "Widening of God's Mercy."

There is a further attempt by Richard at an analogy between the discussion of the weak and the strong in Rom 14. Richard rightly suggests that these passages probably refer to Jewish Christians, who have too many scruples about the food they eat and the day they worship God, versus the Gentiles who have no such scruples. Clearly, Paul identifies with the strong, but wishes to protect the weak as also is the case in 1 Corinthians. But the attempt to then suggest that today the strong are those who have abandoned scruples about same-sex sexual behavior (and related LGBTQ+ advocated behaviors), whereas the weak are those who maintain the teaching that the Bible explicitly gives on such behaviors, is far-fetched. One could just as easily turn this argument on its head. The weak are those who have capitulated to the siren song of our pagan culture about sexual behaviors the Bible does not condone. The strong are those who have remained faithful to the Biblical teaching against the general flow of the American culture. In the end, the attempt at analogies using either Acts 15 or Rom 14 and situations today are strained at best, and frankly unconvincing.

In the final chapter it is argued that what is said in the OT and NT about slaves and slavery is something the church now deems wrong and not to be followed despite what is said in the Bible. The problem with this judgment is it fails to realize that the Biblical dictates and statements about slavery, which is a practice, like patriarchy, that is a result of human fallenness and sin, are all *attempts to limit an existing and ongoing evil, not license it!* Despite the fact that various people over the last two thousand years thought the Bible provided a warrant for enslaving people, this was not the intent of what was being taught. For instance, in the household codes in Col 3–4 and Eph 5–6, Paul must start with a situation that already is in place and exists in the household of new high status Christians with slaves. And, like any good pastor, he must start with them where they are, but not leave them there.

Notice the trajectory of change from Colossians, where there is a remark about equality between masters and slaves (*isotes*), to Ephesians, where we hear that masters are to serve their slaves and treat them with respect, and finally to Philemon, where we see where this trajectory of change is going. The trajectory is moving to "manumission" because Onesimus must be seen by his owner, the Christian Philemon, as "no longer a slave, but rather a brother in Christ." Paul already said in Gal 3:28 that in Christ there is neither Jew nor Gentile, slave nor free, and no male and female. Amen to that. What he did not say or even remotely suggest is that the Biblical standards of sexual morality should be changed to meet the preferences of a pagan culture.

I take it for granted that we are to love and welcome everyone into the church. This does not mean that we are to accept all their ideas, beliefs, and behaviors. They can come as they are, but no one should ever expect to *stay as they are* when they are encountering Christ and the Spirit in the gathering of the church for worship and fellowship and discipleship. To the contrary, everyone, being sinners, should expect to be changed by being part of the body of Christ. What the church should never do is baptize people's sins, of whatever sort, and call it good and acceptable behavior. What actually does the most harm is treating sin and its consequences as if it isn't sin and has no serious consequences.

The message of the church today should be the same today for the sexual sinner as Jesus articulated in His own day, that is, a message which balances mercy and righteousness. "Neither do I condemn you but *go and sin no more*." If the church did an adequate job of making clear that single persons are loved members of the forever family of Christ and should be treated with the same love and respect as traditionally married persons, then we would not need to be citing the verse which suggests it is not good for a human being to be alone. To be an integral, indeed essential, part of the body of Christ and to be loved as such is not to be alone.

In the end do we really want or need a God who is quixotic and changes His mind? How exactly can we trust God and His Word if He keeps changing His mind? How can we even know what God really thinks about crucial matters if this is true? I especially raise this question because both Chris and Richard Hays are raising this issue in regard to God changing His mind AFTER the writing of Scripture on this particular issue. *There is no positive evidence in the Scripture that God changed His mind about sexual ethics, even if you accept the argument that God changed His mind on other subjects unrelated to human sexual behavior.* To the contrary, the critique of same-sex sexual behavior is strong in both the old covenant and the new covenant, in both the OT and the NT.

The argument that after the Holy Spirit inspired the Bible, two thousand years later that same Holy Spirit led the church in a different direction is not tenable. And the argument that we know that God's mind has changed because we have experienced LGBTQ+ folk as good Christians who deserve to be included in anything and everything the church does is entirely an argument from personal experience and not tenable. In short, it is an argument based on assumed analogies. The Scriptural evidence that God changes His mind is lacking and involves a misreading of the key verb *nacham*. The following great hymn sums up the truth of the matter quite well:

Great is Thy faithfulness, O God my Father;
There is no shadow of turning with Thee;
Thou changest not, Thy compassions, they fail not;
As Thou hast been Thou forever wilt be.

*Refrain:*
Great is Thy faithfulness!
Great is Thy faithfulness!
Morning by morning new mercies I see:
All I have needed Thy hand hath provided—
Great is Thy faithfulness, Lord, unto me![6]

---

6. Lyrics by Thomas Chisholm, 1923.

# Appendix Two

# Toward a More Historical Method to Do Socio-Rhetorical Criticism

Methodology is not an indifferent net. It catches what it intends to catch.
—Robert Funk[1]

Many different sorts of methodologies have been applied to the study of the Bible, especially in the last forty or so years. And there are no perfect methodologies. They all have their own focus and limitations as a result of that focus. The use of source, form, and redaction criticism in the twentieth century gradually gave way to an increasing use of the social sciences, and in some case also various forms of rhetorical criticism. A very long time ago, Richard Longenecker told me he was the first one to use the term *socio-rhetorical criticism*. I've been unable to verify this, but what is clear is the phrase became popular and it came to mean different things to different scholars. When Vernon Robbins has used it, he has used it in a broad way to refer to drawing on both ancient and modern sociological methodologies and both ancient and modern approaches to rhetoric. By contrast, when I have used that hyphenated phrase in a series of my commentaries, I have used it to refer to the sorts of rhetoric the writers of the NT could have known and used, and the sort of social history that existed in that era, though I have at times supplemented this by drawing on some of the real gains from applying the social sciences to the NT data. Basically, I have prioritized a historical approach to these matters.

---

1. Funk, "Beyond Criticism in Quest of Literacy," 151.

One of the underlying problems with using a variety of these modern methods is a failure to do the necessary homework on the historical context of the Biblical text, and the resulting failure to ask the sort of methodological questions the original contexts prompt.

For example, in the study of 1 Peter, various scholars have assumed on the basis of some remarks in 1 Peter that the author must be addressing Gentiles. The problem with this assumption is that the material evidence from the various regions in Anatolia mentioned in the prescript shows that Jews in those regions often became very Hellenized, so Hellenized that more traditional Jews like Peter and his coworker Silvanus would view them as pagans, or at least as too compromised as Jews. For instance, the synagogue in Sardis bears witness to just how Hellenized various Jews in that city were. Their lavish synagogue, the largest one we know of in that era, was built right on the main forum area, within sight of the huge gymnasium complex. Notice that in Rev 3 the Christian Jews in Sardis are accused of being mostly spiritually dead, and having "soiled" their clothes (violating OT rules of clean and unclean). Theories about audiences have to take into account the actual material evidence produced by archaeology and the study of ancient contexts as well as inscriptional evidence and texts.

While I don't have a problem with using social scientific models of approach or modern rhetorical models of approach, or canonical methods of approach, or "readings" models of approach, or intertextual methods of approach to the Bible, or a key ideas or themes approach to Biblical theology, in my view, none of these approaches should be undertaken without first assessing the historical givenness of the Biblical text. This is in part what Clifton Black is complaining about when he says,

> German liberal theology's method of doctrinal concepts—grouping thoughts expressed by the NT in alignment with dogmatic topics—betrays "scientific criticism" and provokes caricature of NT writers as systematicians in the modern sense. That method's default setting on canonical documents is likewise misguided: a document's canonization makes no difference for either the Protestant theologian or historical investigator . . . none of its subject matter was born canonical.[2]

---

2. Black, *Biblical Theology*, 18–19. Canonical theology as it is done today by some Protestant scholars is an *ex post facto* approach that is a-historical or in some cases allergic to historical contextual study of the relevant NT texts. This is unfortunate because, as Black goes on to stress, it is not and was not the including of a NT book into the canon which determined its content or intent, and to the extent that the canonical reading of a NT text is at odds with what the text meant in its original historical context it is problematic.

Any time one tries to fit the Biblical data into some procrustean bed, whether it be the sorts of methods mentioned above or more traditional sorts of systematizing, there are problems, because it too often runs roughshod over the actual historical data and the givenness of the text themselves. Consider for example the difference between a social history approach to the NT data, for instance in the work of E. A. Judge, and the social scientific approach to the text, for instance of various members of the "Context Group," and here I'm thinking for example of the work of Jerome Neyrey, Bruce Malina, or John Elliot among others.

Social history is, by definition, the study of the ordinary life of the ancients, whether rich or poor, or somewhere in between. It uses actual historical evidence, including literary and archaeological and inscriptional evidence to draw conclusions about ancient practices of marrying, divorcing, doing business, making and enforcing laws, traveling, relating to the divine, and much more. It does not *assume* that modern studies on cargo cults, or modern analysis of Mediterranean practices of reciprocity, patronage, and honor and shame, or modern approaches to the rhetoric in and of texts, or modern systematic or canonical studies of the Scriptures necessarily comport with ancient praxis, methodologies, belief systems, and the like, nor with the ancient data itself.

While methods such as the study of the NT with the help of social identity theory have often been helpful and have shed some light on ancient concepts of corporate personality or group identity, *it needs to always be checked against and normed against the actual ancient data*. It is one thing to say ancient peoples were not like modern Western individualists, which is true in some ways; it is another thing to suggest that there was not a spectrum of ways ancient people inter-related, including some notable figures that do come across more like radical individualists (e.g., Julius Caesar and later various emperors) who sought to do things their own way, and who sought to establish their own honor in ways that did not always conform to the existing social norms.

When I say the actual ancient data, one of the things I am referring to is not limiting one's study to the literary evidence, which some scholars have been prone to do, but actually working through the vast corpus of ancient inscriptions, as the scholars who have been compiling *New Documents Illustrating Early Christianity* are doing.

This series now runs to ten volumes, and kudos to the SBL Press for publishing the most recent volumes. When one actually works through this vast resource, one quickly discovers that various modern assumptions about ancient cultures do not comport with the actual historical data. It is not true for example that only men upheld the public honor of their families, not least by publishing honorific inscriptions about them, for we have evidence that high status women did this as well. Their life was not confined to protecting the family from shame, nor dealing with in-house or familial matters. The involvement of women in all sorts of business activities in the Greco-Roman world is well documented, never mind in the ANE (see, e.g., Prov 31).

Or consider the fact that modern anthropological assumptions about ancient religions have been brought up short by archaeological evidence, especially that found in southeastern Turkey at Gobeckli Tepe and other nearby sites that date to 8000 to 10000 BC. The anthropological assumption was that religion only appears on the human horizon once there was agriculture to cultivate and village life where people living close to their crops needed some moral ways to relate to each other and acquire the assistance of the gods to produce good crops of wheat and other grains. Alas for this assumption, there were already high places of worship and giving of offerings to the gods long before there was actual village life, and even before the regular practice of growing crops and maintaining agrarian life. Indeed, it was going on before there were written languages, it would appear. There are no inscriptions at all at the vast Gobeckli Tepe site.

As one of the original archaeologists who produced the first major book on Gobeckli Tepe, Klaus Schmidt,[3] said, the high place at Gobeckli Tepe and other nearby sites strongly suggest that human beings were inherently religious from as far back as we can trace the evidence, including before there was writing and written texts. Schmidt saw this as comporting with the Biblical idea of human beings being created in the deity's image and always seeking relationship with one or more gods. Again, the ancient historical evidence itself must be consulted before constructing methodological models that may or may not comport with the empirical evidence.

This brings me more specifically to the issue of socio-rhetorical criticism. My complaint is not that we should not use modern rhetorical studies and modern social scientific studies to illuminate the Biblical text, but rather that historical rhetorical criticism and social history should be examined first and foremost. The essential question to be asked is—What sort of rhetoric could the NT writers have known and used in their composing of their documents? Also, what sort of theories of meaning did they operate with in doing so? Or again one should be asking, What does the literary, inscriptional, archaeological evidence suggest about the social settings into which and out of which these Biblical documents were written?

---

3. Schmidt, *Sie bauten die ersten Tempel.*

If one asks the question why the historical contexts of the Bible are so important, the answer is fairly straightforward—Christianity, like the religion out of which it was born, early Judaism, at its core is a historical religion grounded in certain historic events. It is not primarily a philosophy of life, it is not primarily just some practical wisdom for being happy, healthy, and wealthy, it is not primarily about advocating a new kind of spirituality, nor is it just a set of abstract ideas that one must embrace and believe, though to some extent it involves all these things and more.

At its core Christianity is grounded in historical events that involved historical persons in a particular time and place. It involves divine intervention in human history affecting the lives of ordinary human beings. It was about God in Christ changing human history by transforming the lives of all sorts of people from the least, the last, and the lost, to the most, the first, and the found. It was about being born from above, born again, and receiving the gift of everlasting life. But born into what? Into a relationship with God that was at once both personal and profound, so profound that one became a new creation in Christ.

But none of this would have transpired for anyone if the Son of God had not come, discipled various kinds of people (including tax collectors, fishermen, zealots, teachers, both the well-educated and the relatively uneducated, both men and women), left a body of teachings, died on a cross to atone for the sins of the world, risen from the dead, appeared to various people, both former disciples and at least two persons who weren't His followers earlier (James His brother and Saul of Tarsus), and then empowered them to spread the Good News about Himself and the salvation He provided to all and sundry, by sending them the Holy Spirit after He had departed.

Without all of this, no Christianity would have emerged from early Judaism. As Paul, our earliest witness to the movement that changed the world, says, "If Christ is not raised, your faith is futile; you are still in your sins" (1 Cor 15:17). In short, without an irreducible number of historical events involving and inaugurated by Jesus of Nazareth, there is no Christianity, then or now. This is why the historical context of the Christ event and its immediate effects and sequel must be the first and primary thing one must explore in order to understand the literature we call the New Testament. One's methodology must in the first instance match the very nature of what one is studying, and what one is studying is the Christ event, not merely the later actions of the church in the fourth century AD that recognized which Christian documents belonged in the canon. *The authority of those books did not derive from the church taking an action in about AD 367; it derived from the inspiration of God, and the truth telling of those documents about Jesus and other things from the time their inspired authors wrote them.*

In short, they were holy writ like the OT because God inspired persons to write down the historical story of Jesus and its impact on eyewitnesses and the earliest conveyors of the Good News. This means that Biblical scholars must be many things, including theologians and ethicists, but chiefly they must be good historians, knowing how to study the NT in its original historical contexts.

## Asking the Right Historical Questions

One of the problems with applying certain modern methods to the study of the New Testament is that one fails to ask even basic historical questions. For instance, when one studies the book of Acts from the point of view of narrative theory as practiced by some scholars, the danger is to treat the book as if it were like a work of fiction in which we have an omniscient narrator, and the story must make sense as a story. Alas for this approach, history is often messy, and the narrative will raise various conundrums and may even end abruptly and in an unexpected way, as Acts does. Let me illustrate from personal experience.

On Paul's so-called first missionary journey he goes from Antioch to Cyprus, where Barnabas was from, and they end up in Paphos with a visit to the governor Sergius Paulus, who was certainly interested in miracles and the message of Good News, which to him must have sounded strangely like the imperial propaganda about the Good News of a savior bringing peace to the world. This inscription below is part of a decree made in 9 BC about Augustus, and posted in Priene and elsewhere in the empire. Here's how it reads:

> Since Providence, which has ordered all things and is deeply interested in our life, has set in most perfect order by giving us Augustus, whom she filled with virtue that he might benefit humankind, sending him as a savior, both for us and for our descendants, that he might end war and arrange all things, and since he, Caesar, by his appearance (excelled even our anticipations), surpassing all previous benefactors, and not even leaving to posterity any hope of surpassing what he has done, and since the birthday of the god Augustus was the beginning of the good tidings [εὐαγγέλιον] for the world that came by reason of him.

So when Paul appears before the governor and impresses him with the blinding of Elymas, we hear, "When the proconsul saw what had happened, he believed, for he was amazed at the teaching about the Lord" (Acts 13:12). Even allowing for a bit of Lukan rhetorical flourish here, this confirms Paul impressed the governor. But where would he and Barnabas and Mark go next? We are told they sailed to the south coast of the Asian province, to the ancient Greek city of Perge, but nothing at all is said about them staying and evangelizing there; instead they (without John Mark, who returns to Jerusalem) head directly over rugged mountain territory to a small Roman colony town called Pisidian Antioch, and this begs the question—Why in the world would they do that?

Why not go along the coast to Aspendos, and Tarsus, Paul's hometown, and then back through the Cilician gates to Antioch? Certainly, this would have afforded opportunities for sharing the Good News to largely Gentile audiences. From Perge, it's a good 260 kilometers or 161.5 miles over very rugged, mountainous terrain, taking four weeks or more to traverse it to get to Pisidian Antioch, even if they followed the Roman road called the Via Sebaste. And again, why do that?

There is a good historical answer to this historical question. Sergius Paulus and his family were *from Pisidian Antioch*, as attested by the honorific inscription that Mark Wilson and I found at the small Yalvac (the modern name for the city) museum courtyard gathering mold and gradually wearing away. Here is the very stone we found which mentions Sergii Paulii plural. Later, thankfully they put the stone in the museum as we requested.

In a separate study I have shown there are other honorific inscriptions about both the father and the son in this family, and that they played important governmental roles in that Galatian region, but also in Rome and then in Cyprus. Clearly this family were the favorite and most famous sons of that town and had succeeded in climbing the Roman *cursus honorum*. This leads to the plausible conclusion that the governor of Cyprus urged Paul to go to Pisidian Antioch and share his good news about Jesus, accompanied as it was by miracles the governor had seen. In short, he probably provided Paul and Barnabas with a letter of introduction, and note that according to Acts 13 they were well received, at first, and asked to speak again on the following Sabbath, this time with an audience which included "almost the whole city." Luke says the Jews were jealous that Paul could draw such a large crowd of Jews and Gentiles, and so there was Jewish resistance to his ministry and message, but clearly the Gospel seed had been planted and Paul could return there later.

The historical answer to the historical question—Why a four-week hike to Pisidian Antioch instead of following the easier coastal road with even more cities and villages to be visited?—is provided for us by the connection Paul made with the governor of Cyprus, who likely gave him a letter of introduction to visit the governor's hometown. Like Paul's letters, the Gospels and Acts are documents grounded in ancient history and deserve to be treated according to the conventions of how ancient historical monographs and ancient biographies were written, not how modern ones are. Again, I'm not arguing against applying various modern methods to help us better understand these ancient documents. I am simply arguing in favor of analyzing these texts with full awareness of how ancient historical documents were written, often following both ancient social, historical, and rhetorical conventions, not modern ones. Once one has done justice to the historical contexts of these documents, then there is plenty of time to try other methods and insights to gain understanding of what these documents said and meant in their original context, and for us today as well.

## And So?

For a New Testament scholar to have the scope of knowledge and understanding he or she needs, he or she needs to be something of a general practitioner of the field in regard to both the text and the context of the NT. He or she needs to be committed to relying on historical information about these ancient texts, and modern methodologies must be checked against the actual ancient evidence to see if they comport with one another. If one is teaching either in a college or a seminary situation, it will not be enough to just focus on your area of expertise if this does not help your audiences get a grasp of the basic historical information in the NT. Teaching them to do "readings" of the NT from this or that modern perspective or cultural milieu and context or *au courant* methodology will not suffice to train them how to properly read the Bible, much less do serious research or teach the Bible. As I like to say, a text without a context is just a pretext for whatever one wants it to mean, and in the age of texting and sound bites and the like, there is a great danger of misusing the Bible for agendas the Biblical authors would neither recognize nor endorse.

Never mind the temptations artificial intelligence now presents us with, namely that students can have AI write their term papers without ever having to do proper first-hand research into ancient historical texts and contexts. I was talking recently to a NT scholar who teaches at a Christian college, and he was raving about how bright his students were on the basis of their submitted papers, but then he gave them an in-class exam, and they performed miserably, as if they had learned next to nothing in the class. He discovered upon investigation that those papers had been written with AI doing the lion's share of composition. I myself have seen examples where an AI-generated term paper made up article titles and book titles and sources which *do not even exist!!!* We may be living in a brave new world, where the temptations presented to us from ever advancing technology overwhelms our scholarly ethics and abilities to do honest work that is our own research and writing. Perhaps the warning of the anonymous hand writing on the wall at Belshazzar's feast is still apt—our days are *numbered*, our teaching has been *weighed* and found wanting, and our discipline has been turned over to anonymous artificial intelligence that is writing our students' papers for them. If so, this is even worse than handing over our kingdom to the pagan Medes and the Persians.

Let it not be said that modern historical research into the Bible and its many contexts has become lazy and prepared to allow technology to do all the heavy lifting. If we allow that to dominate our field of historical study, we may soon find ourselves replaced by artificial instructors, with no human check and balance to the content of their lectures or their research and publications. That would not be the "brave new world" of biblical studies; that would be the death knell of the best practices of biblical studies as we know it. This is how historical study ends, not with a bang but a whimper. It is better to be glorious anachronisms than *au courant* artificially intelligent professors.

# Bibliography

Aletti, J. N. "The Rhetoric of Romans 5–8." In *The Rhetorical Analysis of Scripture: Essays from the 1995 London Conference*, edited by Stanley E. Porter and T. H. Olbricht, 294–308. Sheffield Academic Press, 1997.
Alkier, Stefan. "Intertextuality and the Semiotics of Biblical Texts." In *Reading the Bible Intertextually*, edited by Richard B. Hays et al., 3–21. Baylor University Press, 2009.
Arnold, Bill T. *Genesis*. The New Cambridge Bible Commentary. Cambridge University Press, 2009.
Ayars, Matt, et al. *Holiness: A Biblical, Historical, and Systematic Theology*. IVP, 2023.
Baldwin, Sarah Thomas. *Generation Awakened: An Eyewitness Account of the Powerful Outpouring of God at Asbury*. Invite, 2024.
Barclay, John M. G. *Paul and the Gift*. Eerdmans, 2017.
Barrett, C. K. *The Epistle to the Romans*. Hendrickson, 1991.
Barrett, Matthew. "The Immutability and Impassibility of God." The Gospel Coalition. https://www.thegospelcoalition.org/essay/immutability-impassibility-god/.
Barth, Markus. *Ephesians 1-3*. Anchor Bible. Doubleday, 1974.
Bauckham, Richard. *Jesus and the God of Israel*. Eerdmans, 2008.
Beale, G. K., and D. A. Carson. *Commentary on the New Testament Use of the Old Testament*. Baker, 2007.
Bettenson, Henry, ed. *Documents of the Christian Church*. Oxford University Press, 1967.
Black, C. Clifton. *Biblical Theology: Essays Exegetical, Cultural, and Homiletical*. Eerdmans, 2024.
———. Review of *Interpreting Scripture with the Great Tradition: Recovering the Genius of Premodern Exegesis*, by Craig Carter. *Review of Biblical Literature* (July 2022).
Bray, Gerald. *Athens and Jerusalem: Philosophy, Theology and the Mind of Christ*. Lexham, 2025.
———, ed. *Romans*. Ancient Christian Commentary on Scripture 6. InterVarsity, 1998.
Brown, F., et al. *The Brown–Driver–Briggs Hebrew and English Lexicon*. Hendrickson, 1994.
Carter, Craig. *Interpreting Scripture with the Great Tradition: Recovering the Genius of Premodern Exegesis*. Baker, 2018.
Childs, Brevard. *Biblical Theology of the Old and New Testaments*. Fortress, 1993.
Craig, William Lane. *In Quest of the Historical Adam*. Eerdmans, 2021.
Cranfield, C. E. B. *Romans 1-8*. Vol. 1. International Critical Commentary. T&T Clark, 2004.

Cullmann, Oscar. *Christ and Time*. Repr., Wipf and Stock, 2018.
Daley, Brian. *Biblical Interpretation and Doctrine in Early Christianity*. Eerdmans, 2025.
Denney, James. *The Death of Christ*. Tyndale, 1951.
Dodd, C. H. *The Johannine Epistles*. Hodder, 1946.
Dongell, Joseph. *The Most Excellent Way*. Seedbed, 2024.
Elliott, Neil. *The Rhetoric of Romans*. Sheffield University Press, 1990.
Emerson, Ralph Waldo. "Self-Reliance." In *Essays: First Series*, 1841. https://www.gutenberg.org/files/16643/16643-h/16643-h.htm#SELF-RELIANCE.
Feldmeier, Reinhard, and Hermann Spieckerman. *God of the Living*. Baylor University Press, 2015.
Funk, Robert. "Beyond Criticism in Quest of Literacy: The Parable of the Leaven." *Interpretation* 25 (1971) 149–70.
Goldingay, John. *Old Testament Theology: Israel's Faith*. IVP Academic, 2016.
Grudem, Wayne. *Systematic Theology*. 2nd ed. Zondervan, 2020.
Hamilton, Victor P. *Exodus: An Exegetical Commentary*. Baker, 2011.
Hart, David Bentley. *Beauty of the Infinite*. Eerdmans, 2003.
Hays, Richard B., and Christopher Hays. *The Widening of God's Mercy*. Yale University Press, 2024.
Heiser, Michael S. *The Unseen Realm*. Lexham, 2015.
Hirsch, E. D. *Validity in Interpretation*. Yale University Press, 1967.
Hunsinger, George. "Robert Jenson's Systematic Theology: A Review Essay." *Scottish Journal of Theology* 55 (2002) 161–200.
Jenson, Robert. *Systematic Theology*. Vol. 1, *The Triune God*. Oxford University Press, 1997.
———. *Systematic Theology*. Vol. 2, *The Works of God*. Oxford University Press, 1999.
Judge, E. A. *Social Distinctives of the Christians in the First Century*. Edited by David M. Scholer. Hendrickson, 2007.
Kasemann, Ernst. *Commentary on Romans*. Eerdmans, 1994.
Kierkegaard, Søren. *Either/Or, Part II*. Translated by Howard V. Hong and Edna Hong. Anchor, 1959.
Kümmel, W. G. *Romer 7 und das Bild des Menschen im Neuen Testament*. Kaiser, 1974.
Lampe, Peter. *New Testament Theology in a Secular World: A Constructivist Work in Christian Apologetics*. Translated by Robert Brewley. T&T Clark, 2012.
Lewis, C. S. *A Preface to Paradise Lost*. Oxford University Press, 1942.
Longenecker, Bruce W. *Rhetoric at the Boundaries*. Baylor University Press, 2005.
Lyonnet, Stanislas. "L'histoire du salut selon le ch. 7 de l'epitre aux Romains." *Biblica* 43 (1962) 117–51.
Maccoby, Hyam. "Statutes That Were Not Good (Ezekiel 20:25–26): Traditional Interpretations." *Journal of Textual Reasoning (Old Series)* 8 (1999) 4–10.
Marshall, I. Howard. *Kept by the Power of God: A Study of Perseverance and Falling Away*. Wipf and Stock, 2008.
Martin, Dale. *Biblical Truths: The Meaning of Scripture in the Twenty-First Century*. Yale University Press, 2017.
McCall, Thomas H. *Which Trinity? Whose Monotheism?* Eerdmans, 2010.
McGrath, Alistair. *In the Beginning: The Story of the King James Bible and How It Changed a Nation, a Language, and a Culture*. Knopf, 2002.
Mead, James K. *Biblical Theology: Issues, Methods, and Themes*. Westminster/John Knox, 2007.

Mitchell, M. M. *The Heavenly Trumpet*. Louisville: Westminster John Knox, 2002.
Morris, Thomas V. *The Logic of God Incarnate*. Repr., Wipf and Stock, 2001.
Moule, C. F. D. *Christ Alive and at Large: The Unpublished Writings of C. F. D. Moule*. Edited by Robert Morgan and Patrick Moule. Canterbury Studies in Spiritual Theology. Canterbury, 2011.
Nicholson, Suzanne, ed. *Cooperating with the Spirit: Theological and Practical Reflections on the Asbury Outpouring*. Abilene Christian, 2025.
Nikolopoulou, Kassiani. "What Is Anachronism? Definition and Examples." Quillbot, June 27, 2024. https://quillbot.com/blog/anachronism/#:~:text=For%20example%2C%20a%20knight%20wearing,add%20humor%20to%20a%20story.
Oden, Thomas C. *Classic Christianity: A Systematic Theology*. HarperOne, 1992.
Oxford English Dictionary Online. "Aseity." https://www.oed.com/dictionary/aseity_n?tl=true.
Oxford Languages. "Systematic Theology." https://languages.oup.com/google-dictionary-en/.
Pannenberg, Wolfhart. *An Introduction to Systematic Theology*. Eerdmans, 1991.
———. *Systematic Theology*. 3 vols. Eerdmans, 2009–10.
Pelikan, Jaroslav. *The Christian Tradition: A History of the Development of Doctrine*. Vol. 1, *The Emergence of the Catholic Tradition (100–600)*. Chicago University Press, 1971.
Porter, Stanley E., and Dennis Stamps, eds. *Rhetorical Criticism and the Bible*. Sheffield University Press, 2002.
Richter, Sandra L. *The Epic of Eden*. InterVarsity, 2008.
———. *Stewards of Eden: What the Scripture Says About the Environment and Why It Matters*. InterVarsity, 2020.
Sanders, E. P. *Paul and Palestinian Judaism*. Fortress, 1977.
Schmidt, Klaus. *Sie bauten die ersten Tempel. Das rätselhafte Heiligtum der Steinzeitjäger*. C. H. Beck, 2006.
Schreiner, Thomas. *The King in His Beauty: A Biblical Theology of the Old and New Testaments*. Baker Academic, 2013.
Scobie, C. H. H. *The Ways of Our God: An Approach to Biblical Theology*. Eerdmans, 2002.
Shanks, Hershel, and Ben Witherington III. *The Brother of Jesus: The Dramatic Story and Meaning of the First Archaeological Link to Jesus and His Family*. HarperOne, 2001.
Shelton, W. Brian. *Prevenient Grace*. Warner, 2014.
Sleeth, Matthew. *Serving God, Saving th Planet*. Zondervan, 2013.
Smalley, S. *1, 2, 3 John*. Word Biblical Commentary 51. Word, 1984.
Snyder, Howard A. *Consider the Lilies: How Jesus Saves People and the Land*. First Fruits, 2024.
Sprinkle, Preston. "The Widening of God's Mercy—A Review by Preston Sprinkle." *The Bible and Culture* (blog), Oct. 12, 2024. https://www.patheos.com/blogs/bibleandculture/2024/10/12/the-widening-of-gods-mercy-a-review-by-preston-sprinkle/.
Sproul, R. C. *Everyone's a Theologian: An Introduction to Systematic Theology*. Ligonier Ministries, 2014.
Stark, Rodney. *The Rise of Christianity*. Princeton University Press, 1996.
Stowers, Stanley K. *A Rereading of Romans*. Yale University Press, 1997.

Studdert Kennedy, G. A. *The Unutterable Beauty.* Hodder, 1928.

Swamidass, S. Joshua. *The Genealogical Adam and Eve.* IVP, 2021.

Watson, Francis. "'America's Theologian': An Appreciation of Robert Jenson's *Systematic Theology* with Some Remarks About the Bible." *Scottish Journal of Theology* 55 (2002) 201–23.

———. *Text and Truth: Redefining Biblical Theology.* Eerdmans, 1997.

Wesley, John. *Hymns and Sacred Poems.* J. Hutton, 1739.

———. "Last Writing of John Wesley (a Letter to William Wilberforce)." February 24, 1791. https://place.asburyseminary.edu/cgi/viewcontent.cgi?article=1009&context=engaginggovernmentpapers.

Wikipedia. "Diatessaron." https://en.wikipedia.org/wiki/Diatessaron.

———. "Enthymeme." https://en.wikipedia.org/wiki/Enthymeme.

———. "Ethics in the Bible." https://en.wikipedia.org/wiki/Ethics_in_the_Bible.

———. "Mary Magdalene." https://en.wikipedia.org/wiki/Mary_Magdalene.

———. "Systematic Theology." https://en.wikipedia.org/wiki/Systematic_theology.

Wilk, Florian. "Paul as User." In *Reading the Bible Intertextually*, edited by Richard B. Hays et al., 83–99. Baylor, 2009.

Witherington, Ben, III. *The Acts of the Apostles.* Eerdmans, 1997.

———. *Biblical Theology: The Convergence of the Canon.* Cambridge University Press, 2020.

———. *Conflict and Community in Corinth.* Eerdmans, 1995.

———. *Isaiah Old and New.* Fortress, 2017.

———. *Jesus and Money.* Brazos, 2010.

———. *Jesus the Sage: The Pilgrimage of Wisdom.* Fortress, 2000.

———. *Jesus the Seer.* Tyndale House, 1999.

———. *Letters and Homilies for Hellenized Christians.* Vol. 1. IVP, 2006.

———. *Making a Meal of It.* Baylor University Press, 2007.

———. *Paul's Narrative Thought World: The Tapestry of Tragedy and Triumph.* Westminster/John Knox, 1994.

———. *The Problem with Evangelical Theology: Testing the Exegetical Foundations of Calvinism, Dispensationalism, and Wesleyanism.* Baylor University Press, 2005.

———. *Psalms Old and New.* Fortress, 2017.

———. *Sola Scriptura.* Baylor University Press, 2023.

———. *Torah Old and New.* Fortress, 2018.

———. *We Have Seen His Glory.* Eerdmans, 2010.

———. *What Have They Done with Jesus?* Harper, 2004.

———. "The Widening of God's Mercy—Part Four." The Bible and Culture (blog), October 16, 2024. https://www.patheos.com/blogs/bibleandculture/2024/10/16/the-widening-of-gods-mercy-part-four/.

———. "The Widening of God's Mercy—Part One." The Bible and Culture (blog), October 13, 2024. https://www.patheos.com/blogs/bibleandculture/2024/10/13/the-widening-of-gods-mercy-part-one/.

———. "The Widening of God's Mercy—Part Three." The Bible and Culture (blog), October 15, 2024. https://www.patheos.com/blogs/bibleandculture/2024/10/15/the-widening-of-gods-mercy-part-three/.

———. "The Widening of God's Mercy—Part Two." The Bible and Culture (blog), October 14, 2024. https://www.patheos.com/blogs/bibleandculture/2024/10/14/the-widening-of-gods-mercy-part-two/.

———. *Who God Is*. Lexham, 2020.
———. *Women in the Earliest Churches*. Cambridge University Press, 1988.
Witherington, Ben, III, and Darlene Hyatt. *Paul's Letter to the Romans*. Eerdmans, 2004.
Witherington, Ben, III, and Jason Myers. *Voices and Views on Paul*. IVP, 2020.
Wright, N. T. *The Day the Revolution Began*. Harper One, 2016.
———. *Justification: God's Plan and Paul's Vision*. IVP, 2016.

www.ingramcontent.com/pod-product-compliance
Lightning Source LLC
Chambersburg PA
CBHW031356230426
43670CB00006B/556